Evolving Standards of Decency

Politics,
Media &
Popular Culture

David A. Schultz, *General Editor*

Vol. 10

PETER LANG
New York • Washington, D.C./Baltimore • Bern
Frankfurt am Main • Berlin • Brussels • Vienna • Oxford

Mary Welek Atwell

Evolving Standards of Decency

Popular Culture and Capital Punishment

PETER LANG
New York • Washington, D.C./Baltimore • Bern
Frankfurt am Main • Berlin • Brussels • Vienna • Oxford

Library of Congress Cataloging-in-Publication Data

Atwell, Mary Welek.
Evolving standards of decency: popular culture
and capital punishment / Mary Welek Atwell.
p. cm. — (Politics, media, and popular culture; v. 10)
Includes bibliographical references.
1. Capital punishment—United States—Public opinion. 2. Capital
punishment in popular culture—United States. 3. Mass media and public opinion—
United States. 4. Public opinion—United States. I. Title.
II. Series: Politics, media & popular culture; v. 10.
HV8699.U5A89   364.66'0973—dc22   2004014688
ISBN 0-8204-6711-1
ISSN 1094-6225

Bibliographic information published by **Die Deutsche Bibliothek**.
Die Deutsche Bibliothek lists this publication in the "Deutsche
Nationalbibliografie"; detailed bibliographic data is available
on the Internet at http://dnb.ddb.de/.

Cover design by Dutton & Sherman Design

The paper in this book meets the guidelines for permanence and durability
of the Committee on Production Guidelines for Book Longevity
of the Council of Library Resources.

Printed in the United States of America

CONTENTS

Acknowledgments vii

Introduction 1

Chapter One: The Public and Capital Punishment: Past and Present 6
    Historical Background   6
    A Look at Statistics   13
    Changing Public Opinion   17
    Conclusion   22

Chapter Two: "A Random Assortment of Pariahs": The Supreme Court
            Considers the Death Penalty 24
    The Evolution of Evolving Standards   31
    Structural Issues   34
    Categories of Defendants   40
    Divisions within the Court   44

Chapter Three: Real People and "True-Life Novels" 48
    Gary Gilmore: Why Did He Do It and What Did It Mean?   48
        The Context   51
        The System   53
        The Conclusion   55
    The "Boys" Who Killed in Cold Blood   57
        Nature or Nurture?   58
        The Legal Process   61
        The Rope   63
        Two Versions on Film   65

An Eyewitness Account of the Death Penalty in the
United States   67
The Shame of Killing Pat Sonnier   68
"Killing People Is Wrong"   72
Both Sides   73
Adapting *Dead Man Walking*   74

Chapter Four: Novels Transformed into Films   78
If We Must Die, Let It Not Be Like Hogs   79
The Senseless Slaughter of Songbirds   83
Killing a Gift of God   90
What's a Father to Do?   96
Capital Punishment, Not Capital Torture   103

Chapter Five: Killing to Show That Killing Is Wrong: The Death Penalty
in the Movies   111
Just Doing Their Job   112
No Chivalry for Bad Girls   115
Actual Innocence   121
Death by Guillotine   125

Chapter Six: If Words Could Kill: Crime Fiction and the Death Penalty . . .   128
"Them without the Capital Gets the Punishment"   129
One More Texas Execution   132
Money Walks, Rich Folks Never Do No Time   137
There's Just No Point in Giving Up on a Human Being   140

Chapter Seven: The Power of Stories   145

Notes   153

Bibliography   169

ACKNOWLEDGMENTS

Several times during the last few years I have had an opportunity to teach a class on capital punishment. Invariably, the students in those courses have provided insights that helped to shape my own thinking about the subject. Frequently the very best discussions came when we read a novel or watched a movie and shared the reactions prompted by that piece of popular culture. To those experiences I owe the inspiration for this book.

I must single out one special student, Brigittee Jennings, my graduate assistant, who helped with research throughout this project.

As always, my colleagues, friends, and family have been extremely forbearing as I talked out my ideas with them. My husband, Dick Pennock, accepted and supported my preoccupation with the death penalty. Polly Atwell, my daughter, shared the understanding gained through her volunteer work with the National Coalition to Abolish the Death Penalty as well as her sharp editor's pencil.

Finally, it gives one pause to learn about and come into contact with people who put their opposition to capital punishment into action. My admiration for those with the courage and commitment to work for change, especially the NCADP and Virginians for Alternatives to the Death Penalty, is immeasurable.

INTRODUCTION

Imagine a skit on *Saturday Night Live*. A man we'll call "Calvin" is on trial for his life. During the court proceedings the lawyer (we'll call him "Joe, the Sleeping Lawyer") assigned to represent the accused repeatedly falls asleep and slumps over in his chair at the defense table. When he is awake, Joe may consult his notes. However, the entire file he prepared for this capital case consists of 269 words—barely one page of double-spaced type. This lawyer snoozes not only during the current trial; courthouse veterans recall how he slept on other occasions, including during previous capital cases. But judges keep appointing this attorney to represent impoverished capital defendants, despite his habit of napping, and even though nine of Joe's previous clients sit on death row.

In the case being satirized, the defendant, who happens to be gay, is on trial for killing his former lover. His lawyer is known to refer to homosexuals as "fairies," "queers," and "tush hogs." Joe makes no objections when the prosecutor asks questions about Calvin's sexual practices, like whether he likes to "play the man or the woman." Joe remains silent when the prosecutor tells the jury in his closing statement that sending a gay man to prison for life "certainly isn't a very bad punishment for a homosexual."

A Federal District Court judge sets aside the verdict of guilty and the sentence of death and orders a new trial. The state appeals, however, saying that a sleeping lawyer is no different from an intoxicated or drugged lawyer or one with Alzheimer's disease, and after all, representation by such advocates has been found constitutional. The Federal Appeals Court agrees with the state. Two out of three judges on that court thought there was a good chance that even though Joe took numerous naps during the trial, he may not have missed "anything important." Next the governor appears. He enjoys a good nap himself, but he likes to claim that all of the 152 persons executed during his administration had "full access to the courts." When he learns that "adequate assistance of counsel" allows a capital defense attorney to sleep through a trial, he laughs.[1]

Maybe the audience laughs with him. They think, "This is ridiculous. Where does *Saturday Night Live* get these outrageous story lines?"

Now, imagine a serious drama, even a tragedy. The facts are the same. Yet this time as you watch Calvin's story unfold, you have a sense of uneasiness. The comments from the courts and the governor sound ominous. You imagine the defendant moving closer to his date with the executioner and you imagine Joe going back to the courtroom to "represent" another hapless person, too poor to afford a lawyer. Along with the other members of the audience, you are holding your breath for something to introduce a note of justice and sanity to the story. At the last minute, a higher court rules that "Unconscious counsel equates to no counsel at all."[2] The Supreme Court agrees and the movie ends with Calvin about to have a new trial with a new—and presumably alert—attorney.

The case of Calvin Burdine is not a skit from *Saturday Night Live* and it is not a movie. It is a true story that happened in Texas between 1983 and 2002. If the public knew about incidents like this, would it affect their attitudes toward the death penalty? If Burdine's story had been made into a TV comedy or a serious movie, would it have a greater impact on public opinion than it had as a news story?

Popular support for or opposition to capital punishment has been cited in many Supreme Court opinions. As Chapter Two will discuss, the Court looks to "evolving standards of decency" as one way of measuring whether the death penalty offends the contemporary conscience. An assessment of public attitudes is one factor in addressing whether the death penalty should be considered cruel and unusual punishment and thus whether it is unconstitutional.

How does the Court measure public attitudes? It has looked to polls and especially to actions by state legislatures and state courts, as Chapter 1 will examine. One could also argue that novels, television, movies, nonfiction works, and popular journalism offer some insight into how Americans view capital punishment. Of course the vast majority of people will never have any first-hand experience with death row. Unlike our forebears, who might have witnessed a public hanging in the town square, citizens will know about state-sponsored executions from what they read in the papers or hear on the nightly TV news. Therefore, I will argue that for most people in the United States the most vivid encounters with capital punishment come through popular culture. In fact, the entertainment media have raised questions of inequalities in the capital system related to race, gender, and class, examined (sometimes accurately, sometimes not) the legal process, considered the politics of capital punishment, and discussed the execution of the innocent. Without arguing that there is a *direct* cause/effect relationship between popular culture and public opinion about the death penalty, this book will explore how several genres have focused attention on issues surrounding capital punishment. It will encourage students to discuss the issues raised by the real and fictionalized treatment of men and women on death row. It will suggest that the great value of stories in the popular media is their ability to particularize both the victim and the offender, to humanize both, rather than to present them as symbols of good and evil. Such representation can make it possible for many people to move beyond a simple yes or no answer to the question "Do you support capital punishment?" and to draw their response from more information and perhaps, from greater compassion.

Even in the nineteenth century, when the definition of popular culture was significantly different from that of today, Americans drew some of their attitudes toward the death penalty from literature. Publishers produced thousands of copies of sermons written for executions. The "last words" of condemned men (supposedly the statements in which the criminal himself explained where he had gone wrong and repented for his sins) were immensely popular with readers. Well-known poets also took up the issue of capital punishment. In 1843, John Greenleaf Whittier wrote "The Human Sacrifice," an anti-death-penalty poem in which he referred to execution as "the crime of Law." Walt Whitman's "The Dialogue," published in a popular magazine in 1845, was subtitled "A Brief Statement of the Argument for the Abolition of the Death Penalty."

In more recent years, an examination of contemporary popular culture and criminal justice is not a completely original idea. Austin Sarat, for example, has raised the possibility that television and films "could challenge the hegemony of official legal discourse about the death penalty."[3] In other words, the entertainment media can shine a light on issues surrounding capital punishment in a way the courts do not. He suggests further that the survival of the death penalty and some of its apparent popularity may be related to the invisibility of the process. If TV comedians or serious filmmakers had dramatized Calvin Burdine's story, would more people have become aware of deep flaws in the system?

Many scholars advocate a cultural analysis of law, noting the interaction between law and society. In this view, law is more than a "coercive force operating externally to affect behavior and social relations." It is also "a lens through which we view the world and actually conduct social interaction."[4] The legal system creates part of the framework through which we see reality. It helps in formulating our definitions of right and wrong, good and bad. But in the modern world, for many people the "real law" blurs into the law as they see it on television or in the movies. For example, a recent article in the *National Law Journal* reported that experts tell trial lawyers to "take popular culture seriously. It's the stories and images that wind up in the heads of the people you need to reach." Jurors' expectations are influenced by programs such as *Law and Order*, and they are likely to interpret the case before them as an opportunity to "right a wrong." TV shows, books, and films have led jurors to expect lawyers to speak eloquently and to present cases like a screenplay—building to a climax in the closing scene.[5] The fuzziness of the line between the actual legal system and the way it is portrayed may, on the one hand, lead the public to assume that the state's side is always right—that the guilty get the punishment they deserve and that the innocent go free. One of the arguments of this book, however, is that there are many examples where the popular media offer a more nuanced version of reality, one in which the innocent may well be convicted, and one in which the system itself is often seriously flawed.

During the 1950s and 1960s, support for the death penalty in the United States dropped significantly. A variety of theories have attempted to account for this decline, but many cite works of literature such as Arthur Koestler's *Reflections on Hanging* (1956), *Reflections on the Guillotine* by Albert Camus (1959), and *Cell 2455, Death Row*, written in 1954 by condemned inmate Caryl Chessman, as instrumental in sparking the wide-ranging debate about capital punishment. In addition, anti-death-penalty positions by churches and the abolition of capital punishment in virtually all of Western Europe and in Canada and Mexico seemed to make Americans less enthusiastic about executions as retribution for murder.[6]

Current debates about capital punishment are likely to be less concerned with moral issues and more likely to focus on the unreliability of the criminal justice system, its failure to deliver due process (as in the case of incompetent lawyers who do not afford their clients adequate representation), or on the conviction of innocent people, such as those vindicated by DNA evidence. In the late twentieth century and the early years of the twenty-first, the imperfections of the system seem "more demonstrable and more disturbing" than ever before.[7] Studies conducted by Columbia University researchers, for example, indicate that in twenty-six of twenty-eight states, at least 50 percent of capital cases involved significant errors. These flaws included misconduct by prosecutors, incompetent defense attorneys, judicial bias, legal errors, and juror prejudice.[8]

Justice Thurgood Marshall wrote in *Furman v. Georgia*[9] that the criterion for determining whether a punishment is cruel and unusual depends on "whether people who were fully informed as to the purposes of the penalty and its liabilities would find the penalty shocking, unjust, and unacceptable."

In the contemporary world, most people will not read court transcripts or legal journals to learn about the purposes and liabilities of the death penalty. More commonly through popular culture, with its ability to humanize the stories of persons involved in the criminal justice system, Americans come to visualize how victims, families, offenders, and professionals from police to executioners experience the process in which the state determines whether or not to take a life in punishment for crime. From these sources they draw information to decide whether it is "shocking, unjust, and unacceptable." This book will examine fiction—classics and serious works, as well as some conventional detective novels and works of nonfiction that provide glimpses of particular crimes and punishments. It will also review a number of films, some more famous than others, from the last fifty years. It will focus on "serious" popular culture, not tabloids or slasher movies but more substantial works designed at least in part to provoke the audience to mull over contentious issues.

Students of the death penalty would benefit greatly from reading the books and watching in their entirety the movies treated here. I hope *Evolving Standards of Decency* will inspire the interest and energy to carry on the discussion of how capital punishment fits into contemporary American law and culture.

· 1 ·

THE PUBLIC AND CAPITAL PUNISHMENT: PAST AND PRESENT

Public opinion about the death penalty is not static. As with many other issues, policy questions intersect with moral beliefs just as they have since the earliest days of the American republic. The Reverend Jesse Jackson claims that support for capital punishment has ebbed and flowed, based not on enduring principles but depending on how the death penalty was perceived as a "tool of the politics of race and the politics of crime." In his view, public sentiment is again in flux.[1]

This chapter will examine the evolution of these attitudes over several centuries. It will look briefly at the history of capital punishment in the United States, at statistics attempting to identify recent public opinion regarding the death penalty, and at events that seem to have influenced public attitudes. Finally it will consider some examples of issues arising in individual states that highlight questions about the application of capital punishment in the early twenty-first century.

Historical Background

According to Hugo Bedau, the death penalty in America is on the road to extinction. Its decline has been marked by "the end of public executions and mandatory capital sentencing, the concept of degrees of murder, the development of appellate review of capital cases, the decline in the number of annual executions, a reduction in the variety of capital statutes, experiments with its abolition, and the search for more humane methods."[2] From the present perspective, it is clear that for at least one of the factors Bedau cites, the number of annual executions, the decline of the mid-twentieth century was not permanent. During the last quarter of the twentieth century, the numbers on death row increased steadily. However, in 2001, both the total number of death row residents and the number of newcomers sentenced to death decreased.[3] Nonetheless, a look at the history of capital punishment will reveal a narrowing of its use, more legal safeguards in its application, and ongoing debates about acceptable methods of execution.

During the seventeenth and eighteenth centuries, the colonial period in America, most citizens looked to their religious beliefs for an explanation of wrongdoing. The majority held the view that humans were disposed toward evil because of original sin. If an individual man or woman failed to control this tendency and broke the law, he—not the community—was to blame. If the crime was serious (and in the colonial period the list of serious crimes was quite long), execution was a reasonable response. Putting a sinner/criminal to death served the interests of the community, which would be purged of the evil. It also served the best interests of the offender, who would have the opportunity to repent publicly for his sins. His punishment, and perhaps his last-minute contrition, were meant to serve as a deterrent to other potential evil-doers.[4] According to Louis Masur, the ritual of execution was intended to transmit proper values. The overriding theme of the event was to emphasize the preservation of order. Church and state were united in upholding the law and the consequences of breaking it.[5]

Until the time of the American Revolution, while the colonies operated under English law, many infractions from minor property offenses to murder qualified as capital crimes. The Americans, however, actually applied the death penalty much less frequently than their British contemporaries. That may be because a greater need for able-bodied workers in the New World made wholesale executions impractical. Others argue that many in the American colonies came to identify the frequent use of capital punishment with the European systems they rejected as tyrannical and corrupt. In any case, by the late eighteenth century, isolated criticism of the death penalty became more widespread. Many of the Founding Fathers knew the work of the Italian philosopher Cesar Beccaria, who wrote *Of Crime and Punishment*. Beccaria argued that as people became more civilized, punishments should become less severe. Punitive measures that caused physical harm, including death, were themselves barbaric and fostered more violent behavior. In addition, the death penalty was used in an unpredictable and arbitrary way. For all intents and purposes, the only way to correct a wrongful conviction was for a defendant to appeal to the governor for a reprieve or for clemency. Yet such an "appeals process" often depended on whether one had friends in high places. Therefore, if the new United States envisioned itself as an enlightened government, condemning offenders to death seemed corrupt, inhumane, and disproportionate to most crimes. Some even argued that executions fostered crime and would hasten the downfall of the new nation. In the eyes of many public figures, incarceration in prison offered a reasonable alternative. There the offender could be reclaimed and reformed even as society was protected.[6]

By the early decades of the nineteenth century, the states had resolved the debate over punishment to the extent that all had developed both a prison system and a limited list of capital offenses that provided the death penalty only for certain types of homicide and in some cases for a few other crimes.[7] The controversy next shifted to determining the proper place to carry out executions. The rising middle class in the cities expressed disgust with seemingly senseless cruelty and with public displays of rude emotions. They preferred to live as much as possible in "safe, exclusive social settings."[8] Nothing could be more offensive to such sensibilities than the raw intensity of a public hanging.

On the other hand, executions before a community audience were, in the eyes of many people, events of both symbolic and practical importance with a significant place in the popular culture of the nineteenth century. They provided a form of education and entertainment, not only for those who attended in person but also for the reading public. The drama began when the sheriff read the death warrant. To this he might add his own comments. A sermon, often quite lengthy, followed, then a speech by the condemned man, and a hymn. Finally the hood would be placed over the offender's head and the rope placed around his neck. Death might be nearly instantaneous or it might be excruciatingly slow if the hanging was botched because the rope was too short or too long.

Those who observed executions were far outnumbered by people who read the many printed accounts. Execution sermons, the offender's last words, the story of his life and death—all were published and enjoyed wide popularity well into the nineteenth century. If the offender could not or would not utter any memorable last words, publishers had no compunction against composing them. All of these printed materials were meant to teach a moral lesson about the consequences of crime. Yet there is little doubt that they provided entertainment and sometimes even created sympathy for the person being executed. The public spectacle of the hanging was also justified for its ethical message. It was meant to illustrate dramatically that death is the consequence for serious offenses against the community and that the community would come together to enforce social order. At the same time, it was a ritual, set apart from everyday life, designed to separate legitimate violence inflicted by the state from illegitimate violence caused by the criminal.[9]

Whether the crowds who came to view the hanging paid attention to its higher purposes is debatable. Members of the respectable middle class charged that public executions were nothing but an excuse for a day of drunkenness and revelry that disturbed the lives of peaceful citizens. Opponents of the death penalty also argued that hangings, rather than diminishing violence, actually created a taste for blood and vengeance. Businessmen claimed that executions deprived them of a day's labor. More and more the elite stayed away from public hangings and they became less and less "community" events.

By the 1840s, the issue of inflicting capital punishment in public was one thread in a larger discussion of whether to abolish the death penalty altogether. This debate took place within a general reform atmosphere that included movements to abolish slavery, advance women's rights, ban alcohol, encourage healthy eating habits, improve the treatment of the mentally ill, and limit the use of corporal punishment. The period saw the creation of organized reform societies with the purpose of lobbying, petitioning, and holding public meetings to create political pressure that would change law and policy. Members of these societies tended to be middle class—ministers, lawyers, doctors, journalists (and their wives)—who represented the repugnance that many respectable people felt toward violence. One of their goals was to encourage citizens to internalize proper values. They would learn to do this by education, not by force. These groups also noted (as many observe in the twenty-first century) that the death penalty was an embodiment of inequality and privilege. It was the poor and the marginalized who mounted the scaffold for an execution, not the rich and powerful.[10]

Ivan Solotaroff makes the claim that the death penalty is, like slavery, America's "peculiar institution," that both stem from the same desire of one human being to subjugate another.[11] Certainly capital punishment was and continues to be more prevalent in the South than in other regions of the country. Up until the Civil War, slaves were executed at a much higher rate than free persons. A slave accused of a capital offense could be given an expedited trial before a justice of the peace, without a judge or jury. As one slave owner stated, the death penalty was "calculated and designed to put the lawless in fear."[12]

Many of the same men and women who opposed slavery also opposed the death penalty in the mid-nineteenth century, at least in part because they could not accept the state's right to participate in legalized violence and killing. Michigan became the first state to abolish capital punishment in 1847. One incident there seemed to be the decisive factor. Stephen Simmons was charged with beating his wife to death and sentenced to hang. After the verdict, the local sheriff resigned in protest, arguing that Simmons had been too drunk to know what he was doing. A new sheriff, determined to make an example of the offender (and to make a name for himself), ordered a brass band to play at the execution to make it a "celebration" to remember. When Simmons reached the scaffold and was asked if he had any last words, he sang a verse of repentance with great dignity. The crowd wept and filed away in silence.[13] Michigan soon abolished executions.

Only Wisconsin and Rhode Island followed Michigan in eliminating the death penalty in the mid-nineteenth century, and in the 1850s the crisis over slavery and secession occupied the public agenda, sweeping other reforms aside. Following the Civil War, opponents of capital punishment found themselves on the defensive. After President Lincoln was assassinated, those charged in the conspiracy to kill him were swiftly tried and condemned to death. As has often happened with high profile crimes and punishments, the hanging of the Lincoln conspirators was immensely popular.

Rather than eliminating the death penalty, most states gave reformers "half a loaf" by moving executions inside the prison walls. Supporters of capital punishment implicitly conceded that public hangings might disrupt society and offend public delicacy. Moving them out of public view also, however, deprived executions of their educational value—a claim that opponents failed to seize at the time. One could argue that executions became much less an act of the people and much more an act of the government.[14] Privatizing hangings meant in a sense that those responsible for taking the offender's life could be anonymous.

Some scholars argue that the death penalty in America has persisted through many efforts to abolish it because its supporters have been willing to adjust the methods and form of capital punishment to maintain the policy itself.[15] If such a claim can be made for changing the location of executions, a similar argument can surely be made for changing the means of inflicting death. When hanging offended the popular sense of decency, states moved to adopt more technologically sophisticated and supposedly more humane methods—such as electrocution, the gas chamber, and finally lethal injection.

Jesse Jackson has stated that capital punishment "as we know it" is an invention of the twentieth century, a marriage of technology and politics, beginning with the first electrocution in New York in 1890.[16] After experimenting with electrocuting animals in tanks of water and on rubberized tables, authorities decided to rig up a chair as the fatal site for people. Opponents challenged the new method as unconstitutional, a violation of the Eighth Amendment's ban on cruel and unusual punishment. Even before a human being was killed by electrocution, however, the Supreme Court rejected this claim. Reasoning from supposition rather than from evidence, they held that science could develop a way for electricity to "produce instantaneous, and therefore, painless death."[17]

Arthur Kemmler, a convicted murderer, was the first to be put to death with the new technology. It took several jolts to end his life. Some witnesses fainted in horror, others contended that Kemmler "never suffered a bit of pain."[18]

The first death by electricity raised questions that would characterize all modern executions. How could jurors know exactly what they were authorizing when they sentenced a person to death? They would be shown many photos of the crime scene but none of an occupied electric chair, gas chamber, or gurney set up for lethal injection.[19] They would simply have to trust, despite reports to the contrary, that these devices produced "instantaneous and therefore, painless death."

But even with doubts about the pain inflicted by electrocution and even with the association of gas chambers with Hitler and the Nazis, there were only a few notable efforts to abolish the death penalty between World War I and the 1950s. In fact, several states that had eliminated capital punishment in the first decades of the twentieth century reinstated it during a feverish fear of crime in the 1920s.[20] Prominent cases during the twenties and thirties did create some public discussion of the issue. In 1921, Nathan Leopold and Dickie Loeb were found guilty of the senseless murder of twelve-year-old Bobby Franks. Their defense attorney, the famous Clarence Darrow, argued eloquently and successfully that they should be spared from death because of their youth and, implicitly, because their homosexual tendencies constituted a form of mental illness. Nicola Sacco and Bartolomeo Vanzetti, two anarchists who had emigrated from Italy, were executed for a murder and payroll robbery in 1927. Protests against their sentences occurred across the United States and around the world from those who believed Sacco and Vanzetti were being punished not for a crime but for their radical politics. In 1930, eight African-American youths were sentenced to death for the alleged rape of two white women in Alabama. The case of the "Scottsboro Boys" became a world-famous, and notorious, story of racism and capital punishment in the South. Those young men were spared from death only after the United States Supreme Court twice overturned their convictions. In 1937, after a trial that resembled a circus, Bruno Richard Hauptmann was executed for "the crime of the century," the kidnapping and murder of Charles Lindbergh, Jr. Hauptmann maintained his innocence until the end, and many who have studied the matter agree with him. Although each of those high profile cases generated some debate about a specific application of the death penalty, none of them caused a public outcry against the punishment in general.

However, by the mid-twentieth century, scholars raised persistent questions about the purposes of the death penalty. Studies consistently showed that it did not serve as an effective deterrent. Others questioned whether retribution was an appropriate goal of punishment in a civilized society. For these and other reasons, juries outside the South became less likely to vote for capital punishment. However, the death penalty retained its appeal in that region. By the late 1940s, over two-thirds of executions took place in the South. It is hard to argue that these sentences, inflicted disproportionately on African Americans, were not a form of racial control.[21] Racial disparities in the death penalty were prominent among the issues that led organizations such as the NAACP to challenge its constitutionality in the 1960s. We will discuss those cases, culminating in *Furman v. Georgia*, which found the death penalty as applied unconstitutional, in the next chapter.[22]

After the Supreme Court revisited the issue and found some capital statutes constitutional in *Gregg v. Georgia* in 1976, public attitudes about which methods of execution met contemporary standards of decency seemed to change. Witnesses wrote of their shock at the apparent pain caused by lethal gas, others charged that electrocution was violent and painful. In the face of such challenges, most states by the end of the twentieth century adopted lethal injection as a more humane method. This change was not, critics would charge, meant to treat the condemned more decently, but was rather a way to save the death penalty itself.[23] In fact, no one knows whether lethal injection is less painful than other methods. It may simply be a form of "chemical entombment while waiting for heart failure."[24] Robert Jay Lifton is skeptical about the "therapeutic cloak" that execution by means of an apparent medical procedure casts over the reality of death. Lethal injection is supposedly "more tranquil and predictable than the various forms of burning, shooting, strangling, and gassing that in the past have squeezed themselves through the cruel and unusual rubric." It looks like a medical procedure but its apparent painlessness may be misleading, "designed to leach the drama and agony out of the business; to transform it into a form of therapy for society."[25]

The Supreme Court has provided little guidance in the choice of methods of execution. They have either skirted the issue, held that the Eighth Amendment allows botched executions, or deferred to the state legislatures' notion of what conforms to the public sensibility. And indeed, some states have tried to retain obviously painful methods of executions (as Florida did with the electric chair),[26] apparently as a way of symbolizing the community's moral outrage toward an offender.[27] Choosing a less violent means to cause death may be viewed as another example of how Americans have adapted the form of capital punishment to accommodate changing standards of decency. Lifton argues that the use of lethal injection creates the illusion that such a "dire but necessary medical procedure" represents a cure for society. More than previous methods of execution, it obliterates the distinction between healing and killing, making the method more palatable than overtly violent death.[28] Nonetheless, at least one study conducted in California compared a group of subjects who watched a film simulating an execution by lethal injection while the control group watched a nature film. After the viewing, more of those who watched the execution expressed reduced support for the death penalty.[29]

Meanwhile, aside from the discussion of method, during the last quarter of the twentieth century as the United States embraced more conservative politics, the death penalty seemed hugely popular, even invulnerable to challenge. A number of factors may explain this support. Crime rates rose during the 1960s and the public's fear of crime rose as well. For some, enthusiasm for the death penalty was a code for racism. Many people expressed a lack of faith in the criminal justice system to really punish the guilty, believing that too many offenders were given only a "slap on the wrist." Simultaneously, there was a revival of support for the notion that individuals must take responsibility for their own actions, that those who broke the law should receive their "just deserts."[30] In this atmosphere, most politicians were terrified of being called "soft on crime." In 1992, for example, Governor Bill Clinton interrupted his presidential campaign and returned to Arkansas to oversee the execution of Ricky Ray Rector, a brain-damaged African American man convicted by an all-white jury. Rector's mental state was so unsound that he howled, screamed, and barked like a dog while on death row. He clearly did not understand the meaning of his sentence. At his last meal, he left some of his dessert, a piece of pie, uneaten. When asked why, he said he would come back later to finish it.

Stephen Bright, who has defended many death row inmates, claims that a commitment to fairness was a casualty of the war on crime in the seventies, eighties, and nineties. In his view, legislators, governors, and even judges were unconcerned about the conviction of innocent persons. They tolerated woefully inadequate lawyers and allowed jurors to reach decisions without necessary information. In their effort to establish credentials for toughness, politicians did not just support the death penalty, they advocated its expansion.[31] Likewise, governors feared that exercising clemency toward convicted offenders would be political suicide. While the Supreme Court held that commutations and pardons were essential to ensure that the innocent were not executed, such decisions became increasingly rare.[32]

Yet even as elected officials competed to outdo each other in their zeal for putting offenders to death, polls at the end of the twentieth century suggested that the public might not share this enthusiasm, that support for capital punishment might be shallower than it appeared.

A Look at Statistics

Robert Bohm concludes that support and opposition to capital punishment have varied greatly since opinion polling began in the 1930s. During this period the numbers could be graphed as a lopsided V. The earliest polls in 1936 show that 61 percent favored the death penalty. The number dipped to 42 percent, its lowest point, in 1966, and rose to 80 percent in the mid-1990s. Bohm believes that the Supreme Court's *Furman* decision, finding the death penalty as administered unconstitutional, ironically led to an upsurge in pro-capital-punishment sentiment. Perhaps influenced by self-interested politicians, many Americans seemed outraged that the Court could stop the states from executing convicts, even though no one had been executed in the United States for six years before *Furman*. Bohm also claims that variations in opinion correlate with "fear and anxiety engendered by social events," and that the strength of support and opposition are a "psychological barometer of dread and angst."[33] Research on whether more information about the actual workings of the death penalty leads to opposition has yielded ambiguous results, but poll after poll show that support declines when the respondents are provided with alternatives to execution. Recent studies that will be examined later in this section confirm the importance of asking questions beyond the basic "Do you support the death penalty?"

Lifton notes that while "public opinion drives the death penalty," certain groups express greater approval than others.[34] Men, whites, those with higher incomes, and Republicans are more enthusiastic than women, minorities, lower income people, and Democrats. He finds that retribution—making the offender pay for his crime—became a more acceptable reason for support in the late twentieth century. An execution seems to provide an illusion of control and order in a society when many things seem chaotic. On the other hand, Lifton suggests that the support may be "a mile wide and an inch thick." It can diminish when people see the condemned person as an individual, when they are "confronted with a face, a name, and human frailties that, however lurid, bear at least some resemblance to our own."[35]

Radelet and Borg agree that retribution is the most important contemporary justification for support of the death penalty. Many advocates believe that "they (the offenders) deserve it." Retribution provides, in a sense, a moral argument for executing the guilty—they condemned themselves by their vicious actions. Yet capital punishment is opposed by most of those considered "moral leaders." There is a greater consensus among religious spokespersons from mainstream Protestant, Roman Catholic, and Jewish faiths that capital punishment is wrong than there is about any other topic.[36]

Rationales for the death penalty, other than retribution, have been challenged by research. During the 1970s, many claimed it served as a deterrent. Recently, however, 85 percent of studies agree that empirical data show the death penalty has never been, is not, and never could be a superior deterrent to a long prison sentence.[37] Some would claim that only an execution can permanently incapacitate violent murderers. Yet of those whose death sentences were commuted in 1972 with *Furman*, only 1 percent ever killed again. Meanwhile, studies conducted by groups from the General Accounting Office to Amnesty International have concluded that it is "undeniable" that the death penalty is applied disproportionately on the basis of race, ethnicity, and class. Although many citizens are apparently aware of these biases, most do not see it as a reason to oppose the death penalty in theory. Yet the Capital Jury Project has shown that many who actually serve as jurors express lingering doubts about whether death is the appropriate punishment.[38] This latter finding seems to indicate that although a majority will express favorable attitudes toward capital punishment if asked an abstract or global question and many will even admit to injustices in the system, much of that support evaporates when people confront the decision to take an actual human life. Perhaps Donald Hocutt, former executioner for the state of Mississippi, best expresses this ambivalence. "It's funny," he commented, "people love the death penalty. They come up all the time, asking me about executions. Once I get started, though, they really don't want to hear *too* much about it. I never heard a kid say he wants to grow up to be an executioner."[39]

Numerous studies confirm that public enthusiasm diminishes when those sampled were provided with alternatives to death or when they were given more information beyond a yes or no question. Cullen, Fisher, and Applegate examined eight national polls taken from 1995 to 1998. They found that an average of 72 percent of respondents answered "yes" to the question "Do you support capital punishment?" Of those, 57 percent said they would still be in favor if 1 out of 100 executed were actually innocent.[40] However, if offered an option, 60.7 percent chose a life sentence without parole (LWOP) plus restitution to the victim's family, while only 31.6 percent favored the death penalty.[41] Thus the percentages of support and opposition were almost reversed if LWOP were a real alternative. If the offender was a juvenile under the age of 18 at the time of the crime, the proportion supporting LWOP plus restitution climbed to 80 percent.[42]

A study conducted in Indiana in 1992–93 shows a similar pattern. If asked only whether they favored capital punishment, 76 percent said yes, 14 percent said no. But if LWOP was an option, 62 percent chose it over death, while 26 percent still opted for death. The research further showed that 79 percent of respondents agreed that the death penalty was too arbitrary—that some were executed while others went to prison for the same crime. Almost everyone surveyed, 96 percent, believed that laws were needed to protect against racial bias in the criminal justice system. A clue to the original high support for the death penalty may be that most of those questioned believed that a "regular" life sentence would be twenty years or less, and therefore too lenient for a violent murderer.

The same survey also questioned state legislators about their sense of constituents' opinions. It revealed that lawmakers were often mistaken about the public's preferences. Fifty percent of the legislators believed voters would prefer the death penalty, even if LWOP plus restitution were an option. In fact, as noted, with that choice only 26 percent opted for death. Thus this survey, along with similar studies in New York and Nebraska, indicate that politicians are more punitive than the public. Both have misconceptions about the other's views. McGarrell and Sandys conclude that everyone believes that everyone else supports the death penalty, but the consensus is far narrower than it first appears.[43]

A 1997 study of 1,000 Tennessee households explored the issue of gender and support for death sentences. Again, a majority of both men (85 percent) and women (65 percent) answered "yes" to the global question "Do you support capital punishment?" However, more women than men supported life without parole as an option. Women's support declined if they were aware of racial discrimination or if they believed an innocent person might be executed.[44]

In 1991 the United States Senate considered the Racial Justice Act, which would have allowed death row inmates to challenge their sentence if there was a statistical disparity correlated to race in the application of the death penalty in their jurisdiction. Had it passed, the pace of executions would surely have slowed while convicts appealed. The legislation failed, but a study of senators' votes revealed that opposition to the law correlated with states that had higher homicide rates. Even more revealing, the greater the racial disproportion on death row in an individual senator's state, the less likely he or she was to vote to remove the disparity. In other words, the greater the cost of removing the racially discriminatory effects of the death penalty, the less political support there was for addressing the problem.[45] At the very least, this research suggests that members of Congress were willing to accept the likelihood of racial bias in the system, rather than disturb the status quo. The studies previously cited reveal that they, like other politicians, may have overestimated their constituents' devotion to the death penalty. Public opinion polls conducted in 2000 showed that although the majority still supported capital punishment, more than half of those who did also supported a moratorium until the system could be "reviewed for fairness."[46]

How citizens feel about the death penalty is important in many ways. Some contend that the decline in the number of executions reflects public discomfort with the administration of the system.[47] Bohm argues that it is unlikely that the ultimate sentence will be imposed in jurisdictions where most citizens express opposition. On the other hand, assumptions about the popularity of capital punishment sway the way legislators vote, influence prosecutors to ask for death and dissuade governors from offering clemency or vetoing death penalty legislation. And such assumptions have an impact on the way the Court interprets the Constitution.[48]

Although the Supreme Court has repeatedly looked to public opinion to determine whether the use of capital punishment is consistent with evolving standards of decency, the studies cited above provide evidence that an accurate reading of American attitudes is a complex process. Cullen et al. claim that the dismaying reality is that much of the public is ignorant of many aspects of crime and criminal procedures. Single-question polls that seem to reveal punitive attitudes could yield more informed results if citizens were provided with reasons, options, and alternatives.[49] According to Robert Jay Lifton and William Bowers, the Eighth Amendment "requires the Supreme Court to act on its most enlightened interpretation of contemporary values."[50] If that is true, the Court would need to take into account the reservations many Americans express, especially when presented with alternatives to capital punishment.

Changing Public Opinion

Writing in the *New York Times*, columnist Wendy Kaminer summarized the shifts and complexities in public sentiment since the early 1990s. Then, she stated, Americans were preoccupied with the crime rate and had little sentiment for the accused, no matter how he had been abused or treated unjustly. They focused on innocent victims, but rarely thought of "guilty victims," like retarded death row inmates. "The lines between innocence and guilt, victim and predator, were clear." Kaminer claims those attitudes have changed as 94 percent of Americans realize that the innocent are sometimes convicted of murder. If this is true, prisoners can be viewed as people—not just as predators. It may also be clearer to the public that most criminal cases are not simple, but involve degrees of guilt and questions of mitigation. Revelations of numerous wrongful convictions—especially when coupled with extensive police scandals—undermine faith in the infallibility of the criminal justice system to get it right. If, as Kaminer notes, the government can't deliver the mail on time, why should people trust it to select individuals to die?[51]

Jeffrey Kirchmeier, writing in the *Colorado Law Review*, developed a list of events he claims have contributed to a recent movement to stop executions.[52] He describes the sentiment not as anti-death-penalty per se but as concerned that the process does not function properly and makes fatal mistakes. His items include:

- *The release of the book and movie* Dead Man Walking, *described by Radalet and Borg as "the most popular death penalty book of the century,"*[53] *and discussed at length later in this work.*

- *Justice Harry Blackmun's statement that he would no longer "tinker with the machinery of death."* After decades on the bench and years of supporting capital punishment, Blackmun finally concluded that the system could not be made to work fairly and justly enough to take a life. The Supreme Court's opinions on capital punishment will be discussed in the next chapter.

- *The American Bar Association's resolutions calling for a moratorium on the death penalty.* After more than 100 death row inmates were exonerated, the ABA called for a halt to executions by the states and federal government until defendants are guaranteed competent, adequately funded counsel and a full review in the state and federal courts. They have also called for a prohibition on the execution of juveniles. The ABA supports the use of DNA testing to establish guilt or innocence, a requirement that juries be notified if life without parole is an option, and compensation to those who are exonerated. They have advocated that the federal government make some of its funding to state criminal justice systems contingent on the states' providing adequate support for attorneys for the indigent. The ABA has also called for the courts to address racial discrimination in the application of the death penalty.[54]

- *The use of DNA to exonerate innocent defendants.* Between 1976 and 2001, 88 men left death row when they were found to be innocent of the crimes for which they had been convicted. For every seven persons executed during that time, one innocent person was removed from death row or from prison. Although 90 percent of Americans favor public funding for DNA testing, only a few states provide inmates the time and money for such appeals. In fact, despite the growing numbers of vindications when DNA proves that a person *could not be guilty*, thirty-three states require that new evidence be introduced within six months of sentencing. Some, such as Virginia, which allows only three weeks for most new evidence, provide an even shorter window of opportunity. Only seven states permit new evidence to be brought forward at any time.[55] DNA testing has also revealed troubling facts about race and conviction patterns. Of the innocence cases brought in 2000, over two-thirds of them involved African Americans wrongly convicted of rape or rape/murder of whites.[56] Legislation introduced in Congress would make testing available to inmates in federal custody if it were relevant to their claim of innocence, and tie state law enforcement funding to the states' willingness to do the same.[57]

    Although DNA has been a tool for vindicating quite a few innocent persons, many crimes do not turn on such physical evidence and cannot be solved through DNA tests. How would fatal errors in such cases be proven? We cannot assume that wrongful convictions occur only when a technique exists to catch those mistakes.[58]

- *The Illinois moratorium.* On January 31, 2000, Republican Governor George Ryan ordered a moratorium on executions and appointed a commission to examine the state's death penalty system. The decision to suspend executions was the result of publicity that revealed deep flaws in the process. A group of journalism students from Northwestern University saved Anthony Porter two days before his scheduled execution when they found the real murderer and got him to confess. The *Chicago Tribune* investigated every death penalty case since 1977 and revealed that while Illinois had put twelve convicts to death, thirteen innocent men had been sent to death row and later exonerated. They found dozens of cases where lawyers had provided such poor defenses in capital trials that thirty-three of the attorneys were subsequently suspended or disbarred.[59] Before leaving office in January 2003, Ryan spared the lives of all 163 men and 4 women on death row in Illinois.[60]

   In 2001, the governor of Maryland declared a moratorium while a commission looked into the issue of racial bias. Other jurisdictions also reexamined the death penalty. The Nebraska legislature passed a moratorium bill, but it was vetoed by the governor. However, the lawmakers funded a study that found that a Nebraska suspect was four times more likely to get the death penalty if his victim was financially well-off. Resolutions calling for a halt to executions have passed in a number of cities, moratoria have been considered by at least eighteen state legislatures, and moratorium legislation has been introduced in Congress.[61]

- *Media attention to several notable cases.* The case of Karla Faye Tucker in Texas brought widespread attention to the death penalty and led to a discussion of the purpose it serves. Several longtime proponents of capital punishment, including conservative evangelists Jerry Falwell and Pat Robertson, spoke against her execution. The vindication of Earl Washington in Virginia raised questions about race and the reliability of confessions. Even the generally popular execution of Timothy McVeigh was marked by procedural failures in the federal prosecution. Bob Burtman argues that without continued media scrutiny of capital cases, old myths will flourish. Among these myths he mentions the belief that the death penalty is a deterrent, that defendants have adequate representation, that appeals provide all the necessary safeguards, that the innocent are never executed, and that any problems can be solved by minor repairs to the system.[62]

- *Conservative opposition to the death penalty.* In addition to the spokespeople of the Christian right who raised questions about the Tucker case, other former supporters have spoken out. For example, in 2001 Charles Terrell, the former head of the Texas Department of Correction, asked that the state's death row not show a plaque bearing his name because he had developed concerns about the process.[63] In Virginia, a state legislator who had earlier advocated public hanging introduced legislation to end capital punishment. Frank Hargrove explained that he had changed his position because his conscience bothered him. He feared that innocent people were executed, and he believed that life without parole was a viable alternative.[64]

- *Adding life without parole.* Like Representative Hargrove and like those Americans cited in the polls discussed above, many people would argue that LWOP protects society from dangerous killers. Unlike the death penalty, it is not irreversible.

- *Studies about mistakes.* A number of analyses, especially those done by James Liebman of Columbia University, have examined the high rates of reversal in capital cases. Liebman looked at 5,000 death sentences between 1973 and 1995 and found that more than 68 percent of those cases were reversed by appellate courts. He further discovered that the counties with the highest capital sentencing rate had the highest error rate (71 percent) and those with the lowest capital sentencing rate had the lowest error rate (41 percent). One might conclude that haste and an interest in quantity rather than quality processing explains that fact. The study also showed that reversal rates were twice as high in cases with white victims and higher in jurisdictions with frequent, partisan elections of judges. In general, Liebman's research seems to indicate that truth is most jeopardized in places where capital prosecutions proceed carelessly, without adequate preparation or safeguards, motivated by political rather than public safety concerns.[65]

- *International pressures to end capital punishment.* The international trend is toward abolition and the American position has become more isolated. Since 1976 when the United States reinstated the death penalty, more than seventy nations have eliminated it.[66] Turkey, long known for its tough approach to crime, in 2002 prohibited executions to meet a precondition for membership in the European Union, which adamantly opposed capital punishment as a human rights issue. The United States is one of only two nations, along with Iran, that execute persons who were juveniles at the time of their crime. China, which had formerly been part of that group, recently abolished the death penalty for juveniles.

- *The presidential candidacy and election of George W. Bush.* The 2000 campaign put the national spotlight on Texas, the national leader in executions. Although more than 150 persons were put to death during Bush's tenure as governor, he claimed to be confident that all were guilty and that all "had full access to the courts." But quite a few stories raised questions about due process in Texas. For example, Texas has no public defender system. Individual counties assign counsel and pay for them, sometimes raising property taxes to fund an individual case. Harris County, the death penalty capital of the world, spent $26 million on prosecutions and $11.6 million on defenses in 1998. Defense counsel are appointed by elected judges for whom a speedy trial with few objections is often more desirable than a vigorous representation of the accused. Bush vetoed a bill that would have provided for independent commissions to appoint defense counsel. The Board of Pardons and Paroles, the only body that can grant clemency, does not actually meet. They communicate by fax.[67] A study by the Texas Defender Service says that the quality of appointed lawyers for the appeals stage is as bad as those for trials. They call the appeal system "broken."[68]

Negative publicity during the presidential campaign may have led the next Texas governor, Rick Perry, to support the Fair Defense Act. It still allows county judges to appoint defense attorneys, but it sets minimum standards and provides for funding, reporting requirements, and state monitoring. And although Texans still favored the death penalty in 2001, their support was not without reservations. Sixty-six percent opposed executing the mentally retarded; 76 percent favored a moratorium on executions affected by DNA evidence; and 65 percent acknowledged that Texas had probably executed innocent persons.[69]

All in all, Kirchmeier's points may be seen as part of a larger trend of lessened confidence that capital punishment works. *The Economist* finds "cracks in the apparently solid phalanx of support" for the death penalty, based on mounting evidence that the system works so badly it "makes a mockery of the notion of justice."[70] The press carries many such stories, but a few will suffice to illustrate the point here.

After a death sentence was thrown out in Pennsylvania in 2001, the NAACP Legal Defense Fund noted that prosecutorial misconduct is more pervasive than is generally realized. In this case, the prosecution tampered with evidence by whiting out exculpatory statements by the defendant's wife before handing the materials over to the defense. They did not pass along neighbors' statements implicating someone else. Instead they convicted a retarded African American man with a ninth-grade education who did not even understand why he was being given a new trial. The errors were uncovered eleven years after the original death sentence by a privately funded group, the Defense Association of Philadelphia.[71]

Many questionable cases come out of Texas, where more than two dozen people on death row are foreign nationals, eighteen of them from Mexico. In 2002, Texas executed a Canadian and two Mexican citizens, despite appeals to uphold the 1963 Vienna Convention, which was signed by the United States and which would prohibit such sentences.[72] Texas, which has never executed a white person for the murder of a black person, put Napolean Beazley to death in 2002. Beazley, an African American who was 17 at the time of the crime, was convicted by an all-white jury, with a white judge and prosecutor. One juror commented that the "nigger got what he deserved." Another, a repairman, would not fix appliances belonging to African Americans. In addition, the victim's son, a federal judge from Virginia, "assisted the prosecution" throughout the case.[73] These cases got some attention in the national media, but David Dow argues that most executions are not newsworthy in Texas. Instead, they are so common, so mundane that large newspapers no longer send reporters to death row. One might ask, who is being deterred if no one is paying attention?[74] What purpose is the system serving if death has become routine?

Conclusion

The examples from Texas and Pennsylvania illustrate something important about capital punishment in the United States. There is no one death penalty. The policy is implemented at the state level and, more importantly, at the local level. Prosecutors, judges, and jurors within a jurisdiction determine how and when a person is sentenced to death. Thus there are great differences in capital sentences between Houston and Dallas, between Philadelphia and Pittsburgh, and between Memphis and Nashville. Because the death penalty is implemented locally, there are a variety of points for public opinion to influence policy—at the level of state legislation, but also in the choice of prosecutors and judges.[75] Barbara Norrander notes that just because national polls show that a majority supports capital punishment (and even those numbers are ambiguous if alternatives are offered), public officials should not assume that the same is necessarily true for their area. She further argues that state institutions are embedded in a culture of an earlier era. In other words, capital legislation may have been passed when public opinion was different from what it is today. Policymakers need to find the links between current and past policies and contemporary opinion. They should keep track of how the standards of decency are evolving in their area.[76]

Lifton sees the local differences in the application of the death penalty as a return to the pre-*Furman* situation. He believes that the variations among the fifty states and from county to county, dependant on the makeup of juries and the competence of attorneys, create conditions that are just as arbitrary as those the Supreme Court found unconstitutional in 1972.[77]

Even if this is so, few commentators predict that the Court will return to its *Furman* perspective and abolish the death penalty any time soon. For one thing, the current makeup of the Court is much more conservative and much more likely to defer to the states than the Court of the 1970s. Since that time, it has surrounded the death penalty with "an arcane set of rules that are applied haphazardly."[78] But even with the complex legal framework that regulates executions, the one issue that has the potential to dismantle the structure is the question of actual innocence. Banner argues that if anything could tip the scales against the death penalty it would be the execution of a highly sympathetic and apparently innocent person.[79] *The Economist* agrees that in the event of several cases with incontrovertible proof that states had put innocent people to death, public opinion would be likely to shift definitively against it.[80]

The next chapter will look at the Supreme Court's death penalty jurisprudence since the 1970s. It will examine why the Court found flaws in *Furman* and how it has rebuilt the structure since *Gregg v. Georgia*. It will focus on the Court's use of public opinion in considering "evolving standards of decency" and will consider Justice Blackmun's claim that it is hopeless to "tinker with the machinery of death."

· 2 ·

"A RANDOM ASSORTMENT OF PARIAHS": THE SUPREME COURT CONSIDERS THE DEATH PENALTY

The Eighth Amendment to the Constitution forbids the use of cruel and unusual punishments. The words are simple, but exactly what is prohibited is not so obvious. In the contemporary world a significant number of people argue that the death penalty itself violates the Eighth Amendment. Others would claim that the framers of the Constitution had no qualms about capital punishment. To support this point they cite the Fifth Amendment's guarantee that no one could be deprived of *life*, liberty, or property without due process of law. It is not illogical to read that provision to mean that the deprivation of life would be permissible, if due process were followed. Likewise, the Fifth Amendment's restriction on double jeopardy, providing that no one should twice be forced to risk *life* or limb, implies that one risk of life for a crime is acceptable. Indeed, some legal scholars, including Supreme Court Justice Antonin Scalia, argue that the Eighth Amendment should be read to mean exactly what it meant to the founders, claiming that they did not intend to restrict the use of death itself as a punishment.

When the Constitution was written in the late eighteenth century, "cruel and unusual" included the idea that the punishment should be proportionate to the crime and that punishments not authorized by law were prohibited. In other words, the other branches of government could carry out only the sanctions authorized by the legislature. They could not make it up as they went along. However, in applying the legislated punishments, the courts and the executive enjoyed wide latitude. The Eighth Amendment could also be read to forbid punitive measures that were unnecessarily painful or too oppressive.[1]

Exactly how those punishments were defined seemed to be based on a general notion that the sensibilities of a republic placed a high value on human dignity.

Ultimately, the responsibility for defining "cruel and unusual" rests with the courts, especially the United States Supreme Court. Yet for more than a century, the justices considered few cases that addressed the issue. The idea that the death penalty itself might be unconstitutional because it violated the Eighth Amendment was not brought before the Court until the middle of the twentieth century. There are several reasons for this. The Court, for the most part, assumed that the forbidden cruel and unusual punishments were the obvious tortures and barbaric cruelties that offended any modern civilized community. Everyone knew that boiling in oil or drawing and quartering would not be permitted under the U.S. Constitution. In addition to recognizing a general consensus that there were outer limits to the humane treatment of offenders, the Court stayed away from most discussion of capital punishment because its methods and application were considered matters for the individual states to decide. Until the post–World War II era, the Eighth Amendment, along with the rest of the Bill of Rights, was seen as binding on the federal government but not on the states.[2]

A 1958 decision, *Trop v. Dulles*, although it did not deal with the death penalty, provides the first clear statement from the Court that "cruel and unusual" should be measured against public opinion.[3] The case involved Army Private Trop, who "deserted" his unit for one day in 1944 and was picked up while returning voluntarily to his base. He was convicted of desertion, sentenced to three years at hard labor, and given a dishonorable discharge. Eight years later when he applied for a passport, Trop learned that a dishonorable discharge for wartime desertion meant that he had lost his American citizenship. The law that authorized deprivation of citizenship for wartime desertion was the subject of the Court's opinion. In finding the provision unconstitutional, the Court spelled out the major premises of modern capital punishment jurisprudence. It held that the "basic concept underlying the Eighth Amendment is nothing less than the dignity of man," and that although its words are not precise, *"their scope is not static. The Amendment must draw its meaning from the evolving standards of decency that mark the progress of a maturing society"* (italics added). Thus the Court provided a new test for determining whether a specific penal procedure violated the Constitution, and it indicated that the criteria were dynamic, reflecting changing, and presumably more refined, beliefs about human dignity. "The provisions of the Constitution are not time-worn adages or hollow shibboleths. They are vital, living principles. . . ."

Virtually every Eighth Amendment and capital punishment case that followed *Trop v. Dulles* would invoke the notion of "evolving standards of decency" and wrestle with how to measure those standards.[4] The National Association for the Advancement of Colored People (NAACP) was one group involved during the 1950s and 1960s in bringing cases challenging the application of the death penalty. Among other things, they raised the claim that racial bias in capital sentencing violated the evolving standards. The signal that at least some justices were willing to look at the death penalty in those terms came in 1963. *Rudolph v. Alabama* concerned a black man sentenced to death for the rape of a white woman, a punishment all too common in the segregated South. The Supreme Court declined to hear Rudolph's case, but in a rare procedure, three members of the Court wrote a dissent to that denial of certiorari.[5] Justices Arthur Goldburg, William O. Douglas, and William Brennan questioned whether executing a man for rape violated evolving standards of decency. They cited trends both in the United States and around the world indicating that a death sentence for rape ran counter to standards of decency "more or less universally accepted." Although only a third of the Court expressed those sentiments in 1963, the *Rudolph* dissent contained the seeds of some significant future jurisprudence, including the relationship between race and the application of the death penalty and the issue of how to measure standards of decency. Should the Court consider only public sentiment within the United States or should "universally accepted" beliefs be included in defining the standards?

Between 1963 and 1972, when the Court issued what was arguably one of its most important and most complex decisions in *Furman v. Georgia,*[6] the NAACP was busy assembling arguments against the death penalty. Among other things, they developed and presented social science research on racial bias and arbitrariness in its application. They also attempted to block all executions (a de facto moratorium) while the constitutional issues were being litigated.[7] In fact, no state executed a convict between 1967 and 1977.

In 1972, the Court heard three death penalty cases grouped under the title *Furman v. Georgia.*[8] Furman was a black man who had shot a white homeowner, apparently by accident, during a robbery. The other two cases from Georgia and Texas involved rapes in which the offenders were black and the victims white. No injury aside from the rape had occurred in either case. All three defendants were sentenced to death. Each justice wrote a separate opinion and, although a majority of five members of the Court found that the death penalty as administered was unconstitutional, the explanations for their holdings varied greatly. Meanwhile, four Justices found no constitutional flaws with the system of capital punishment. Our major interest is how they reconciled their positions with the notion of evolving standards of decency.

Among those who voted to uphold the death sentences, Chief Justice Warren Burger did not find evidence that the public opposed them. He wrote that for a punishment to be considered "inordinately cruel," it must be "so perceived by the society so characterizing it." Just because capital punishment was rarely inflicted, one could not assume that the public had made such a moral judgment. Nor, in response to those who claimed that the death penalty was arbitrary and discriminatory, did Burger think it proper to assume that "only a random assortment of pariahs" was sentenced to death.

Justice Lewis Powell, who also voted to uphold the Georgia law, grappled with the evolving standards issue. He allowed that both standards of decency and due process unfolded over time and cited as evidence the fact that certain crimes and certain criminals were no longer eligible for death. But to Powell (as to many other justices), the only objective ways to assess contemporary standards were through the actions of legislatures and the decisions of juries. Neither, in his view, had found capital punishment per se to be cruel and unusual, and therefore unconstitutional. Without that endorsement from lawmakers and jurors, Powell believed, the Court could not move further.

In 1972, Justice Harry Blackmun agreed with Powell. After expressing his personal distaste for capital punishment, he argued that the Court could not decide the issue for the public. He did, nonetheless, endorse the notion of evolving standards by citing a strong statement from Thomas Jefferson. "Laws and institutions must go hand in hand with the progress of the human mind. As that becomes more developed, more enlightened, as new discoveries are made, new truths disclosed, and manners and opinions change with a change of circumstances, institutions must advance also and keep pace with the times. We might as well require a man to wear still the coat that fitted him when a boy, as civilized society to remain forever under the regime of their barbarous ancestors." Later in his career on the bench, Blackmun would retract his support for capital punishment, concluding that the system could never be sufficiently reformed to meet the requisite standards of fairness.

On the other hand, by 1972 Justice William Brennan had concluded that capital punishment was, by definition, unconstitutional. He believed that evolving standards of decency were the starting point of the argument. Punishments that were degrading to human dignity violated the standards and were therefore cruel. Degrading punishments were not just those that caused pain, but those that treated people as less than human, "as objects to be toyed with and discarded." Such treatment was inconsistent with the premise that "even the vilest criminal remains a human being possessed of common human dignity." If contemporary society rejected a punishment, that was an indication that the punishment did not comport with human dignity. The test of society's acceptance or rejection? According to Brennan, it was not just the laws on the books but actual practice, not the availability of a procedure but its use. As for the death penalty, there was widespread authorization for its use but Americans apparently felt a "deep-seated reluctance to inflict it." He argued that its "rejection could hardly be more complete without becoming absolute." For him, capital punishment failed every constitutional test. It was unusually severe. There was a strong possibility of its arbitrary and biased use. It was substantially rejected by the contemporary society, and it accomplished no greater purpose than less severe punishments. In Brennan's view, standards of decency had already evolved to the point where the death penalty was not acceptable. It remained only for the Court to formalize that position by declaring it unconstitutional.

To Justice Douglas, the definition of cruel and unusual was not "fastened to the obsolete but may acquire meaning as public opinion becomes enlightened by a humane justice." He focused particularly on those who were sentenced to death under the existing system. Douglas found they were outcasts, members of unpopular groups "whom society is willing to see suffer though it would not countenance general application of the same penalty across the board." His opinion is complex and raises some troubling issues. Douglas seems to be saying that enlightened opinion rejects capital punishment for the majority but is willing to tolerate it for those against whom prejudices persist. The logic of his argument is that the Court must prod the evolving standards in the right direction, making them more inclusive.

Thurgood Marshall, the first African American justice on the Supreme Court, reiterated that the cruel and unusual clause must be continually examined "in light of contemporary human knowledge." He held that capital punishment was excessive and that it served no valid purpose that a lesser punishment might not serve as well. But even if it were not excessive and even if it served a valid purpose, it would be unconstitutional "if popular sentiment abhors it." In that case, "if citizens found it morally unacceptable," the death penalty would take its place with those punishments banned since the adoption of the Eighth Amendment. Marshall then went on to make an ingenious argument for public rejection of capital punishment. He acknowledged that public opinion polls showing a favorable view had some validity, but he argued for probing more deeply. He saw more than a question of whether the "mere mention [of the death penalty] shocks the conscience and sense of justice of the people." That was clearly not the case. But, he inquired, if people were *fully informed* about the death penalty, would they find it "shocking, unjust, and unacceptable?" He argued that an informed public would reject "purposeless vengeance." They would not tolerate a system whose burden falls upon the "poor, ignorant, and underprivileged and members of minority groups least able to make their complaints." Inertia should not be mistaken for support. "So long as the capital sanction is used only against the forlorn, easily forgotten members of society, legislators are content to maintain the status quo, because change would draw attention to the problem and concern might develop. Ignorance is perpetuated and apathy soon becomes its mate." If, however, the average citizen had all the facts, he or she would find capital pun-ishment "shocking to [the] conscience and sense of justice." Retention of the death penalty in Marshall's view did not prove that it conformed to contempo-rary standards of decency, but rather demonstrated that most people were not aware how much the system deviated from those standards.

Justice Marshall was not naïve. He had experienced prejudice and intoler-ance throughout his own life and had observed its force in the lives of count-less other African Americans. Yet he argued eloquently that racial and class bi-ases in the administration of capital punishment would offend the white majority to the point that they would reject it, if they knew how flawed the system was. To a considerable degree, this book takes up a thread of Marshall's claim as it argues that for most Americans, knowledge about the failings in the system will come, not from reading scholarly research about it, but from the humanizing force of popular books and movies.

The results of *Furman* were numerous. For the inmates on death rows around the country it meant that their sentences would not be carried out. They remained in prison but dates with the executioner were cancelled. The decision was followed by a series of rulings that bolstered the rights of the ac-cused in criminal proceedings. To supporters, the Court was standardizing criminal procedure to ensure its evenhanded application, trying to minimize the effects of racism, and to some, promoting social change through an inno-vative reading of the Constitution.[9] For others who were more conservative, *Furman* was an outrage and a call to action, definitive proof that the Supreme Court had gone too far in favoring "criminals." Stuart Banner says that the death penalty became a "terrain of cultural argument," a symbolic way for pol-iticians and the public to "get tough on crime" and to hold offenders morally responsible.[10] Polls showed a rise in support for capital punishment after 1972. Many state legislatures rushed to get new laws on the books that would meet the constitutional objections of *Furman*.[11] Evolving standards of decency would become the test by which the new laws and procedures were measured.

The Court had found the laws at issue in *Furman* arbitrary and capricious, allowing too much discretion to juries, and permitting the consideration of unacceptable factors such as race. North Carolina was one state that tried to meet these concerns by making the death penalty mandatory for certain of-fenses. To the majority of the Supreme Court in *Woodson v. North Carolina*, this approach violated contemporary standards of decency.[12] They cited evidence that juries had historically rejected mandatory sentences as too harsh and as failing to take into account the circumstances of an individual case. Jurors often dealt with this dilemma by nullification. If required to sentence a sympathetic defendant to death, they simply found him not guilty. In the Court's eyes, such a practice showed a repudiation of mandatory death sentences, proof that they violated the community's standards. The justices also held that death was inappropriate for a "substantial portion of first degree murderers." A law making it mandatory "departs markedly from contemporary standards respecting the imposition of the punishment of death and thus cannot be applied consistent with the Eighth and Fourteenth Amendments' requirement that the State's power to punish be exercised within the limits of civilized standards."

On the same day they ruled against the North Carolina law, the Court upheld a new Georgia capital statute, again invoking the contemporary standards of decency.[13] The majority in *Gregg v. Georgia* read the eagerness of thirty-five states to create new death penalty laws since *Furman* as significant evidence that the punishment itself did not violate public sensibilities. They also found that the relative infrequency of capital sentencing by juries did not indicate reservations about the policy but a sense that death should be reserved for the worst cases. They interpreted the isolated use of the death penalty as a sort of endorsement. In addition, the Court stated that even if capital punishment did not actually serve to deter crime or to protect the public, retribution toward the offender was acceptable as a justification. A death sentence could serve as an "expression of the community's belief that certain crimes are themselves so grievous an affront to humanity that the only adequate response may be the penalty of death." Finally they deferred to the theory of federalism, holding that each legislature can evaluate the moral consensus in its particular state. Thus in *Gregg v. Georgia* the Court proclaimed that the states had succeeded in fixing the flaws in the old capital statutes that had placed them at odds with the contemporary standards of decency. Either that or the standards had evolved away from an aversion to the death penalty to approval of it in a period of five years. Three members of the Court, Chief Justice Burger and Justices Byron White and William Rehnquist, expressed a less optimistic but more ominous view in their concurrence. In response to the argument that no government could administer the death penalty without discrimination or mistakes, they acknowledged that "mistakes will be made and discriminations will occur which will be difficult to explain." But they seemed to imply that the Court would not interfere with the states' enforcement even in the face of such errors and biases.

Justice Marshall's dissent reiterated his view that the constitutionality of the death penalty rested on the opinion of informed citizens. He discounted the rush to enact new capital sentencing laws as indicative of contemporary standards because the American people still knew little about the death penalty. "The opinions of an informed public would differ significantly from those of a public unaware of the consequences and effects of the death penalty." The latter might be less willing to tolerate the mistakes and discriminations mentioned by White, Burger, and Rehnquist.

Marshall also found the majority's endorsement of retribution as a purpose of capital punishment contrary to the Eighth Amendment. "To be sustained under the Eighth Amendment, the death penalty must comport with the basic concept of human dignity at the core of the Amendment; the objective in imposing it must be consistent with our respect for the dignity of other men . . . Under these standards, the taking of life 'because the wrongdoer deserves it' surely must fail, for such a punishment has as its very basis the total denial of the wrongdoer's dignity and worth."

Gregg was a 7–2 decision. From that point forward, the Court has operated on the assumption that the death penalty per se does not violate evolving standards of decency. It has constructed an elaborate body of capital punishment law that provides for a process of guided discretion in choosing who will die. It frequently calls on the notion of evolving standards when looking at the application of the death penalty to particular groups or for particular categories of crimes.

The Evolution of Evolving Standards

One of the earliest such cases finally addressed the question of whether the death penalty for the rape of an adult woman violated the Constitution. In *Coker v. Georgia* the Court found that as Georgia was the only state that treated rape as a capital crime in its new post-*Furman* law, such legislation no longer conformed to standards of decency.[14] All other state legislatures had rejected the opportunity to continue to sentence rapists of adult women to death. The Court believed this reflected a public consensus that the punishment was disproportionate to the crime. It is ironic that the issue of race was not raised in *Coker*. This was one of the rare capital convictions for rape where both the victim and the offender were white.

Another situation where execution could seem disproportionate to the crime is felony-murder. An accomplice is sentenced to death even though he did not actually kill anyone. Rather he participated in a crime in which someone was murdered. Does such a policy comport with the Eighth Amendment? Does it violate standards of decency? In 1982, the Court considered this question in *Enmund v. Florida*.[15] Earl Enmund drove the getaway car for a robbery that resulted in the murder of an elderly couple at their farmhouse. Nothing placed Enmund near the shooting or indicated that he had any intention of killing anyone. The majority of the Court found that Florida's law permitting the execution of an accomplice who did not kill or intend to kill unconstitutional. They reasoned that society had rejected such punishment and cited as evidence the fact that only eight states considered such limited participation in a murder as a capital offense. In addition, they found that juries overwhelmingly rejected the death penalty in such cases. Other than Enmund, only two out of 789 death row inmates in the nation had been sentenced without being physically present when the murder was committed. The Court majority did not rely only on the behavior of legislatures and juries, however, noting that "it is for us ultimately to judge whether the Eighth Amendment permits imposition of the death penalty on one who aids and abets but . . . who does not himself kill, attempt to kill, or intend that a killing take place or that lethal force will be employed. We had concluded, along with most legislatures, that it does not." Thus while five justices considered the usual measures of contemporary standards, they also acknowledged that they had a responsibility beyond checking the public pulse to apply the Constitution as they believed it should be applied.

Justice Sandra Day O'Connor wrote the *Enmund* dissent in which she read the support for felony-murder in a way that differed from the majority. In her calculation, "nearly half the States" would permit Enmund's execution. (Thus she found more than eight, but less than a majority.) "These legislative judgments indicate that our 'evolving standards of decency' still embrace capital punishment for this crime." O'Connor's argument raises the question of how few or how many states should be used as the measure of evolving standards. Can the Court arbitrarily decide what meets the test of contemporary standards? Or does it actually decide on a constitutional interpretation and then simply choose a way to read public sentiment that supports that view?

Five years later, Justice O'Connor had the opportunity to write for the Court in another felony-murder case, *Tison v. Arizona*.[16] This time Raymond and Ricky Tison were sentenced to death for participation in a kidnapping and robbery in which four members of a family were killed. Neither shot the victims. Their father, who had broken out of jail and had apparently done the shooting, died of exposure in the desert. The Court upheld the Tison death sentences and distinguished the case from Enmund. On the one hand, Justice O'Connor found that Raymond and Ricky's participation in the murders was greater than Enmund's and therefore, they were "more guilty." She also used the same statistical arguments as in the previous case, indicating that contemporary standards would support the punishment. The Court noted that only eleven death penalty states did *not* have felony-murder laws. The dissenters, on the other hand, found that if non-death-penalty states were included, three-fifths of the states did not allow the death penalty for those who neither kill nor intend to kill. Again, the two sets of justices were at odds over how to read the contemporary standards.

The dissenters made another point about evolving standards, suggesting that although *Tison* may have coincided with popular sentiment that called for vengeance based on the heinousness of the crime, such motives for punishment were anachronistic. "The urge to employ the felony-murder doctrine against accomplices is undoubtedly strong when the killings stir public passion and the actual murderer is beyond human grasp. And an intuition that sons and daughters must sometimes be punished for the sins of the fathers may be deeply rooted in our consciousness. Yet punishment that conforms more closely to such retributive instincts than to the Eighth Amendment is tragically anachronistic in a society governed by our Constitution." An anachronism, by definition, fails to reflect contemporary standards. It is something from an earlier time, superimposed on the present where it does not belong.

Yet the desire to avenge victims was a popular one. If such feelings were anachronistic and should have been rejected by a modern civilized society, the Court seemed more willing to take them into consideration when it ruled in *Payne v. Tennessee*.[17]

Payne concerned the admissibility of victim impact statements. In determining whether to sentence a person to death, a jury considers two sets of circumstances, aggravating (those that add to the seriousness of the crime) and mitigating (those that help to explain the offender's behavior). Can statements from the survivors or relatives of the victim be included among the aggravating factors? Should the decision to execute a person be influenced by pain caused to people whose existence he may not even know about? In the case of *Payne*, a young mother and her daughter had been murdered. The victim's mother was allowed to testify that the victim's other child, a small boy, missed his mother and his sister and often asked for them. The Court held that if a state legislature decided a jury should hear testimony about the victim, such statements were not unconstitutional. Justice O'Connor's concurrence referred to a "strong societal consensus" in favor of victim impact evidence. Justice Scalia's concurrence takes that point even further. He argued that the victims' rights movement proved that the public's sense of justice demanded that the defendant be held accountable, even for the unanticipated consequences of his actions. Commenting on the *Payne* decision, Austin Sarat finds that it reflects a political climate where vengeance and emotionalism are admitted to the capital process, in complete opposition to the Court's intention in *Furman*. Victim impact statements, in his view, personalize criminal justice and force jurors to identify with either the victim or the offender.[18] They reflect a popular desire for retribution, which may be a regressing rather than an evolving standard of decency.

The dissent in *Payne* makes some similar points. Justice Stevens wrote that victim impact statements have a "strong political appeal but no proper place in a reasoned judicial opinion." He continued, "Given the current popularity of capital punishment in a crime-ridden society, the political appeal of arguments that assume that increasing the severity of sentences is the best cure for the cancer of crime, and the political strength of the 'victims' rights movement,' I recognize that today's decision will be greeted with enthusiasm. . . ." Stevens, however, considered the decision a great tragedy because of "the danger that the 'hydraulic pressure of public opinion' has played a role in . . . [the Court's] resolution of the Constitutional issue. Today is a sad day for a great institution."[19] He would agree with those who see victim impact statements as a sort of referendum on the murdered person's worth tilting the jury toward a death sentence. If jurors do not vote for the death penalty, the victim's family might interpret this as devaluing their loved one.

As with *Tison*, the dissenters in *Payne* were dismayed at what they saw as the Court's willingness to interpret the Constitution in a way that caved in to popular outcries for vengeance. The Court in these decisions seems to wrestle with the hard task of distinguishing, for the purpose of defining evolving standards, between reasoned public opinion and intense public emotion.

Structural Issues

Another way of looking at the death penalty debate involves returning to Justice Marshall's formulation. If citizens were really informed about the problems with the capital punishment system, would their enthusiasm evaporate? It they knew about structural flaws in the system related to race and class, would they reject it? The Court has considered some of these weaknesses in the structure of capital punishment with mixed results.

In 1987 the justices ruled on what is considered the most powerful challenge to racial disparities in the sentence of death. *McCleskey v. Kemp* involved the question of whether race was a factor in the administration of the death penalty in Georgia.[20] Warren McCleskey, who was black, had been sentenced to die for the shooting of a white police officer. His appeal was based largely on a massive statistical report, the Baldus study, showing among other things that the killer of a white person was more than four times more likely to be sentenced to death than the killer of a black person. Thus the race of the victim appeared to play an impermissible role in deciding which offenders lived and which died. McCleskey argued that this bias in the system violated his constitutional right to equal protection.

The majority of the Court disagreed. They held that McCleskey would need to show that racial bias had existed in his own case, not just that it infected the system as a whole. (This approach was in direct contradiction to *Furman*, which found that systemic flaws rendered the death penalty unconstitutional.)

They also noted that although the Baldus study showed a "discrepancy that appears to correlate with race," it did not constitute an "unacceptable risk of racial prejudice." Finally, they observed that if McCleskey's claim of racial bias were taken to its logical conclusion, the whole criminal justice system would be thrown into question. The Constitution, Justices Powell, Rehnquist, White, O'Connor, and Scalia determined, did not require that all discrepancies be eliminated in order to permit capital punishment.

Justices Brennan, Marshall, Blackmun, and Stevens dissented. They argued that analysis of the statistical data showed that by any imaginable standard, the "risk that race influenced McCleskey's sentence is intolerable." They were certain that "we should not be willing to take a person's life if the chance that his death sentence was irrationally imposed is more likely than not." Suppose people were willing to tolerate a few racial disparities in the justice system? The Court was expected to do more than just reflect popular opinion. "Those whom we would banish from society or from the human community itself often speak in too faint a voice to be heard above society's demand for punishment. It is the particular role of courts to hear these voices, for the Constitution declares that the majoritarian chorus may not alone dictate the conditions of social life. The Court thus fulfills, rather than disrupts the scheme of separation of powers by closely scrutinizing the imposition of the death penalty, for no decision of a society is more deserving of 'sober second thought.'" Here the dissenters noted again that sometimes the Court needed to go beyond—to lead rather than follow—public opinion in the interest of protecting the minority from the tyranny of the majority.[21] Suppose the public knew what the Court learned in *McCleskey*, that decisions about the death penalty were correlated with race, would they reconsider their support? Sadly, one person who did reconsider his support was Justice Lewis Powell, who had voted with the five-member majority to reject McCleskey's claim. After his retirement from the Court, Powell told his biographer that if he could do it over, he would cast his vote the other way.[22] As things stood, however, *McCleskey* was the last time the Court considered racial bias and its implications for capital punishment. Later studies have shown that the anomalies revealed in the Baldus study are replicated throughout the system.[23]

If one can argue that race plays a role in who is sentenced to death, few would dispute the point that class is also a factor. One frequently hears the comment, "There are no millionaires on death row." Instead, virtually every person sentenced to death could be classified as "poor." Few had the money to hire private attorneys. Rather, they depended on the state to supply them with legal representation. Most Americans are aware that if one cannot afford an attorney, one will be appointed. What most may not know is what the Court considers adequate representation.

Ineffective assistance of counsel is frequently the grounds for appeal in death penalty cases. A 1984 decision, *Strickland v. Washington*, remains the standard for determining whether the defendant's lawyer provided representation that meets the constitutional standard.[24] The *Strickland* rule has two parts. The defendant has the burden of proof that the lawyer's performance was inadequate. He must demonstrate that his attorney made errors that a reasonable advocate would not make. In addition, the defendant must show that the mistakes were harmful to his case, that they affected the outcome and actually prevented him from having a fair trial. The *Strickland* standard sets the bar very high for finding assistance ineffective. As discussed in the introduction, many shocking performances by lawyers have been tolerated in capital cases.

Burger v. Kemp in 1987 provided an early example of the application of the *Strickland* standard.[25] At Burger's sentencing hearing, his court-appointed counsel introduced no mitigating evidence. During the appeal process, the lawyer defended this behavior as an intentional strategy. He claimed he had made a "reasonable professional judgment" that the defendant should not have a psychological examination and that no witnesses could assist his case. A majority of the Court accepted this rationalization. The four dissenters found the attorney's behavior "outside the range of professional competence." He did not present evidence that the defendant was an adolescent with psychological problems. Most importantly, he decided not to invite Burger's former mentor, a black attorney, to testify, arguing that such a witness might make an unfavorable impression on the jury because of his race. The dissenters were most offended that the defense attorney made no effort to investigate this racial bias. In *Burger v. Kemp*, the Court seemed to signal that the expectations for legal representation are minimal.

In 1989, *Murray v. Giarratano* addressed another question of representation. Do inmates sentenced to death have the right to counsel for post-conviction appeals?[26] At the time, Virginia provided death row inmates with access to the law library and with "unit attorneys" who served the entire correctional facility, but not with personal lawyers after the initial appeal. Giarratano, along with others under sentence of death, argued that these provisions were insufficient in view of the complexity of death penalty law, the limited time available to them, and the distraction of preparing for death at the same time they needed to pursue appeals. The majority of the Court held that the Constitution requires only that counsel be provided at trial, not after trial when the proceedings are civil in nature. The special constraints relating to capital punishment, especially the greater need for accuracy because of the finality of the outcome, apply only at the trial. There, the Court held, there were sufficient safeguards to "assure the reliability of the process." Justice Kennedy noted in concurrence that the states must have wide discretion to determine how much legal assistance to provide after the trial and initial appeal. He seemed to suggest that there was no national benchmark, no evolving standard.

With decisions like *Burger* that held appointed counsel to a very low standard, and *Giarratano* that limited access to counsel after conviction, the constitutional right to an attorney for death row inmates was in danger of becoming a mere formality. The dissenters in *Giarratano* found this a cause for concern. They maintained that it was fundamentally unfair for a capital defendant to be expected to initiate post-conviction appeals "without counsel's guiding hand." Since the 1930s, the Court had held that capital defendants had a greater access to counsel than others because death is qualitatively different from any other punishment. The "grim deadline" faced by those on death row was unlike any other sentence. Obviously the chance to rectify faults in the initial trial required scrutiny by someone trained in the law. Without such expertise, the appeals process became a sham. The dissenters turned to evolving standards—what did other states do about providing attorneys for appeals? They found that only five death penalty states did not have a system for appointing counsel for collateral appeals and that only Virginia and Nevada had actually executed people without provision for appeals counsel. Thus, at the time, thirty-one death penalty states did provide counsel as Giarratano requested. That would seem an excellent example of the kind of test of evolving standards the Court chose to use in other cases.

Since *Giarratano*, things seem to have gotten worse for defendants needing appellate counsel. The federal government has defunded the death penalty centers that provided experienced defense attorneys for capital appeals. Some states may be involved in a "race to the bottom" when it comes to providing appellate attorneys. Alabama, for example, requires that those under capital sentence file a *proper pro se petition* in order to be assigned counsel. It comes close to a mockery of justice to think that death row inmates, without legal help, can put together the exact petition that the state requires. If such an unlikely event occurs, and an attorney is appointed, he or she will have only limited access to the client and will receive a maximum of $1,000 for the entire case.[27]

A 2002 case, also out of Virginia, provides further evidence that a majority of the Court are satisfied with minimal legal representations for death penalty defendants. The attorney who was appointed to represent the accused in *Mickens v. Taylor* had previously represented the victim.[28] The judge who appointed him as lawyer for Mickens knew this, the attorney knew it, but Mickens the defendant did not know. He only found out about his counsel's previous association with the victim when a clerk gave his appeals attorney the wrong file by mistake. Mickens appealed, of course, on the grounds that he was denied effective assistance of counsel because his lawyer had a conflict of interest. To many observers, this conflict was obvious. Who would go out and hire a lawyer who until yesterday was representing their adversary?

Five members of the Supreme Court did not see that conflict. They applied the *Strickland* standard and held that Mickens did not show that having the same attorney as the victim had harmed his case. He could not prove that the lawyer's performance was adversely affected by his previous association with the victim. Mickens's death sentence stood.

The four dissenters were incredulous. They could not say whether Mickens would have been sentenced to death without the conflict, but they knew that he did not receive the legal representation the Constitution guarantees. Foisting the victim's lawyer on the accused was not just capricious; it "poisons the integrity of the judicial system." They assumed that the attorney had taken the case for the money and for the publicity. Attorneys with such faulty ethics were unlikely to be deterred in the future because the Court's ruling blamed the client for his ignorance about the lawyer's history. Justices Breyer and Ginsberg wrote a separate dissent arguing that the conflict of interest was egregious. The fact that it was a capital case made the injustice worse. The state of Virginia through the judge had created the conflict; the defendant should not have to prove harm. The state "seeks to execute a defendant, having provided that defendant with a lawyer who, only yesterday represented the victim. A death sentence so obtained would invariably diminish faith in the fairness and integrity of the criminal justice system."

We might return to Justice Marshall's formulation. Would the public support execution if they were more aware of how the Court has interpreted the right to counsel? Would such cases diminish their "faith in the fairness and integrity" of the capital system? Many legal ethicists were severely troubled by the Mickens case. They argued that effective assistance of counsel must mean lawyers who "comply at a minimum with professional rules of conduct." Speaking for the ethics experts, Lawrence J. Fox told the *National Law Journal* that the justices in the majority did not recognize that "the devastating effects of a conflicted representation can never be demonstrated because you've got an impoverished record that is a result of a conflicted representation." The case seems to reveal the very different attitudes toward the death penalty among the members of the Court. The Chief Justice and Justices O'Connor, Kennedy, Scalia, and Thomas seem "impatient for executions to proceed unless there is a plausible showing of innocence," not just a procedural problem. The usual dissenters, Justices Stevens, Souter, Ginsberg, and Breyer, are "anxious to take every extra step to ensure there are not improper proceedings."[29]

The cases discussed above and many others illustrate that the problems with lawyers in capital proceedings are not just a series of poor performances by individuals, but severe flaws in the whole system that provides legal services to the indigent.[30] Penny White, a former judge, provides further support for the argument that the issues are systemic. She argues that the *Strickland* standard means that even if counsel is deplorable, a judge may deny relief based on the assumption that the jury would have sentenced the defendant to death anyway. How would a judge be certain of this? When Congress attempted to address the issue of attorney competence by establishing minimal standards, the National Association of District Attorneys opposed it. Their position suggests that prosecutors hope to take every advantage to get a conviction, despite the lack of decent representation and the "poverty and powerlessness" of the accused. A poorly prepared defense attorney means fewer questions about prosecutorial misconduct, whether this misconduct involves attempts to keep minorities off juries or appeals to fear, hate, and intimidation in closing arguments.[31]

Another issue that involves fairness and public opinion is what a judge must tell a jury about alternatives to a death sentence. We have shown in Chapter 1 that surveys indicate a substantial decline in support for capital punishment when life in prison without parole (LWOP) is offered as an option. Should jurors be informed if LWOP is an choice in the case before them? In *Simmons v. South Carolina* the Court said yes.[32] Here the prosecutor tried to stack the deck. He knew that the defendant would be ineligible for parole if he was sentenced to life, but he argued nonetheless that the accused posed a threat of future dangerousness unless he was sentenced to death. The judge refused to let the defense attorney mention that his client was ineligible for parole, and when the jury asked the meaning of "life sentence," the judge would not clarify the term. In this case, a majority of the Supreme Court held that Simmons's right to due process had been violated. The prosecutor intentionally misled the jury and "misunderstanding pervaded the jury's deliberations." It could be argued that the players in the courtroom—the judge and the prosecutor—intentionally tried to thwart the will of the legislature (which provided the option of LWOP) and the jury (who sought clarification about the meaning of a life sentence). Perhaps the prosecutor and judge realized that standards of decency had evolved away from the outcome they desired and they tried to push things the other way.

The Supreme Court seemed to change directions in *Weeks v. Angelone* when they upheld the death penalty in a 5–4 decision.[33] Again the jury was confused. They asked the judge to clarify whether finding one aggravating circumstance meant they *must* choose the death penalty or if they could choose life without parole. Rather than answering the question, the judge pointed them to a paragraph in his original instructions. As the jury already had a written copy of those instructions, they were asking the judge to explain the alternatives. After he refused, they deliberated for two more hours and returned a verdict of death. When the jury was polled about the sentence, a majority of them were in tears. It was clear that a number of jurors did not want to vote for death, but they believed the judge's instructions required that result. The failure to explain that there was an alternative seems terribly unfair. How can a jury's decision be a reflection of the community's standards if the members of the jury are not given all the information they need to reach that decision?

Categories of Defendants

Another example of the Court's attention to evolving standards of decency involves questions of whether the execution of certain categories of defendants—the insane, the mentally retarded, juveniles, the factually innocent—violates those norms. On the one hand, the issue of insanity seems fairly clear. If a person is judged legally insane at the time a crime is committed, he would be found not guilty by reason of insanity. Such a defendant would not be punished but sent to a mental facility. Likewise, if someone is judged incompetent to stand trial, his case will be postponed. However, the matter of people who are considered mentally ill but not insane when they commit a crime is much more problematical. Mental illness is generally viewed as a mitigating circumstance, but how it affects the outcome of a case will vary greatly. The Court has, however, determined in *Ford v. Wainwright* that a person who was sane at the time of his crime and his trial but subsequently became insane could not be executed.[34] Justice Marshall wrote for the majority that executing an insane person not only violated contemporary standards, it also ran counter to English and American common law tradition and offended basic humanity. No punitive purpose would be served if the state were to kill an insane person. Even retribution became meaningless if the offender did not comprehend what was happening to him. Marshall cited the lack of a single state statute authorizing the execution of the insane as proof of the evolution of the standard. It must be noted that despite the ruling in *Ford v. Wainwright*, the question of whether a state may medicate an inmate to make him "sane" enough for the death penalty to be carried out remains unresolved.

The Court has considered the question of executing the mentally retarded several times in the last two decades, most recently in 2002 in *Atkins v. Virginia*.[35] Thirteen years earlier in *Penry v. Lynaugh* the Justices found insufficient evidence of a national consensus that it was cruel and unusual to put the retarded to death.[36] In the interim, a number of state legislatures voted to ban the execution of the mentally retarded. The Court found these prohibitions a "consistent trend" in public sentiment. They noted that a punishment may violate the Eighth Amendment depending not on the standards at the time the Bill of Rights was adopted but on the standards that currently prevail. "The dignity of man" underlies the prohibition against cruel and unusual punishment and that phrase takes its meaning from evolving standards of decency. They also cited procedural problems involved in cases with retarded defendants. Given the greater likelihood of error because such defendants would not understand the process or would confess in their eagerness to agree with authority figures, the increased chance of wrongful conviction was unacceptable.

The three dissenters, Chief Justice Rehnquist and Justices Scalia and Thomas, could not disagree more. They argued that the Bill of Rights means precisely what it meant to the founding fathers. In a very acerbic dissent, Justice Scalia questioned the very notion of evolving standards.[37]

Some of the same issues that relate to the mentally retarded also pertain to whether juveniles should be subject to the death penalty. In 1989, the same day it decided *Penry*, the Court by a vote of 5 to 4 found in *Stanford v. Kentucky* that the execution of someone who was sixteen years old at the time of the crime did not violate the Eighth Amendment.[38] Justice Scalia wrote for the majority, holding that American society "as a whole" did not reject the policy, that because a majority of capital punishment states permitted such punishment, it did not violate evolving standards. Although juries rarely sentenced juveniles to death, this fact demonstrated to the Court's satisfaction that juries found it acceptable—in those rare cases. The argument that juveniles could not vote, drink legally, enlist in the army, or marry only demonstrated a consensus that the majority of youths were immature. But criminal justice laws are meant to be individualized. Therefore it did not contradict the consensus view to execute the occasional (presumably more mature) juvenile killer. Nor was scientific evidence of more impulsiveness among juveniles considered relevant. Finally, the Court rejected the argument that virtually every other democratic country prohibited the execution of juveniles as unrelated to American values. In *Stanford*, the only measure of evolving standards that seemed to matter to the majority was a tally of death penalty state laws.

The four dissenters found it relevant that a majority of states (if non-death-penalty states were counted) and the rest of the world rejected the execution of juveniles. If nothing else, *Stanford* demonstrates again that calculating evolving standards of decency is a very inexact science.

In 2002, Justices Stevens, Ginsberg, and Breyer voted to issue a stay of execution for Toronto Patterson, who was seventeen at the time of his crime, so they could once again hear arguments on the constitutionality of the death penalty for juveniles. As at least four votes are required for the Court to consider a case, Patterson's appeal was denied. However, many observers consider that, barring drastic changes in the membership of the Court, they will look at a juvenile death penalty case relatively soon. It seems significant that a third of the justices think that Patterson raised a "sufficiently plausible (constitutional) claim to warrant a hearing."[39]

Some may argue that being under the age of seventeen or having an IQ below 70 should not spare a guilty person's life. Few would argue that wrongfully convicted innocent persons should be put to death, whether or not their trial met the minimum standards of due process. If anything meets the standard of legal procedures that "shock the conscience" and violate the Constitution, surely executing the innocent causes that shock. Yet arguably the Court's 1993 decision in *Herrera v. Collins* creates the potential for the state to kill innocent people.[40]

A Texas jury convicted Herrera in the killing of two police officers. Ten years later, he claimed that new evidence had emerged proving that he was "actually innocent." In a 6 to 3 decision, the Court denied Herrera's appeal. They found, among other things, that Herrera had had a fair trial, that the Texas law prohibiting the introduction of new evidence more than thirty days after sentencing did not deny him due process, and that if he had claims of innocence, he should take them to the governor and ask for clemency. The criminal justice system needs "finality." According to the Court, Herrera's claim fell far short of the high threshold required for reopening his case. Three of the majority, Justices O'Connor, Kennedy, and White wrote concurrences stating that the execution of an innocent person would be "constitutionally intolerable" and unconstitutional. This was true whether the criterion was "contrary to contemporary standards of decency," "shocking to the conscience," or "offensive to a principle of justice so rooted in the traditions or conscience of our people as to be ranked as fundamental." But they also held that "at some point in time, the State's interest in finality must outweigh the prisoner's interest in another round of litigation." If that point came before the defendant had a chance to bring forward his claim (perhaps because he had an inadequate attorney), then it was clearly possible that an innocent person could be put to death.

That possibility did not seem to bother Justices Scalia and Thomas, who also wrote a concurrence claiming that there was no constitutional right to "demand judicial consideration of newly discovered evidence of innocence brought forward after conviction." If that rule "shocks the dissenters' conscience . . . perhaps they should doubt the calibration of their consciences, or better still, the usefulness of 'conscience shocking' as a legal test." From that concurrence, many have seen a willingness among some justices to allow the execution of innocent persons as merely a collateral cost of maintaining an efficient system.

The three dissenters, Justices Blackmun, Stevens, and Souter, thought the majority was overly eager to do away with any obstacles to the "States' power to execute whomever and however they please." But such haste threatened constitutional protections. The dissenters were certain that "just as an execution without adequate safeguards is unacceptable, so too is an execution when the condemned prisoner can prove he is innocent. The execution of such a person . . . comes perilously close to simple murder." They also noted that clemency was not a reliable remedy for wrongful convictions. Constitutional rights should not depend on the "unreviewable discretion of an executive officer of an administrative tribunal." The majority opinion was much more optimistic about the value of clemency, although their evidence consisted of a 1932 study that showed that in forty-seven out of sixty-five cases of actual innocence, clemency provided relief. The fate of the other eighteen innocent defendants was not revealed, nor was the likelihood that modern governors would grant clemency, even to the innocent.

Many comments on the *Herrera* decision maintain that the Court valued finality over justice, that they were more concerned with procedure than with truth.[41] In the opinion of some observers, the justices have grown tired of appeals from death row. The Antiterrorism and Effective Death Penalty Act (AEDPA), passed by Congress three years after *Herrera*, further curtailed the appeals process for death row convicts. The law raised the standard for federal courts to consider claims of actual innocence from "clear and convincing evidence" to "probable" evidence of innocence. It also required a higher level of deference to the decisions of state courts.[42] At the same time, Congress cut funding for the death penalty resource centers that had provided counsel for indigent condemned persons. To some, the combination of these events is destined to result in the execution of some who are innocent. Stephen Bright, who has represented many capital defendants, argues that the defenders of the death penalty concede (as Justice Scalia seems to) the "inevitability of executing the innocent." That fact forces responsible supporters to rethink their support. Does an execution accomplish retribution if the wrong person is put to death? What benefits to society outweigh the cost of executing someone who is innocent?[43]

The possibility of executing an innocent person arose again in 2002 when a federal district court decided *United States v. Quinones*.[44] In that case, Judge Jed S. Rakoff declared the Federal Death Penalty Act (FDPA) unconstitutional. He held that evolving standards of decency demanded due process. In his opinion, the FDPA violated procedural due process because it deprived the innocent of an adequate chance to prove their innocence. It also violated substantive due process because it created an undue risk of executing an innocent person. In view of dozens of recent exonerations of wrongfully convicted defendants, the public was more aware of the danger of convicting and sentencing people who were not guilty. These exonerations resulted from DNA tests, recanting witnesses, and new investigations. Yet the FDPA permitted convictions on types of evidence that had been shown to be unreliable—uncorroborated accomplice testimony and single eyewitnesses. It also allowed circumstantial evidence to be weighted as heavily as direct evidence. All in all, Rakoff found that "[t]he unacceptably high rate at which innocent persons are convicted of capital crimes, when coupled with the frequently prolonged delays before such errors are detected (and then only fortuitously or by the application of newly developed techniques), compels the conclusion that execution under the FDPA, by cutting off the opportunity for exoneration, denies due process and indeed, is tantamount to foreseeable, state-sponsored murder of innocent human beings."

The decision in *United States v. Quinones* was reviewed by a federal appeals court and Judge Rakoff's ruling was overturned. Nonetheless, his reasoning about due process and evolving standards captures a significant theme in public discourse—the sense that if there is a real risk of punishing the wrong person, the death penalty system may be inconsistent with contemporary expectations about justice. David Dow rightly notes that the likelihood of executing an innocent person is not the whole problem but only a symptom of a larger problem with the death penalty system.[45] Yet undeniably, by the turn of the century the public was more aware of flaws in the system. As the ruling in *Quinones* suggests, the review process has become so constricted that the "risk of executing innocent people increased exponentially." According to defense attorneys Mandy Welch and Richard Burr, that risk is greater than at any other time in United States history, despite the "public outcry" against wrongful convictions.[46]

Divisions within the Court

The whole question of the constitutionality of the death penalty is marked by ambiguity and contradiction and, one could argue, a lack of consensus. The Supreme Court has, on the one hand, created a complex body of capital law that regulates the application of death sentences. On the other hand, it has moved toward less scrutiny and more deference to state processes. While some justices have criticized the death penalty itself, others seem willing to accept even the problems, such as killing someone who is not guilty.

For several members of the Supreme Court the more experience they have with death penalty cases, the less rational the system appears. One good example is Justice Harry Blackmun. He personally opposed capital punishment, yet voted to support its constitutionality in both *Furman* and *Gregg*. Blackmun struggled with the issue until the early 1990s, when he finally conceded that the system could not be made to work fairly. In a dissent from the Court's decision not to hear *Callins v. Collins* in 1994, the Justice spelled out his disillusionment. He announced that he would "no longer tinker with the machinery of death."[47]

Blackmun refused to "coddle the Court's delusion" that the death penalty was fair and that no regulation was needed. Yet he saw his fellow justices moving to deregulate the entire procedure, to replace constitutional requirements with "aesthetics," and to abdicate their duty to provide judicial oversight. The Court had been right in *Furman*. Even if most people desire it, and the Constitution appears to permit capital punishment, it is "beyond dispute that if the death penalty cannot be administered consistently and rationally, it may not be administered at all." In other words, the Constitution sets a higher standard than public opinion demands. It requires a justice system without bias, prejudice, or passion. Blackmun noted that at the time of *Gregg*, the federal courts conducted substantial reviews of state court decisions (and found many errors). By the 1990s, there were "unprecedented and unwarranted barriers" to such review. *Herrera v. Collins*, decided the year before *Callins v. Collins*, may have been a last straw for Blackmun. He was appalled that only five justices, "a bare majority of the Court," were willing to say that executing an innocent person violated the Eighth Amendment. He concluded that the Court had come to prefer finality to the reliable determination of guilt.

Justice Scalia's response to the Blackmun opinion reveals the deep division on the Court. Although Scalia acknowledged that some members of the Court had "passionate and deeply held" views on the death penalty, there was no excuse for reading them into the Constitution. In this instance, Scalia would defer totally to public opinion. If the people decide that brutal deaths can be deterred through capital punishment or if they determine that such crimes are avenged by capital punishment, the creation of "false, untextual, and unhistorical contradictions" in the Eighth Amendment should not prevent them. Presumably execution of the innocent is one of these "false contradictions" in the Eighth Amendment.

Observers have noted the stark differences among members of the current Court on the issue. Edward Lazarus sees a huge gap between those like Scalia "who do not want to look again at the troubling realities of the capital punishment system and those anxious to pursue the legal conclusions to which those realities point them."[48] In the latter group are Justices Stevens, Souter, Ginsberg, and Breyer. As they had more experience with capital punishment, all three moved from "complacency to active skepticism." Like Blackmun, they did not undergo a moral conversion but came to a realization that there is a "flaw at the heart of the system." The flawed system includes the insidious role of race and the "moral certainty" that the quality of one's attorney is the single most important factor in whether one is sentenced to death. But for the majority of the Court, Lazarus argues, the public demand for retribution takes precedence over questions of due process. They want to rely on an elaborate set of rules and to relegate their enforcement to the states and not look too closely at the results.[49]

It is also intriguing that both women justices have expressed concerns about the death penalty in comments outside the Court. It is perhaps not surprising that Ruth Bader Ginsberg stated that she had "yet to see a death case among the dozens coming to the Supreme Court on eve-of-execution applications in which the defense was well represented at trial."[50] Justice O'Connor's speech to the Minnesota Women Lawyers in 2001 was more unexpected, as she usually votes to uphold death sentences. However, in that forum, O'Connor expressed "serious questions" about the administration of the death penalty. She noted that "if statistics are any indication, the system may well be allowing some innocent defendants to be executed." She suggested minimum standards and adequate compensation for defense lawyers and concluded that people in Minnesota must "breathe a sigh of relief every day" not to have the death penalty.[51]

O'Connor is often considered the "swing vote" in 5 to 4 decisions, so her views have exceptional weight. She is the only member of the Court who has served in elected office, as a legislator and judge in Arizona. She has often expressed particular deference to state legislatures as being "more attuned to the public will and more accountable" to their constituents than the courts. Justice O'Connor frequently has the last word in deciding "to what standards of decency society has evolved." She could become the "dispositive vote" regarding the death penalty, depending on how she reconciles the concerns expressed in Minnesota with her sense of deference to the acts of legislatures.[52]

As this chapter has discussed, since the mid-1970s, the Court has ruled in dozens of death penalty cases and laid down numerous rules. Yet scholars have noted that this regulation has had "almost no rationalizing effect."[53] Carol and Jordan Steiker write that the Court created an "absurdly arcane and minutely detailed body of constitutional law," which has left an "unacceptable burden" on the states' use of capital punishment. Perhaps the Court then lost interest in trying to figure out how to administer all this complexity and "turned its back on regulating the death penalty," no longer concerned with its arbitrary and discriminatory application. Or perhaps it shared a false sense that the intricate legal structure really does prevent arbitrary or unjust executions.[54] Chief Justice Rehnquist and Justices Scalia and Thomas often propound their belief in federalism, in constraints on interference with states, and in judicial self-restraint. Hugo Bedau is skeptical of this claim, and suspects that they really believe in the "substantive merits of capital punishment." Whatever the rationale, he concludes that it is impossible to build and police thirty-eight death penalty systems to make them fair and efficient.[55]

Until recently, however, it seems that the public believed there were sufficiently stringent regulations to prevent wrongful convictions. Judges and juries shared a mistaken belief that the power to inflict death was "safely circumscribed." Because so many had a hand in the capital process, moral responsibility could be diffused and people could believe that mistakes would be caught before it was too late.[56] But as the comments from Justice Ginsberg and Justice O'Connor demonstrate, such confidence is misplaced.

If more Americans become aware of flaws in the system, and if Justice Thurgood Marshall was right that most people will not accept systematic injustice, then standards of decency could evolve to demand a reversal of capital punishment policy. Over the last several decades, the Court has examined the issue many times and often "tinkered with the machinery of death." Yet with few exceptions, it is not constitutional law that influences public opinion about the death penalty, but high profile cases in the news, movies, television, and books that make the issue real and tangible.

The next chapter will look at books dealing with real cases that have captured the public's imagination and at the films made from those books.

REAL PEOPLE AND "TRUE-LIFE NOVELS"

S tories of capital punishment have been told in books and in movies. Some of those that leave the most powerful impression are told in both genres. The decision to make a novel or a work of nonfiction into a film involves multiple factors, but surely among those considerations is a calculation of whether the public will be sufficiently interested in the story to buy a ticket or, in the case of TV movies, to tune in. This chapter will look at books from several genres—the journalistic fiction or "true-life novels" of Norman Mailer and Truman Capote, which include the highly acclaimed works *The Executioner's Song* and *In Cold Blood,* and the memoirs of Sister Helen Prejean and Mikal Gilmore, *Dead Man Walking* and *Shot in the Heart.*[1] Chapter 4 will examine the widely read novels *To Kill a Mockingbird* and *A Lesson Before Dying,* along with two best-selling John Grisham works, *A Time to Kill* and *The Chamber.*[2] It will also include Stephen King's *The Green Mile,* an immensely popular story first published in serial form.[3] Each book was adapted into a commercial film, and it can be argued, exposure to these works has given millions of Americans the opportunity to confront the death penalty.

Gary Gilmore: Why Did He Do It and What Did It Mean?

Take the story of Gary Gilmore. There were two real murders and one real execution in Utah in 1977. But the telling of this tale has lasted for more than two decades. Gary Gilmore's story is interesting from many angles. It was the subject of two prize-winning and critically acclaimed books. Both books were later made into television films. In addition, because Gilmore's was the first execution after the Supreme Court reinstated the death penalty in *Gregg v. Georgia*, his life and death filled the pages and airwaves at the time it happened. It provides an excellent place to begin the study of the modern intersection between popular culture and the death penalty.

Few people on death row capture the interest of major authors like Norman Mailer. Fewer still have brothers who are journalists, able and willing to tell their stories. Because of these fortuitous circumstances, people have the opportunity to become acquainted with Gary Gilmore. More especially, they have a chance to try to understand what led him to death row.

In Gilmore's case, there was no claim of innocence. He murdered two young men in the course of robberies. Gary Gilmore was not wrongfully convicted. Rather, assuming that one does not believe that some people are just born bad, the interest in this narrative stems from the rare opportunity to understand the environment that helped shape a man who took the lives of others and who was eager to forfeit his own.

Norman Mailer dreamed of writing a novel "big enough to take on American life."[4] At over one thousand pages, *The Executioner's Song* is such a work, offering readers a chance to examine facets of American culture by adding the novelist's perceptions onto the world of real people and events. Some critics fault such books for "establishing a total equivalence between what's real and what's plausible."[5] For our purposes, though, the distinction between real and believable is not as important as the ideas about capital punishment conveyed through the writing or film.

Utah is crucial to the setting of all the works on Gilmore. In a review of *The Executioner's Song*, Joan Didion remarks on the "vast emptiness at the center of the Western experience."[6] Many other reviewers refer to the regional atmosphere, implying some symbiotic relationship between the American West and violence, a sense that somehow the frontier culture still prevails. But, especially in Mailer's book, one gets a sense not so much of a Wild West full of action as a region of ugliness, aridity, and boredom. It is the desert West that provides the physical setting for Gilmore's last months. Didion describes a life there that could seem incomprehensible to residents of the urban East. "People get sick for love, think they want to die for love, shoot up the town for love, and then they more on, move away, forget the face. . . . People get in their cars at night and drive across two states to get a beer, see about a loan on a pickup, keep from going crazy because crazy people get committed again, and can no longer get in their cars and drive across two states to get a beer."[7] The first half of *The Executioner's Song* weighs the reader down with that sense of pointlessness and inevitability. From the moment Gilmore arrives in Utah, he moves inexorably toward self-destruction, oppressed by the flatness of the environment. After spending most of his life in reform school and prison, he finds the outside world so unfamiliar that at first he cannot make change, buy a beer, or talk decently to a girl.

As Didion notes, many of Mailer's characters don't seem to believe that outcomes can be influenced. This attitude adds to the sense of inevitability in *The Executioner's Song*. The women especially "move in and out of paying attention to events, of noticing their own fate."[8] It is disastrous when Gilmore falls obsessively in love with Nicole Baker, who is such a woman. The crises in that relationship trigger, although they do not explain, Gilmore's seemingly meaningless murders.

In addition to being situated within the aridity of the desert, the story needs to be seen squarely within the Mormon culture that dominated life in Utah. It was a community in which Gilmore was totally out of place. For Mailer, Gilmore's inability to conform to social norms contrasted with the rectitude of the Mormons, especially the two young men he killed. Likewise, in both the book and film versions of *Shot in the Heart*, the Mormon church is most significant, especially as it exercised great influence on Bessie Gilmore, the mother of Gary and his brothers. Even though she disassociated herself from the church for many years, the worldview Bessie passed along to her sons was marked by the fear and superstition she learned in the Mormon community. She told her children about the notion of blood atonement—the Mormon belief that a wrongdoer must be required to shed his blood as a penance. Gary Gilmore chose to die by firing squad, a death many believe he saw as a form of blood atonement.

Dreams and premonitions implicitly linked with Mormonism frame the written version of *Shot in the Heart*. The book begins with a dream in which Mikal Gilmore, Gary's brother, sees the family moving between the darkness inside a house and the darkness outside. It ends with a dream in which he watches Gary's trial. Although in the dream Mikal tries to testify that his brother was the victim of beatings and abuse, the judge finds that information irrelevant. Instead, the court condemns both Gary and his child to death. They believe the child is contaminated by "bad blood."[9]

Clearly, while Mailer has looked at the story of Gary Gilmore on the broad canvas of its meaning in American life, Mikal Gilmore focused on the "bad blood," on how his family produced a man who was executed for murder. His book is a dissection of dysfunction. In fact, one reviewer called it a contribution to the literature of child abuse.[10] The film made from Gilmore's book draws on an even smaller canvas. Except for flashbacks to family history, it is set almost entirely in the state prison where the brothers meet during the last six days before Gary's execution.[11] As one reviewer remarked, *The Executioner's Song* "reflected the storm around Gilmore; *Shot in the Heart* rests firmly in the quiet dread of the eye."[12]

The Context

Although Mailer and Mikal Gilmore approach the story from different angles, both address the question of why Gary Gilmore committed the two murders that cost his life. Both suggest that the answer is found in the family, with its "webwork of dark secrets and failed hopes,"[13] and in the brutalizing experience of decades in prison. As Frank Gilmore, the oldest brother, remarks, Gary's twenty-two years in the "animalistic prison system" turned him into an animal. Frank believed that if you take any kid with problems and put him in "outrageous horror house reformatories and prisons," the kid would turn out to be just like Gary.[14] In interviews with Gary Gilmore that formed a major portion of Mailer's book, Gilmore explained that he was different after reform school. After that experience, "a kid knows stuff"; he identifies with the criminal element.[15] Gary told Mikal another story. There was a boy in reform school, he said, who was afraid and couldn't stand up to the abuse. One night that boy asked if he could crawl into bed with Gary because he was so scared he wanted to disappear into nothingness where no one could hurt him. Gary held him during the night but in the morning the frightened boy was dead.[16] Mikal feels certain the "dead boy" was the side of Gary that showed vulnerability. As a teenager he had advised Mikal to learn to be hard, to take things and feel no pain. "Let people beat you, kick you. If you don't give in, they'll kill you."[17] Frank thought that Gary never learned that lesson, in prison or at home. "Gary always fought back—and he got hit harder."[18]

It was certainly within his family where Gary first experienced brutality. His life started with insecurity. Frank Gilmore Sr. was a con man, on the run from his scams and from some horrible past deed (presumably murder). Gary happened to be born in Texas, but because of his father's fear of detection, he was given a false name. His birth certificate read "Fay Robert Coffman," a combination of Frank's mother's name and that of a son by another marriage. As Gary later noted, he was never officially born, but he would officially be put to death. To complicate matters, Frank Sr. thought from the beginning that Gary was not his son. The suspicion triggered episodes of abuse. He beat his wife in front of the children. Once he left her and Frank Jr. at a filling station in a remote town in Iowa. Shortly thereafter, the baby Gary was found on a park bench where his father had abandoned him. That was just the start of a life that Mikal called a "history of destruction." He believed that "each moment made a difference and there were just too damn many of them that were bad."[19]

When the family settled in Portland, Oregon, where Frank Sr. ultimately made a decent living in a legitimate business, he seemed to turn his deviance into more brutality toward his family. All the sons except Mikal (who was born much later than the others) endured horrible beatings, usually for the most trivial of reasons. The father's behavior was thoroughly inconsistent, even irrational. When Gary did get into trouble with the juvenile authorities, the father defended his son and blamed the system, thus forgoing any intervention to address the family's dysfunction. More importantly, he may well have given his son the message that the justice system was illegitimate.

Although in his last days on death row, Gary would claim that his mother had always loved him, Mailer and Mikal tell a different story. Bessie admitted that she never wanted children, but that she had them because her husband wished to. "If only we had stayed that way forever, without kids." Once, when her husband was in prison, Bessie returned to her family's home in Utah with Gary and Frank Jr. There she repeatedly beat the boys and so neglected them that her own parents called the child protective agency. She took the children and ran away to a motel. It was, strangely, the same motel where Gary robbed and murdered the clerk thirty years later. Bessie's life seemed to be ruled by fear and superstition. She insisted that several of their homes were haunted and maintained that a ghost entered Gary. Like many women who experience domestic abuse, Bessie stayed in her marriage despite the damage to her children and herself for the "sanctity and unity of the family . . . nothing is worse than sundering your family's integrity. The family—and the privacies of its authority—must be preserved."[20] Whatever the reason, she is surely one of the women Didion describes as not believing that events can be influenced.

Every reviewer of *Shot in the Heart* links the horrors of the Gilmore family with Gary's crimes. *Maclean's* describes an atmosphere of "mayhem . . . a family tale so fraught with violence, misplaced love, loss and doom that it resembles a Greek tragedy."[21] *The Economist* says that the execution was "the logical conclusion of the family's awful history."[22] Mikal Gilmore told *People* magazine that he would like people to remember Gary as a "case study for the things you should not do to a child's heart."[23] None of the accounts of Gary Gilmore's life mention the physical links between chronic child abuse, brain damage, and violent behavior. It is quite possible, however, that he could also make a case study for that process.

Both *The Executioner's Song* and *Shot in the Heart* can be seen as making arguments for the brutalizing effects of prison. Gary was incarcerated virtually every day from the age of fourteen to his death. He not only failed to learn how "normal" people live, he fought the system. He later claimed that because he made trouble, the guards pulled out his teeth. He was then given ill-fitting dentures that caused constant discomfort and pain for the rest of his life. Because he complained about the teeth, he was put on mega doses of the drug Prolixin, with horrible physical and mental side effects. Although none of these episodes justifies the murders he committed after his release, they help to explain why he was not "rehabilitated" by the prison system, why when he talked with Mikal, Gary referred to his "rage." The experiences in prison may also explain why he insisted on execution rather than a life sentence.

A few words about the film version of *The Executioner's Song* are in order.[24] Of the works considered, it pays the least attention to the long-term reasons for Gary's crimes, but focuses instead on the months leading to the murders. The film suggests that Gary was unable to adjust to life in Utah after prison. It shows him lacking in patience and impulsive, with a maniacal laugh. He abuses pills and alcohol and steals for no reason. His love for Nicole Baker is intense, but marred by impotence and jealousy. Shortly before the murders, he seems ready to burst with violence. He drives recklessly, yells, and hits Nicole and her children.[25] The film seems accurate in portraying Gary as a dangerous man with a very short fuse. Yet by offering little to account for the rage, the portrait remains superficial.

The System

Another area to examine in the Gilmore saga is the portrayal of the criminal justice system as the case proceeded from arrest through the courts. Mailer's book provides the most detail in this area and emphasizes the Mormon character of Utah justice. He describes the police detective who questioned Gary for an hour and a half with no lawyer present. The officer knew he was "cutting corners on Miranda close enough to send the whole thing up on appeal." But the detective wanted a confession, even if it would be inadmissible in court. By using the "good cop" technique, including a discussion of the Mormon religion, he believed he was instilling confidence and making a connection with the suspect. Gary bragged that he had committed as many as a hundred robberies before. He knew how to do it without getting caught, implying that perhaps this time he purposely let himself mess up. When asked if he would have gone on killing if he had not been arrested, Gary said he thought so. When asked why he killed the two men, Gary responded, "I don't know . . . I can't cope with life." The detective was "bolstered" by the conversation. He had never gotten a confession from a hard-core criminal before.[26]

The state decided to ask for the death penalty because of the "cold blooded" crimes and based on Gilmore's prior record of violence in prison, escape attempts, and "failed rehabilitation." If given a life sentence, the prosecutor argued, Gary would try to escape, or he would be a hazard to the guards and other inmates. Attempts at rehabilitation would be hopeless. The only possible defense his court-appointed attorneys could come up with was insanity, perhaps because of the overdoses of Prolixin. Gilmore not only refused this strategy, he also refused to allow his lawyers to call his girlfriend Nicole either in the guilt or the mitigation phase of the trial.

Jury selection took only one day, amazingly short for a death penalty case. The prosecution's case was weak—they could not use the confession, they did not test blood found at the scene, they had no fingerprints on the gun, and the stolen money was not produced in court. They relied mostly on witnesses' testimony. But the defense put on no case whatsoever. Not surprisingly, the jury reached a guilty verdict in one hour and twenty minutes.

During the second phase of the trial, aggravating and mitigating evidence was introduced to determine whether capital punishment was appropriate, as prescribed in *Gregg v. Georgia*. The prosecution emphasized Gary's future dangerousness. They also claimed that based on what he had done to the victim's family, he had forfeited his right to live. In mitigation, Gilmore's lawyers argued that he needed treatment, that everyone has a right to life, and that parole was far in the future. When, to no one's surprise, the jury opted for death, Gary showed no affect.[27]

Normally, a death sentence would lead to automatic appeals, but the Utah death penalty law did not require mandatory review. Thus much of the rest of Gary Gilmore's short life revolved around a legal argument—should he appeal his sentence and challenge the constitutionality of the Utah law? In other words, the decision to appeal was in his hands, and he consistently refused every attempt to persuade him, including Mikal's arguments in the last days before the execution.

Gilmore had grounds to challenge his sentence as, among other things, the state had introduced evidence of another murder in the guilt phase of the trial. There was also good reason to think that the Utah statute, by not providing for mandatory appeal of death sentence, did not meet the Supreme Court's standards set down in *Gregg*. As the American Civil Liberties Union attorneys argued, if one execution took place under a defective law, it would be harder for the courts to later find it unconstitutional. They also made the case that if Gilmore were put to death, it would touch off a major wave of executions. It would demystify capital punishment and end the national moratorium on state-sponsored killing that had been in place for more than ten years. Gary remained impervious to the pleas of the ACLU and became infuriated when the NAACP tried to persuade him to appeal. As a white man, he did not need their help, he said. Ultimately, the ACLU tried to delay the execution without Gilmore's cooperation by making the argument that taxpayers' money was being used to carry out an unconstitutional law. Although a lower court judge issued a stay, the Supreme Court refused to consider the argument.[28]

On film, *The Executioner's Song* is not very effective in presenting the legal issues surrounding Gary Gilmore, but that is probably not its purpose. The movie spends a mere two minutes on the trial, showing only the prosecution's side, no defense or mitigation. It also portrays Gilmore as behaving badly in the courtroom. The ACLU attorney, wearing a grotesque wig, appears stupefied when she argues before the Board of Prisons. All in all, the film seems to suggest that the legal process is either meaningless or foolish.[29]

The Conclusion

In both books and both movies, one knows from the beginning that ultimately Gary Gilmore will be executed. All address to some extent the question of who benefited from his death. Death penalty supporters would be relieved that the punishment could be used again. According to Mikal Gilmore, the courts had thrown aside due process, as though everyone was "caught up in the novelty, the excitement, the vicarious deadliness of the event, and nothing could stop it."[30]

Mailer's book details the media feeding frenzy that surrounded the execution. Clearly, the first man put to death after the moratorium would sell newspapers and provide TV journalists with a big story. Gilmore, a man Mailer describes as a "mediocrity enlarged by history," was pictured on the cover of *Newsweek*. Perhaps with less attention, he might have been able to quietly change his mind and appeal. As things developed, Gilmore was "trapped in fame and it gave him a bizarre strength."[31] Journalists entered a bidding war for the exclusive rights to a "hot property," interviews with Gary and his family. Larry Schiller, who ultimately "won" the war and who provided the raw material that later became Mailer's book, paid handsomely for the story—more than $100,000, which ultimately went to some of Gary's family and friends. At one point, Mikal Gilmore asked Schiller if he was working to see Gary executed in order to have an ending to his story. Schiller replied that if Gary were not killed, it would demonstrate how the "public gives an event importance, but they can take away that importance."[32] As a reviewer of *Shot in the Heart* on film commented, Gilmore was "bizarrely charismatic," the "prime exhibit in the national pop-culture freak show."[33]

Mikal Gilmore seemed appalled that his brother's approaching death was the source of tawdry commercialism. He believed that the court-appointed lawyers, the journalists, and even his uncle were using Gary to line their pockets. If there were any doubts, they were banished when the uncle produced "Gilmore Death Wish" T-shirts and brought them to the prison.

But it could be argued, and Mikal Gilmore seems to make this argument, that Gary Gilmore himself benefited the most from his execution. He apparently welcomed the prospect of death, although there are different explanations of why this was so. Mailer quotes a letter from Gilmore to his girlfriend Nicole in which he explains that he does not want to "rot in prison," to grow old and bitter convinced that he's "an innocent victim of society's bullshit."[34] Mailer also gives considerable attention to Gilmore's belief in reincarnation, a notion Mikal Gilmore barely mentions. He contends that his brother was simply determined to die. He put the state of Utah and the death penalty advocates on the spot. They became "not just his allies, but his servants; men who would kill at his bidding, to suit his own ideals of ruin and redemption." He thinks that some people hated Gary "because he seemed to figure out how to win, how to escape."[35] Given the story Mikal told, Gilmore's desire to escape from his life is completely plausible. In any event, Gary convinced Mikal that he truly wished to die, that if he were not executed he would find a way to commit suicide, and so Mikal agreed not to enter an appeal on his brother's behalf. He came to think that Gary had worked out in his mind some sort of "atonement." He wanted death as his "final scenario of redemption, his final release from the law."[36] As a reviewer for *New Statesman* explained, it was almost as if Gilmore "killed two random strangers in order to recruit the state as his accomplice in the self-destructive psychodrama that he had lived since childhood. He was never truer to his Mormon ancestors than when choosing to shed blood for the remission of sin."[37] At the very least, these accounts leave an ambiguous answer to the question, what was gained by the execution of Gary Gilmore?

Mailer's book and the film based on it follow the story of Gilmore's death by firing squad. It appears that the state spent little time arranging for an appropriately solemn setting. The execution was carried out in a small building on the prison grounds, formerly used as a cannery. Although the blind for the shooters had been meticulously prepared, Gilmore was seated in an old office chair, surrounded by sandbags and backed by a filthy mattress to keep the bullets from ricocheting off the walls. The room was full of police and bureaucrats who had apparently been invited en masse. The director of corrections "danced around, greeting people" in a white cowboy hat.[38] In the film, Gilmore walks through the snow in a sleeveless shirt to get to the execution site. He too makes conversation before the hood is put over his head. Although the press reported that his last words were "Let's do it," Mailer claims that he spoke last to the Catholic chaplain. "Dominus vobiscum" (The Lord be with you), Gilmore allegedly said to the priest. He answered, "Et cum spiritu tuo" (And with you too). According to Mikal Gilmore, his brother's last words could have been a statement of despair or one of hope, "There will always be a father."[39]

One might approach *The Executioner's Song* and *Shot in the Heart* with a sense that these works describe not flaws in the workings of the death penalty, but instead a success story of how, with little wrangling in the courts, the right man was executed for heinous crimes. And yet even this case is not that simple.

Although Norman Mailer has often been criticized for romanticizing violence in his writings, here he avoids that. Instead he humanizes Gilmore, his family, his friends, and the victims. If not all the characters are likeable, they are complex individuals. Mikal Gilmore accomplishes this humanization as well by making the reader see his brother not just as a murderer, but as a man—with a whole life behind him—who committed murder. As Marcelle Clements wrote of *Shot in the Heart*, perhaps Mikal succeeded "where his brother failed, in harnessing the forces of the media to defend a point of view—which is, simply, that violence always has a context."[40]

The "Boys" Who Killed in Cold Blood

Norman Mailer admitted that he had read *In Cold Blood,* Truman Capote's "nonfiction novel," before he wrote his own true-life novel, *The Executioner's Song.* And, although each work tells a story of senseless, brutal murders that led to executions, and each is enhanced by the author's reconstruction of events, Mailer vehemently denied that he stole the idea from Capote. In fact, he faulted *In Cold Blood* as a description of crime from the outside, in which Capote "decided too quickly" to blame the crime on heredity, "that in their genes his killers were doomed and directed to act in this fashion; there was no other outcome possible."[41] An examination of Capote's book and the two film adaptations will afford an opportunity to test Mailer's criticism.

According to a widely repeated anecdote, one morning in 1959 Truman Capote noticed a small article in the *New York Times* reporting the apparently motiveless murders of a prosperous Kansas farmer, his wife, and two teenaged children. The event and the community's reaction, he thought, might provide the subject for an experiment he had been eager to try, the nonfiction novel. Capote traveled to Holcomb, Kansas, the site of the murders. At first he intended only to tell the story of the immediate victims and the town's need to punish the guilty, experience retribution, and return to normality and stability as soon as possible. It became clear that the community's formerly "unfearful" life could be restored only when the crime was solved.[42] This was true not only because the small town seldom saw violence but also because the victims, the Clutter family, were model citizens. As one local woman described the reaction, "Feeling wouldn't run half so high if this had happened to anyone *except* the Clutters. Anyone *less* admired. Prosperous. Secure. But that family represented everything people hereabouts really value and respect, and that such a thing could happen to them—well it's like being told there is no God. It makes life seem pointless. I don't think people are so much frightened as they are deeply depressed."[43] Besides, the murders had been brutal. Each member of the family had been bound with ropes and shot. In addition, Herb Clutter's throat had been slashed. A high school English teacher, among the first at the crime scene, described his response, "The suffering. The horror. They were dead. A whole family. Gentle, kindly people, people I knew—*murdered*. You had to believe it, because it was really true."[44]

How to explain such a horrible crime unless whoever did it was some sort of creature, alien or less than human? The term "animal" figured often in talk of the crime. The chief investigator, Alvin Dewey, looked repeatedly at photographs of the scene like a child trying to "find the hidden animals" in the picture. The sister of Perry Smith, one of the killers, tells how she needed to keep her distance from him. He "lived in the wilderness," apparently uncivilized, like a beast.[45]

Capote successfully juxtaposes the extravagant theories of the crime developed by the investigators and members of the community with the actual story of Dick and Perry, the murderers, as they make their incompetent way on the road. Fear often leads people to envision a villain who is both all-powerful and less than human. Yet "the boys," as these young men in their late twenties were called, were more bumbling than menacing. When the fugitives were finally apprehended and brought back to Kansas, the townspeople gathered outside the courthouse. There were some reporters, whom Capote called "professional spectators." Otherwise, the "congregation" in the square might have been there for a pep rally or a parade. High school students chanted cheerleader rhymes, mothers pushed babies in strollers, fathers carried children on their shoulders. Members of a Boy Scout troop, a bridge club, and a veterans' organization were present. It seemed to be a gathering of the "good people" against the villains. However, when Richard Hickock and Perry Smith arrived with their police escort, "the crowd fell silent, as though amazed to find them humanly shaped."[46] They did not look that different from anyone else in the town square, yet they had apparently committed a crime that defied rationality.

Nature or Nurture?

One critic has noted that because the murderers seemed to have no meaningful purpose to their crime, they were both more ordinary and more disturbing. They did not kill for financial gain (the robbery netted $40, a portable radio, and a pair of binoculars) or for revenge in the usual sense of the term. They were not "criminal masterminds," they were not even very competent. Agent Dewey was perplexed because the crime seemed to be a "psychological accident, virtually an impersonal act; the victims might as well have been struck by lightening."[47] He found it "ludicrously inconsistent" to slaughter four people "for a few dollars and a small portable radio."[48]

Yet the book must explore the reasons for the murders, and despite Mailer's comment that Capote attributed the crimes to heredity, the actual explanations are much more complex. Richard (Dick) Hickock came from a struggling but loving farm family. He had been a high school athlete with an IQ of about 130. Unable to afford college, he took laboring jobs, married at nineteen, and had several children. By the time of the Clutter murders, he had been twice divorced and had returned to live at his parents' home. Capote found Dick's face remarkable in that it "seemed composed of mismatching parts. It was as though his head had been halved like an apple, then put together a fraction off center."[49] In his early twenties, his face and his life were destabilized by an automobile accident that seemed to distort both his appearance and his judgment. Hickock's father traced his son's delinquent behavior to the crash, noting that he was "not the same boy" afterward. Somehow, in Mr. Hickock's eyes, the accident got Dick started on his favorite illegal activity, passing bad checks. When he was caught for "hanging paper," Dick was sentenced to seventeen months in prison. "That was the ruination of him," his father said. "He was a plain stranger to me. You couldn't talk to him. The whole world was against Dick Hickock—that's how he figured." Hickock's mother blamed her son's crimes totally on Perry Smith. "That friend of his. That's what happened. One look and I saw what he was. With his perfume. And his oily hair."[50]

But perhaps Hickock's sense of resentment toward those more fortunate than he predated both his accident and his incarceration. Even as a child he had hated to see people with things he was unable to have. Once he had stolen some seashells a friend brought back from a trip to the ocean and crushed them with a hammer. "Envy was constantly with him; the Enemy was anyone who was someone he wanted to be or who had anything he wanted to have." He especially hated "big-shot bastards."[51] Hickock also seemed to struggle with a fear that he was not "normal." He claimed on the one hand, that the only reason for going to the Clutter house was to get the money for "a regular life with a business of his own, a horse to ride, a new car, and 'plenty of blond chicken'."[52] Yet he also had a sexual interest in female children, a taste that was clearly not "normal," which may have had something to do with his scheme to rob the Clutter farm. In Hickock's own statement to the psychiatrist who examined them during the trial, "It seems to be an impulse. . . . I knew there would be a girl there. I think the main reason I went there was not to rob them but to rape the girl. Because I thought a lot about it." It was the one reason he stayed in the Clutter home, even after he realized there was no safe and no money. "I did make some advances toward the Clutter girl when I was there. But Perry never gave me a chance. I hope no one finds this out but you, as I haven't even told my lawyer. . . . I'm afraid of my people finding out."[53]

Dick, like his parents, believed the automobile accident was responsible for his personality change. "I have had sickness. I think caused from the car wreck I had. Spells of passing out, and sometimes I would hemorrhage at the nose and left ear. . . . Not long ago I had a piece of glass work out of my head. It came out the corner of my eye. My dad helped me get it out."[54] A young man who felt he never had the chances he deserved, a serious head injury and probably damage to his nervous system, and exposure to the prison culture—these seem to be the ingredients that combined to place Dick Hickock at the Clutter murders. Whether he actually killed any of the victims is another matter. Hickock maintained that Perry killed them all, and while Smith confessed to all four murders, he claimed he did so to spare Hickock's parents.

Every commentator notes that Truman Capote was much more interested in Perry Smith than in Dick Hickock. A number of them claim that the author was in love with the young man with slicked-back hair, short stumpy legs injured in a motorcycle accident, and tiny feet. There was little that could be called "normal" in Perry's early life. His parents made their living on the rodeo circuit and privately carried on what seemed to be a mutually abusive relationship. After they separated, Perry and his siblings lived with their mother, at the time a prostitute who brought clients home in the presence of the four children. Later, Perry spent his time in orphanages or on the road with his father, often living in a car while they traveled prospecting for gold. His memories of childhood were marked by abuse from nuns in the orphanage, who beat him for wetting the bed and called him "nigger" for being half Indian, and by neglect from his father , who never allowed him to go to school and who belittled his interests. At sixteen, he joined the Merchant Marine and later served in the army in Korea. Although he spent four years in the military and earned a bronze star, he never made corporal because, in his words, he "wouldn't roll over" for the "queens."[55]

During the rough spots in his life, Perry often dreamed of a huge yellow parrot who avenged the wrongs against him, lifted and enfolded him in its wings, and carried him to paradise. The fantastic bird first appeared to slaughter the nuns who had beaten him, but the dream recurred even as Perry waited for his trial in the Clutter case. That time he imagined that he cut his wrists, which brought the parrot to lift him up above the sheriff and those who would punish him. Although Capote does not offer an explanation for the parrot image, it seems to be the sort of savior an abandoned child would imagine—a large, powerful, but beautiful creature who would avenge and protect. In his study of Capote's work, William Nance claims that the reader's feeling for Perry derives not from his "dynamic badness" but from "his amoral, pathetic blending of violence and aspiration." He is "a childlike dreamer, a romantic wanderer," a murderer by "psychological accident."[56] The dream of the yellow parrot embodies both the childlike and the violent elements in his personality.

There is no doubt that Perry was capable of violence. Dick thought his partner was a "natural killer—absolutely sane, but conscienceless and capable of dealing, with or without motive, the coldest-blooded deathblows."[57] During questioning by the detectives, Perry described why he didn't leave the crime scene when it became clear there was no money to steal. "It was like I wasn't part of it. More as though I was reading a story. And I had to know what was going to happen. The end. So I went back upstairs. . . ."[58] Later Perry explained to an old friend who visited him in jail that he committed the murders not because he was afraid of Dick or because he was afraid of being identified for the break-in. "Not because of anything the Clutters did. They never hurt me. Like other people. Like people have all my life. Maybe it's just that the Clutters were the ones who had to pay for it."[59] Thus Perry offers an alternative to Dick's description of a "natural killer." His murderous quality came not from nature, but from nurture—or more accurately, the lack of nurture. As Capote stated in an interview, Perry committed the murders out of an accumulation of disillusionments and reverses. He "found himself in a psychological cul de sac. The Clutters were such a perfect set of symbols for every frustration in his life."[60] In the film version the symbolism is made abundantly clear when Mr. Clutter's face merges with that of Perry's own father.

The Legal Process

The trial of Richard Hickock and Perry Smith took place in 1960, twelve years before the Supreme Court found the death penalty as administered unconstitutional in *Furman v. Georgia* and fifteen years before revised death penalty statutes were approved by the Court. In their case, the justice system reached the expected result, but in the process raised some significant questions. As they could not afford private attorneys, the court appointed lawyers to defend the "boys." Hickock's attorney "accepted his task with resigned grace," while Smith's contended that he had no desire for the case but no choice other than to take it.[61] Neither lawyer had much experience with criminal trials; in fact, an observer noted that Smith's attorney was "more at home with land deeds than with ill deeds."[62] The county attorney determined to ask for the death penalty. He cited the violence and lack of mercy toward the victims and claimed that execution was the only way to protect the public, as there was no such thing as life without parole in Kansas.[63] The defense lawyers decided not to ask for a change of venue, despite the strong local feelings about the murders. They claimed the location would not matter, as the sentiment toward the killers was the same all over the state. However, they did ask for a postponement immediately before the trial because Hickock's father was ill and might not be able to testify. Another and possibly more compelling reason was that the Clutters' property was to be auctioned off just a week before the trial began. The sale, where all the murdered family's belongings would be displayed for the public, was like another funeral in reminding the community of the victims. In any event, the judge refused to postpone the trial.[64] It began as scheduled, with the seating of an all-male jury. Every one was a family man, each was involved in one of the local churches. The selection took only four hours. When asked his position on capital punishment, one juror replied that he was "ordinarily against it. In this case, I'm for it." He was seated anyway.[65]

Over several days, the state put on its case. They showed photos of the crime scene and the bodies of the Clutter family. The Kansas Bureau of Investigation agents testified concerning their inquiries and the confessions of the two defendants. Floyd Wells, Hickock's former prison cellmate, explained that he had told Dick about the Clutter farm and the family's wealth. That testimony established premeditation—Hickock had been planning the robbery for months.

In response, the defense's case lasted only ninety minutes. Mr. Hickock told of his son's car accident and the changes in his behavior. The best case for the defense would have involved consideration of the physical and mental traumas that might have distorted the men's sense of reality. But because Kansas used the M'Naughton Rule to determine a defendant's sanity, the defense psychologist was only allowed to answer "yes" or "no" when asked if the men knew right from wrong. If the answer was "yes," the court was not permitted to consider anything else about the defendants' mental state.

In *Reflections on Hanging*, published around the same time as Hickock and Smith's trial, Arthur Koestler explained the limitations of the M'Naughton Rule. It was developed in 1843, before the word "psychiatry" had been invented, "before Darwin had published *The Origin of the Species*, before it was realized that man has a biological past, has 'animal' instincts and impulses . . . an explanation, and at least partial excuse for his actions. Nor was it realized that childhood, education, and social conditioning are largely responsible in forming character, including criminal character. . . . Yet even at that date the M'Naughton Rules were an anachronism, condemned by the majority of the medical, and the more enlightened of the legal profession."[66] Nonetheless, in 1960 Kansas judged a person's criminal responsibility by a yes or no answer to "Did he know right from wrong?"

In writing *In Cold Blood*, Capote described the events in the courtroom as they were limited by invoking the M'Naughton Rule, but he devised a way to provide the reader with more insight into the defendants' real mental state. Although Dr. Jones, the psychologist, was limited to one-word answers,

Capote tells what the doctor would have said if he could. He would have explained that Dick had no tests to determine brain damage after the accident, and that he showed signs of a severe character disorder. He would have said that Perry grew up without direction, love, or moral values, that he manifested paranoia and poorly controlled rage.[67] The court might have learned of recent scholarly work on "senseless murders" that identified "individuals disposed to severe lapses in ego-control which make possible the open expression of primitive violence, born out of previous, and now unconscious, traumatic experiences." In all such cases, *extreme* parental violence (such as Perry experienced) led to defects in ego formation and impulse control.[68]

The jury had none of that information, and after the defense put on its brief case, they heard closing statements. The state retained Logan Green, an expert criminal lawyer with legendary dramatic and rhetorical talents, as a "special assistant" to the county attorney. For some reason, he was permitted to be the "last act on the program," after the defense and even following the judge's instructions to the jury. Green called up the image of the doomed family, including Nancy Clutter begging for her life, and reminded the jury that the defendants had not shown the victims the mercy they wanted for themselves. He quoted the Old Testament message of retribution. He argued that sending Dick and Perry to prison would not protect the community. They could escape or be released on parole and "the next time they go slaughtering it may be *your* family." Finally, Green challenged the jury. "Some of our enormous crimes happen because once upon a time a pack of chicken-hearted jurors refused to do their duty."[69] With that ultimatum, the jury took only forty minutes to find Hickock and Smith guilty on all counts. As each charge was read, the jury foreman replied, "Guilty of murder in the first degree, and the punishment is death."[70]

The Rope

Five years passed before the two men were executed on April 14, 1965. During that time their appeals reached the Supreme Court three times. Each time the high court rejected them. Some would claim that nonetheless several important constitutional issues were raised. Was the trial held in such a hostile atmosphere that due process and seating an unbiased jury were impossible? What about the juror who admitted in voir dire that he favored capital punishment in *this* case? Were the defense attorneys competent to represent their clients? Did they collude with the prosecution? Why did they not request a change of venue? Was it permissible to admit confessions made without attorneys present? The murder weapon, a shotgun, was taken from Hickock's parents' home without a warrant. Was it lawfully seized? Those legal questions were enough to earn three stays of execution but not enough to warrant a new trial or to prevent the ultimate punishment.[71]

Both men were executed on the same day. No one seemed to recall why Hickock went first. It might have been a coin toss, or perhaps they followed alphabetical order. When twenty people arrived to attend the executions, they saw two ropes hanging side by side in a dimly lighted old warehouse where building materials were stacked against the walls. No chairs were provided; everyone stood to watch the proceedings.[72] The hangman, imported from Missouri, wore a cowboy hat to shield his face. He was paid $600 for the two executions. Agent Dewey had expected a more dignified setting. Instead, the witnesses stood around making "self-consciously casual conversation." As with the execution of Gary Gilmore, the contrast is dramatic between the momentousness of the event when the state deprives a person of his life and the seedy, even sordid, setting in which it is done.

When Hickock entered with the chaplain and guards, he was wearing the harness that would attach to the gallows structure. For whatever reason—hubris, manners, shock—he shook hands with the KBI agents and said, "Nice to see you." He stated that he had no hard feelings toward his executioners, expressed his hope of going to a better place, and hung for twenty minutes before the doctor pronounced him dead. A reporter in the crowd wondered, "Do they feel it or do they get to take something to ease the pain?" No drugs, his colleague responded. That would be against the rules.[73]

Smith followed, and although Capote attributed the response to the second hanging to Agent Dewey, it more likely reflects the author's own reaction. Smith came in chewing gum, apparently to control his nerves. In his last words, Perry stated that he did not believe in capital punishment. "Maybe I had something to contribute." An apology, he said, would be meaningless and inappropriate, but he apologized anyway. Then there was the "thud-snap" of a broken neck and the crowd could look up to see his "childish feet, tilted, dangling." We are told that Dewey, like the majority of law enforcement officers in his day, thought capital punishment was a deterrent to violent crime, and "if ever the penalty had been earned, the present instance was it." Hickock, he thought, was worthless, but Smith had the "aura of an exiled animal, a creature walking wounded."[74]

Had the book ended there it would have left unresolved questions— whether the state is justified in taking lives with no consideration of the offenders' mental state, without even knowing if any mitigating circumstances existed, whether the "present instance" really warranted execution. But Capote seemed compelled to send the reader off with a sense of the rightness of it all. In the last few pages, Agent Dewey meets Nancy Clutter's friend Susan at the cemetery. They both find assurance that normal life will, as it should, go on. Brian Conniff claims that the scene, which is "pure fiction," misleads by suggesting that the story's meaning is found in the cemetery, rather than on the gallows.[75]

Some claim that Capote needed executions to complete the book, that if he cared so much about Dick and Perry's best interests he might have provided money for appeals instead of buying them magazines to read in prison.[76] Smith's defense lawyer said in a later interview that although Capote had a real sympathy for the men and "hated to see them done in," he was actually "draining their brains."[77] He conducted over two hundred interviews with Smith and Hickock, wrote to them twice a week after their trial, and sent them reading material. His relationship with them was intimate, in the sense that he became their confidant. After the execution, Capote cried for two days.[78] Yet to some critics, the writer's exploitation of the condemned men for the purposes of his best-seller was obvious. The *Saturday Review* commented, "Capote got two million and his heroes got the rope."[79]

Two Versions on Film

Two years after Dick Hickock and Perry Smith "got the rope," their story was made into a powerful and critically acclaimed film.[80] Shot in stark black and white, with an ominous musical score by Quincy Jones, the movie has the feeling of a post-World War II film noir. As with the films about Gary Gilmore, *In Cold Blood* evokes the open spaces of the American prairie. Buses, trains, cars, and tumbleweeds travel across the flatlands—just as Dick and Perry traveled after the murder of the Clutter family. Like the nonfiction novel on which it is based, the film has a documentary quality. A number of scenes were filmed at the Clutter home, the actual site of the crime. The two actors chosen to play Dick (Scott Wilson) and Perry (Robert Blake) bear uncanny resemblances to the real killers. Although for the most part the movie follows the book quite closely, there are several points of difference. Dick's family appears to be living in stark poverty. The character playing his father is shown in a shack, with rags on the windows for curtains. With this setting it is easier but less accurate to explain Dick's crimes as growing from a grudge toward society in general, and toward the successful (like the Clutters) in particular. He comes across as a cool, cynical con man. He explains to Perry that there is one law for the rich and one for the poor; that the national pastimes are cheating and stealing. He is motivated by a desire for money that, presumably, will open some of the doors his poverty has closed to him. Perry is treated as a more complex individual. His participation in the murders is part fluke (if he had made contact with another friend, he would never have met up with Dick) and partly the outcome of his horrible upbringing. Perry claims to have loved his father, yet it is his father's face superimposed on Mr. Clutter when Perry kills him and on the hangman who kills Perry. If there is a real villain in this piece, it is "Tex" Smith.

As Perry's family was abusive and Dick's was poverty-stricken, "the boys" create a sort of dysfunctional family of their own. Dick, although clearly heterosexual, calls Perry "honey" and says they will stay together "till death do us part." Their flawed family of two stands in contrast to the victims' ideal family.

The trial in the film parallels the real events in court in important ways. The film shows no case for the defense, analogous to the one hour presented by the actual defense. Green's speech with all its emotional fervor is theatrical enough for the movie. Like the Mormons in the story of Gary Gilmore, the attorney calls on the Bible to justify the shedding of blood in atonement for murder.

Although some critics find it a heavy-handed device, the film includes a character who serves as narrator or sort of one-man Greek chorus in the last portion.[81] The shadowy character, whose voiceover interprets events, provides a psychological profile of "the killer." He is someone who felt physically inferior, sexually inadequate, who could not tell fantasy from reality. He had a violent childhood, and although he would feel an urge to kill before actually committing a murder, he would not mind if he gained nothing from the crime. The profile fits Perry like a glove. At a later time, the narrator explains that together Dick and Perry complemented each other and became a third person. This new character is the one who committed the murders.

At the end of the film, the shadowy figure offers a comment on the executions. Four innocent and two guilty persons have been killed. The deaths sell newspapers, give politicians a subject for speeches, garner attention for police and parole boards. Everyone passes the buck. Then there's another murder. "Maybe this [hanging] will stop it," says a naïve young journalist. "It never has," concludes the narrator.

Thus the movie succeeds in presenting the reality of the crime without glamour or undue sympathy for "the boys" who did it. Yet in a rather obvious way it does raise questions about the death penalty, slightly different questions than those raised in the book. Whereas the latter leads the reader to wonder whether the criminal justice system functions as it should, the movie asks whether capital punishment accomplishes anything other than simple vengeance.

By contrast, the television film *In Cold Blood* made in 1996 is both more overt and more superficial in its analysis.[82] Anthony Edwards's Hickock is a cynical, bullying con man who lives in the moment and is obsessed with women, especially with rather violent sex. As Perry Smith, Eric Roberts is not only too good-looking and too clean-cut, he is almost sweet. His killing of the Clutters is unexplained by his character or by the disconnected references to his family story. Whereas Capote's book and the earlier film portray

Perry's father as abusive and threatening, in the TV film he is an eccentric old codger dressed in a cowboy suit.

The crime itself takes on a specifically sexual dimension as Dick is shown in the act of raping Nancy. Perry "saves" the girl, speaks comfortingly to her about horses, hands her a teddy bear and then, apparently, shoots her, sending her brains all over the wall. The only motive for the shooting in this version seems to come from some perverted competition between the two men to determine who "had the guts to do it" and Dick's determination to "leave no witnesses."

With one exception, the TV film does not show the trial, nor does it note anything about irregularities in the justice system. It moves quickly from the interrogation to brief scenes of the men in their prison cells to the execution. The only exception is a cameo of Dick's mother testifying that her son was a good boy. Next we see Perry telling Agent Dewey that he wants to take the blame for all four killings to spare Dick's mother the pain of thinking of her son as a murderer—another offhand indication that Perry isn't all bad.

The execution scene follows the descriptions in the other versions fairly closely, although the warehouse where it takes place seems huge rather than small and disorderly. However, hangings in Technicolor lack the starkness of the black and white film. Where in the original movie the viewer is left with the notion that Hickock and Smith were also killed "in cold blood," the later version focuses on the appropriateness of the outcome. It suggests that they were just bad and that no further explanation is necessary, an attitude summed up by Agent Dewey's wife. The day after the execution she reads aloud a newspaper article that offers a psychological explanation for the killings (similar to some of what Capote worked into the trial testimony). Mrs. Dewey throws the paper aside and remarks contemptuously, "That's a joke."

If, after that comment, there is any doubt that the killers deserved to be executed, the scene shifts to a dreamlike moment where Nancy Clutter and her horse frolic happily in the river. The sun sparkles on the water. In the spirit that characterized some criminal justice policy in the 1990s when the film was made, one could see the ending as a visual message that executions brought good to society. Retribution restored the community as it was, innocent and happy. The ambiguity of the earlier film was gone.

An Eyewitness Account of the Death Penalty in the United States

According to Jeffrey Kirchmeier, *Dead Man Walking* by Sister Helen Prejean ranks with a handful of extremely significant anti-death penalty books, including Beccaria's *Of Crime and Punishment*, Koestler's *Reflections on Hanging* and

Reflections on the Guillotine by Albert Camus. He even compares it to *Uncle Tom's Cabin*, a book so influential in stimulating anti-slavery feeling that President Abraham Lincoln called its author, Harriet Beecher Stowe, "the little lady who started this big war."[83] Kirchmeier attributes the book's impact to its evenhandedness, its concern for the victims as well as for the defendants, and Sister Helen's effective exposition of her own "journey" to understand and oppose the death penalty. He further claims that the commercial success of the book and the film made the death penalty a marketable subject for popular culture.[84]

Another reviewer notes that Sister Helen took as her mission Justice Thurgood Marshall's notion that if people knew the truth about capital punishment, they would consider it shocking and unacceptable. To further the education process, copies of *Dead Man Walking* were sent to members of the Supreme Court.[85] Raymond Schroth compared the book to *Silent Spring*, which had inspired the environmental movement. Not only might the message reach the Supreme Court, he predicted, but someday Americans might look back at the death penalty with the shame they now feel toward slavery.[86]

The account of Prejean's personal acquaintance with capital punishment grew out of her religious commitment to take on the struggles of the poor. Joining in those efforts "inevitably means challenging the wealthy and those who serve their interests." To do so, she came to understand how *systems* inflict pain and hardship. In other words, in her own learning process Sister Helen realized that injustice is not just the work of malicious or selfish individuals. If unjust systems are responsible for inflicting pain and hardship, it is not enough to be personally kind, it is necessary to work to change the system.[87] Thus *Dead Man Walking* may be read both as the stories of two men on death row and Sister Helen's work with them and also as a critique of the political and economic structures that enclose those stories. Unlike the works considered previously where authors created "novels" out of real events, Sister Helen makes every effort to report what actually happened as truthfully as possible. Her critique becomes persuasive to the reader because Prejean's own reactions to what she learns and experiences are so real and believable.

The Shame of Killing Pat Sonnier

Sister Helen's first encounter with a death row inmate came when she agreed to write to Elmo Patrick (Pat) Sonnier, a young white man convicted for the rape and murder of a teenaged couple. Through Pat, Sister Helen became aware of class biases in the criminal justice system as well as the deep flaws in the application of the death penalty. Like Dick Hickock, Pat noted that there were no rich men on death row. In fact, in the film Sister Helen first establishes rapport with him by commenting that both she and Sonnier live among the poor, she in a housing project and he in prison.

The familiar link between poverty and poor legal representation is obvious in Pat's case. Although he and his brother Eddie were both convicted of rape and murder, and it is even likely that Eddie actually did the killing, the latter got life in prison while Pat was sentenced to death. Sister Helen found that Pat's attorney provided "shamefully inadequate counsel."[88] Yet Louisiana did not provide legal representation for indigent defendants who wished to appeal their cases. It was only because Sister Helen found a first-rate death penalty specialist, Millard Farmer, who was willing to take on the case that Pat was able to challenge his sentence. In both the book and the movie, Farmer serves as the expert who educates Sister Helen, and, by extension, the readers and viewers, about the flaws in the criminal justice system. A good attorney is critical to everything that happens to a defendant. Farmer implies that if the accused has a poorly qualified lawyer it gives the district attorney an incentive to go to trial and even to ask for the maximum penalty, whereas with a "top notch defense attorney," the state is much more likely to plea bargain rather than risk losing in court. He points out that the process works like a series of turnstiles: a defendant can keep going forward toward the death chamber but it is impossible to go back and fix mistakes if the original lawyer did not raise the issue at trial. Thus, although there were questions about Pat's interrogation, about comments the district attorney made during the trial, and about the state's excessive use of peremptory challenges, the original attorney did not object at the time, and those issues could not be raised on appeal. Farmer noted that in the days immediately after *Gregg v. Georgia*, the federal courts had monitored such errors, but, by the 1990s they tended to defer much more to the states. The courts, in his view, were "so interested in speeding up executions that it doesn't seem to matter if they're running roughshod over people's constitutional rights."[89]

Racism in the form of punishing crimes against white victims more severely than those with black victims also distorts the system of capital punishment. According to *Dead Man Walking*, predominantly white judges and jurors are more outraged if whites are murdered and more willing to execute their killers than if the victims were black. Sister Helen found that although 90 percent of homicide victims in Louisiana were black, 75 percent of those on death row were there for killing a white person. The nun encountered the same phenomenon when, working with victims' family members, she found that among forty murders with African American victims, only one or two of them even went to trial. She and Farmer conclude that race, poverty, and geography determine who gets sentenced to death. It is likely to happen when the victim is white, the defendant poor, and the local district attorney wants the political advantage of a capital conviction.[90]

The systematic race and class biases in the criminal justice system form the basis for Prejean's opposition to capital punishment at the same time as she condemns the crimes and empathizes with the survivors. "I would not want my death avenged—*especially by government*—which cannot be trusted to control its own bureaucrats, collect taxes equitably, or fill a pothole, much less decide which of its citizens to kill."[91] The comment becomes more powerful as Sister Helen later reveals the corruption that marked the decisions of the state Pardon Board, whose members took bribes and whose chairman eventually went to prison. Likewise, Governor Edwin Edwards (who went to prison for graft after *Dead Man Walking* was published), claimed to dislike the death penalty. However, not wanting to risk his political career or take personal responsibility for "deciding which citizens to kill," he put capital appeals as far from himself as possible by claiming he was forced to rely on the Pardon Board's findings.

Nor did many within the Catholic Church acquit themselves well when it came to capital punishment. Although the United States Conference of Bishops issued a statement opposing the death penalty, the archbishop of New Orleans wrote a formal opinion that Catholics could, in good conscience, support it. When two Jesuit priests testified against the execution of an indigent black man, the archbishop sent two other priests to argue the opposite side.[92] In addition, the Catholic chaplain at the prison where Sister Helen visited did everything he could to make her life difficult. He criticized her for not wearing a nun's habit (although such attire had been optional for more than twenty years) and asserted that women were too emotional to serve as spiritual advisers. He claimed that Prejean was naïve, easily taken in by the convicts, and that Pat Sonnier might have "lost his soul" because he did not receive the last rites from a priest. That too, the chaplain believed, was Sister Helen's fault.[93] Unlike the "naïve" nun, the chaplain seemed neither to question the system nor to perceive the humanity of the men caught up in it.

But the chaplain, the archbishop, the political figures, and even the lawyers were all peripheral figures compared to Pat Sonnier. Unlike Gary Gilmore or Perry Smith, Pat had not suffered a violently abusive childhood, although his life was far from easy. His parents had fought and separated. His father took him to a bar and bought him drinks when Pat was twelve years old. They were so poor that the Sonnier brothers often had to go out and shoot a squirrel or a rabbit for food. He'd gotten into some trouble as a juvenile and had been sent to prison for stealing a truck. (His accomplice, a cousin whose family had hired a lawyer, got probation for the same offense.) At the same time, Pat had a strong work ethic and deep affection for his family. Sister Helen found him "human and likeable." Pat comes across as someone who has had a lot of bad luck and made some very wrong choices, but who, if his financial profile had been different would certainly not be on death row, labeled a "monster."

It is the personhood of the condemned man that is *Dead Man Walking*'s most powerful argument against the death penalty. Without romanticizing the violence he committed and while insisting that he take responsibility, Sister Helen shows Pat Sonnier to be someone worth saving, in both senses of the word. If there was any doubt of his fundamental humanity, he ended his life with dignity. He thanked the cook for his last meal, refused the "nerve medicine" that would "relax" him, and noted how degrading it was for a grown man to be dressed in a diaper. Like Gary Gilmore, he expressed relief that he would be free: "no more life in a cage." His last words asked forgiveness "for what me and Eddie done, but Eddie done it." Sonnier's life ended by raising the question of whether, although the state executed a man who committed a violent crime, they may have executed someone who was not a murderer.

Millard Farmer, a veteran of capital punishment litigation, found the execution repellent. His words echoed Thurgood Marshall. "How shameful. A few witnesses deep within a prison in the dead of night to watch a man killed. If most people in Louisiana saw what the state did tonight, they would throw up."[94] Among those who did know what the state did, no one wanted to take responsibility. The staff of the Department of Corrections were just "doing their job." Those involved in the execution carried out a drill, like doing an exercise. When Prejean asked the head of the Corrections Department what had been accomplished, he confirmed the words of the journalist from *In Cold Blood*, "Zero, absolutely nothing."[95]

Later she talked with another officer in charge of death row who admitted that after an execution he could not eat or sleep. Speaking of the condemned men, he stated, "I don't excuse what they've done, but I talk to them when I make my rounds. I talk to them and many of them are just like little boys inside big men's bodies, little boys who never had much chance to grow up. After the electrocution, I just can't square it with my conscience, putting them to death like that . . . a man who can't defend himself." That officer eventually yielded to his internal conflict. He took a transfer from death row, retired at the first opportunity, and soon after was the victim of a heart attack.[96]

The futility and inhumanity of capital punishment did not bother some within the criminal justice system. Prejean quoted a district attorney who admitted that the death penalty was not a deterrent. But even if it was not, he said, "All we've lost is the life of a convicted criminal." A life that he believed he could dismiss as "disposable," "not as human as you or I."[97] Prejean's book is, from beginning to end, a challenge to that way of thinking.

"Killing People Is Wrong"

The second convict who became Sister Helen's advisee may have seemed more "disposable" than Pat Sonnier. With Robert Lee Willie, there was no doubt that he actually raped and killed in an eight-day rampage that extended across several states. He expressed racist views and claimed to be an admirer of Adolph Hitler. Willie fit the death row profile. His family was poor and dysfunctional, with a father who spent most of his time in prison. Willie himself was raised behind bars, like Gary Gilmore. And, although he was a killer, Willie's case can also demonstrate flaws in the system. One could identify the political uses of the death penalty. Willie had been tried, convicted, and sentenced in federal court to three life terms for his crimes. Yet the state of Louisiana was able to bring him back and charge him with capital murder in state court for one of those offenses. President Ronald Reagan, running for reelection at the time, personally called the victim's father and *promised* that Willie would be brought to Louisiana and sentenced to death.

Willie's story revealed the continued arbitrariness of the death penalty. His accomplice, who was tried at the same time, in the same courthouse, with a different lawyer, got life in prison. It demonstrated the disadvantages of being poor and being stuck with inadequate representation. Willie's state-appointed counsel failed to prepare any witnesses at his trial and offered no evidence in mitigation at the sentencing hearing. He did not object when members of the jury pool overheard the accomplice's lawyer claim that Willie was the killer.[98]

Sister Helen's work with Robert Lee Willie involved encouraging him to lose his hate and anger, to take responsibility for his own acts, and to go to death with repentance. His last words indicate that she succeeded. He spoke first to Mr. and Mrs. Harvey, his victim's parents, who had been enthusiastic about the execution. "I hope you get some relief from my death." Willie continued, "Killing people is wrong. That's why you've put me to death. It makes no difference whether it's citizens, countries, or governments. Killing is wrong."[99]

Once again the reader faces the contradictions raised by Willie's death. What was accomplished? Prejean notes that now another person was dead and another mother had to bury her child. In an interview with Peter Jennings on ABC she mentioned that the presence of the victim's family at an execution seemed to emphasize that the death penalty was personal vengeance. Its supporters claimed that capital punishment was a noble act on the part of the state. Such alleged nobility was belied by the secrecy with which executions were actually carried out. She stated again that if the state did not kill in secret, if the torture and violence of executions were unmasked, "we would be embarrassed."[100]

Both Sides

Dead Man Walking is notable for the attention and respect it pays to the families of victims and to their suffering. Sister Helen refuses to take sides, to fall into the thinking that if she ministers to the condemned man she cannot also grieve for the losses he caused. Her position stands—consciously—in opposition to politicians who would tell the public that they must care either about the victim or about the killer, as if treating the latter as a human being showed disrespect for the people he injured. Because Sister Helen will not make that either/or choice, the reader is free to see both sides.

Besides exemplifying the ability to care for "both sides," Prejean reveals hypocrisy in the way the criminal justice system treats some victims as valuable and others as if they were just as "disposable" as the condemned men. She brought together a survivors' group in inner city New Orleans. These poor African American families had lost loved ones to murder. Yet most had never even been interviewed by an investigating officer; many had never seen any official documents such as an autopsy report or even a death certificate. Needless to say, in most cases they did not have the "closure" of knowing that their child's killer had been punished. Meanwhile Sister Helen read reports of district attorneys so solicitous of white victims that they visited the families at home and held press conferences to express their outrage.[101]

Among the families of Sonnier's and Willie's victims, Prejean encountered a range of responses, from working to forgive the killer to wanting to see him "fry." Vernon Harvey, the stepfather of Willie's victim, was the most vehement. He could not rest until "justice was done," assuming that the execution would restore life in some way. Perhaps he felt that if his daughter's killer did not die, her memory would be betrayed. But what if Willie, like his accomplice, had been sentenced to life in prison? Sister Helen believed that he would have faded away into anonymity. Perhaps then the Harveys could have gone on with their lives, rather than standing immobilized like deer in the headlights. As if was, they could think only about the revenge that the "state has promised them." They follow the appeals, and "wait and wait, reliving the murder again and again. And the hope is that when Willie's death does come, it will ease their pain and their loss. At least they will have justice."[102] She does not minimize the Harveys' grief; rather she believes that the state has misled them by promising a comfort they will not feel, even after the execution occurs.

Reviewing *Dead Man Walking*, Hilary Holman states that Sister Helen's reactions to the death penalty are convincing. She cites the desperation of Vernon Harvey, still angry and dissatisfied even as, after Willie was dead, he spins out fantasies of crueler methods of execution. Harvey still grieves and rages, but now he has no object to focus on. "Even vengeance has not been served."[103] Thus, Prejean has demolished the last justification for the death penalty—the need for retribution. Aside from the deep biases and flaws in the system, the failure of deterrence, the moral problems with states taking human life, capital punishment falls short even of providing closure to the victims' families.

Adapting *Dead Man Walking*

Few people predicted that a nun's memoir, her journey into the reality of capital punishment, would become a best seller. Unlike *The Executioner's Song* and *In Cold Blood*, it was neither the work of a famous writer nor the story of an infamous crime. Translating the book into a commercial film meant some changes in the story, making it more linear and a bit less didactic.

In the movie, Pat Sonnier and Robert Lee Willie become a composite character, Matthew Poncelet.[104] Sean Penn, with a devilish goatee, slicked-back hair, and a sinister look in the early scenes, plays the condemned man; an understated Susan Sarandon has the role of Sister Helen. However, making two men into one dilutes some of the book's power. The written version was more successful in showing how both a generally decent man who was probably not a killer and a harder person who definitely murdered suffer from the systemic flaws in the death penalty. But Matt's story clearly raises the issue of inadequate counsel. Like Sonnier and Willie, he gets death while his partner gets life in prison. (A writer in the conservative *National Review* called it a "clever move" to give the guiltier accomplice a life sentence. He apparently thought it was a fictional plot device, rather than a reflection of the importance of a decent lawyer.)[105] The economic biases in the criminal justice system as well as its use for political purposes also affect Matt. He mentions that the governor, who is running for reelection, has overseen the execution of two black men and suggests that it's time to put a white convict to death. In the background of the film, one sees billboards and hears radio ads advocating "get tough" policies as part of political campaigns. At the Pardon Board hearing, the district attorney pulls out all the stops calling for Poncelet's execution. He calls him a "heartless killer" and claims that justice for the "sweet girl" who was his victim is long past due. He mentions how the families of the murdered teenagers will never see their weddings, their grandchildren, and so on. He tells the Board to "steel their spines," as if its politically appointed members were likely to falter because a poor defendant was able to demonstrate the flaws in his conviction. Matt's lawyer is not given a very good script before the Pardon Board either. He uses the occasion to lecture on the death penalty, especially the cruelty of lethal injection. Although that is something about which the film wishes to educate the audience, discussing it at that point interrupts the flow of the story. While the district attorney asks the Pardon Board for "simple justice," that is, proceeding with the execution, Sister Helen's role is to demonstrate that killing Matt does not accomplish what the state has promised.

"Simple justice" would suggest that the process somehow restores a sense of rightness, that things will resume their proper place. Yet if there is one emotion that dominates *Dead Man Walking* it is grief, a sense of irrevocable loss. The families of the victims continue to mourn for their children, but while one father tries to go beyond the hate to forgiveness, the other parents want only retribution. They turn their grief into rage at Matt, and to some extent at Sister Helen because she refuses to make a choice between the respectable victims and the murdering "scum." And yet, like Vernon Harvey in the book, they are not satisfied by witnessing the execution. Matt's family is also devastated by loss. His mother, inarticulate and inept, is broken-hearted. Her life and her younger sons' lives will never be restored to normality either. Matt comes to understand that his actions have caused all this sadness, and after accepting that, he is able to go to his execution without hate and with dignity.

The execution scene is dramatic. Unlike Sonnier and Willie, who were electrocuted, Poncelet is put to death by lethal injection. After he is strapped to the gurney, he asks forgiveness of the boy's father, and then, quoting Robert Lee Willie, says "Killing is wrong, no matter who does it, me, you, or your government." The gurney is, at that point, in an upright position, showing Matt with his arms pulled outward as if he were being crucified. While the vials of lethal fluids empty, scenes of the murders for which he is being put to death are superimposed over the death chamber. Finally, in an ambiguous moment, the images of the two young victims are reflected, smiling, in the window of the execution chamber. Are they happy that "justice is done," are they welcoming the repentant Matthew to the anticipated "better place," or are they, perhaps, judging those who take yet another life?

The execution does not end the film. Matt's family buries him, and again their grief is obvious. The father of the young man Matt killed stands in the background. He admits that he still feels hate. "I don't have your faith," he says to Sister Helen. She replies that it isn't faith, but work that will find the way out of hate. In the movie's last scene, Sister Helen and the father pray together. In a sense, the "work" needs to go on at all levels—experiencing personal transformation, consoling those who mourn, and trying to fix the flaws in the system.

There are critics, such as Austin Sarat, who argue that *Dead Man Walking* is strictly limited in the questions it raises. He finds that it focuses too much on the individual and his responsibility and not enough on the legal problems with the death penalty or the social causes of crime.[106] He further claims that such movies assume the legitimacy of capital punishment and invite us to justify its use.[107] Apparently he means that by presenting the view that Matthew needed to take responsibility and repent for his behavior, the film was somehow holding him accountable and therefore justifying his execution. To some extent, Sister Helen did take the existence of capital punishment as a given and thus tried to help Matt prepare for his death, but at no time does the film seem to be on the side of those who actually advocate or even support the death penalty. Victoria Rebeck finds a somewhat different theme. She thinks that the movie is less about the politics of the death penalty than about the courage to accept responsibility and to love even the unlovable. It is not only Matt who must take responsibility; Sister Helen must also see what is required of her.[108] By contrast, those who work in the criminal justice system and "pass the buck" for its failures are not accepting their responsibilities. Christy Rodgers finds that with the "unremitting focus on the actions and motivations of individual characters," the social evil of capital punishment loses its systemic quality. In her view, the film suggests that if bad characters are converted or neutralized, injustice, oppression, and prejudice will be neutralized.[109] On the other hand, she believes that the execution scene was crudely drawn to make the point that state-sponsored killing and individual killing are both wrong. To undercut the "sterile" lethal injection with the bloody murders served no other purpose than to make the point that execution equals murder.[110] Rodgers seems to find fault with the film both for its emphasis on the individual story and for its generalizations about capital punishment.

David Dow contrasts *Dead Man Walking* with real life. He believes its message, conveyed through the story of a rather vile character, is that platitudes and easy answers are false. He compares the film's use of gory footage to the Supreme Court's use of grisly details in their opinions. The Court, he asserts, does that simply to make readers totally unsympathetic to the offender, so unsympathetic that they will be willing to allow unconstitutional violations of his rights. In the movie, viewers do not want to see Matt treated unjustly, even if his only endearing quality is that he loves his family and they love him. That quality takes him out of the realm of "monsters" and makes him human.[111]

Another reviewer, Brian Johnson, notes that the film is successful because it does not proselytize. Because Matt is neither innocent nor terribly sympathetic, it forces the audience to consider whether the state should kill *anyone*, even a violent criminal, in cold blood. Johnson sees the lethal injection scene as making a link between murder and execution as two sides of the same coin. In fact, the scene demonstrates that no killing is more premeditated and cold-blooded than an execution.[112] Whether or not that message constitutes proselytizing, it is almost identical to Capote's theme in tying together Smith and Hickock's crimes with the state putting them to death in cold blood.

Sister Helen Prejean's accounts of her experiences with men condemned to death in her book, the movie, and later an opera, [113] have given her a great deal of credibility in discussing the issue of capital punishment in the United States. The people she originally wrote about, Pat Sonnier and Robert Lee Willie, by their own admission committed terrible crimes, yet she was able to explain their stories in a way that humanized them and portrayed the death penalty as unacceptable. It is unfortunate that Sister Helen was not able to reach so wide an audience with the story of Dobie Williams, a death row inmate to whom she ministered in the late 1990s. She believed that Williams, a poor black man accused of killing a white victim, tried before an all-white jury, with a lawyer who put on no defense, was truly innocent. Williams fit the death row profile perfectly, and in Prejean's opinion, was "railroaded to death" because a white person had been killed in a small racist Southern town and someone had to pay for it. As his execution approached, Dobie grew in faith and love, even for those who had wronged him. Sister Helen believed his death was truly a crime.[114] Yet she maintained her position that ultimately innocence or guilt is not the issue in the struggle against the death penalty. Rather the real argument is that the state should not kill people, even the guilty.

The books and movies examined in this chapter have considered the stories of men who, in most cases, committed the acts for which they were put to death. But they have also raised the issue of whether the state, in taking their lives "in cold blood," has itself betrayed human values. In addition, every example has revealed serious flaws in the criminal justice system, flaws directly related to social and economic class. Finally, each work has raised the question: What was accomplished by this execution?

Putting Gary Gilmore to death ended the miserable life of an unhappy man. It also, amidst great fanfare, triggered the restoration of capital punishment as a feature of American life. The execution of Perry Smith and Dick Hickock satisfied the public demand for their lives in return for the lives of the Clutter family. Despite the rosy epilogues in the book and the TV film, their deaths did not restore innocence to the community. More likely, the film's anonymous narrator correctly pointed out that the death penalty would not prevent the next murder. *Dead Man Walking* in all its incarnations makes it plain that capital punishment does not heal, it only widens the circle of grief. All of these representations of state executions could lead one to agree with the Louisiana Director of Corrections. On the positive side, they accomplished "zero, absolutely nothing."

·4·

—

NOVELS TRANSFORMED
INTO FILMS

The previous chapter looked at books and movies drawn from actual cases. They told of men who were found guilty and sentenced to death for murder "in real life." The stories are compelling both as they explore human emotions and as they bring to light glitches in "the machinery of death." This chapter will focus on fictional narratives dealing with the death penalty. Each of these narratives became a commercial film. The five novels and films were chosen because they have, in one or both genres, enjoyed great popularity with the reading and viewing public. *A Lesson Before Dying* and *To Kill a Mockingbird* have been the choice of teachers and librarians around the country, not only for classroom assignments but also for citywide reading programs.[1] Two novels by lawyer and best-selling writer John Grisham, *A Time to Kill* and *The Chamber*, deal with capital cases. Likewise, Stephen King's 1996 work *The Green Mile* sold millions of copies in serial form and as a complete book. It then became a successful movie.

It may be startling at first to realize that these works of fiction, set in the 1930s and 1940s as well as the 1980s, address many of the issues raised in the nonfiction pieces from the post-*Furman* era. All deal specifically with matters of race and class as those factors interact with the criminal justice system. In four of the five stories, the defendant is poor and black. In the fifth, he is a member of the Ku Klux Klan. Contemporary readers and viewers will note legal and social changes since the period in which the works were set. They will also note that questions of the fairness of the system and its accuracy in determining guilt or innocence persist. As in the earlier works, through these books and movies the accused—even the aged racist in *The Chamber*—become real, individual human beings with stories that deserve our attention rather than "monsters" who must be expunged from society. All five stories are set in the South: two in Louisiana, two in Mississippi, one in Alabama. Historically and at present, the death penalty has been inflicted much more frequently in the Southern states. Fiction writers who live and write about the South would likely see capital punishment as a more established fact of life. Likewise, the racial themes in these novels have particular resonance given the history of slavery and segregation in the region. Although racial disparities in the application of the death penalty have occurred around the country, the overt appeals to racism portrayed in these novels and films seem more familiar in the Southern setting.

Finally, it is important to distinguish between how essentially nonfiction works like those discussed in the previous chapter and the novels considered below deal with a subject like the death penalty. While the books by Mailer, Gilmore, Capote, and Prejean address legal and justice issues head-on, fiction writers are more likely to examine the process of condemning a person to death as part of a complex depiction of human experience. In other words, these novels are not "about" the death penalty. They include a confrontation with the issue of state execution, but that issue is only one among the many threads woven into each story.

If We Must Die, Let It Not Be Like Hogs

Within its first ten pages, the themes emphasized in this chapter emerge in Ernest J. Gaines's *A Lesson Before Dying*.[2] From the beginning it is obvious that Jefferson, a poor, young, uneducated black man, is not afforded due process when he is tried for the murder of a white storekeeper. His conviction is a foregone conclusion, his attorney is a disgrace, his death sentence comes as no surprise. What does unfold in the novel is the meaning of Jefferson's death to him and especially to the African American community in rural Louisiana.

Most of the novel is told in the voice of Grant Wiggins, the "teacher." Wiggins is an educated man in the midst of the plantation society that persisted in rural Louisiana even in the late 1940s. His day job is teaching in the one-room schoolhouse that also serves on Sundays as the black church. After the trial, Grant's aunt and Jefferson's godmother assign the teacher the critical task of helping Jefferson to see himself as a man before he goes to the electric chair. This project is necessary because both the segregationist society and especially the justice system have stripped Jefferson—and by extension other black men—of any notion that he is a human being entitled to dignity and respect. Philip Auger describes Grant's assignment as redefining Jefferson from "the identity given him by the white dominant culture, hog, to a new identity, man."[3]

Grant was not present at Jefferson's trial, but he knew how it would proceed without being there. A white man had been killed, two robbers died at the scene, one (Jefferson) was captured. "He too would have to die."[4] The prosecution had one version of the events, the defendant another. Jefferson's story was that after watching the shooting he "wanted to run but he couldn't run. He couldn't even think. He didn't know where he was. He didn't know how he had gotten there. He couldn't remember a thing he had done all day."[5] He didn't have any idea what to do. He could not call for help, as he had never dialed a telephone in his life. Instead, he snatched a bottle of liquor, took a drink, and grabbed the money in the cash register, even though he knew stealing was wrong. At that moment, several white men entered the store. From their perspective, which became the prosecution's version, Jefferson had been involved in the killings and robbery and was found taking a drink to celebrate the mayhem he had caused.

In the 1931 Scottsboro case *Powell v. Alabama*, the Supreme Court ruled that states were constitutionally required to provide defendants in capital cases with competent legal representation.[6] Jefferson had an attorney. The lawyer's argument to the all-white jury that they should spare the life of the accused, while it is odious, reveals the mind-set of those called upon to decide whether he would live or die. The attorney said that Jefferson, even though he was over twenty-one years old, was not a man. "I would call it a boy and a fool. . . . Do you see a man sitting here? Look at the shape of this skull, this face as flat as the palm of my hand. Do you see a modicum of intelligence?. . . . What you see here is a thing that acts on command. A thing to hold the handle of a plow, a thing to load your bales of cotton, to chop your wood, to pull your corn." Jefferson's lawyer noted that his client did not know the months of the year, nor could he recognize the names of Keats, Byron, or Scott. He could not quote the Constitution or the Bill of Rights. "What justice would there be to take this life?" the defense counsel asked. "Why I would as soon put a hog in the electric chair as this."[7] Thus Jefferson's lawyer pleaded for his life by arguing that, in human terms, it was worthless. The jury returned from their lunch break with a guilty verdict.

Grant believed himself ill-prepared to build Jefferson's sense of self-worth. He was acutely aware that his job consisted of drilling children in what white folks told him to teach. By implication, his job was to assist in maintaining, not challenging, the status quo, in a sense to ensure that black people remained as ignorant of "culture" as Jefferson's lawyer had described. Grant was not expected to show too much intelligence in the presence of whites. Correct grammar and pronunciation would be interpreted as "getting above himself." In such an environment, what was the purpose of helping Jefferson? "Suppose I reached him and made him realize that he was as much a man as any other man; then what? He's still going to die. The next day, the next week, the next month. So what will I have accomplished? What will I have done? Why not let the hog die without knowing anything?"8

During Grant's early visits with Jefferson in the segregated jail, his efforts did seem hopeless. The condemned man was silent and defiant, his face a total blank. He refused to eat the food his godmother cooked for him and refused to respond to Grant's attempts at conversation. Once he got down on hands and knees and ate without using his hands, like a hog. He feared he was being fattened up to be killed. "Hogs don't worry. Hogs just know."9 During another visit he decided he wanted a gallon of vanilla ice cream for his last meal. "Eat it with a pot spoon. A whole gallona ice cream. . . . Ain't never had enough ice cream. Never had more than a nickel cone."10

A breakthrough occurs when Grant brings Jefferson a radio. The music seems to establish a connection with human society that becomes clear during the next visit when Grant delivers some pecans and peanuts sent by the schoolchildren and Jefferson tells him to thank them. Such simple courtesy links him again with the human family. Finally, in the last period before Jefferson's death, Grant persuades him to write his thoughts in a little note-book. Despite being almost illiterate, Jefferson demonstrates his dignity and humanity through the written words.

The transformation of Jefferson from "hog" to man does more than pre-pare him to walk to his death with dignity. It allows him to become a symbol of heroism to the entire African American community. Grant muses on the need for black heroes as he considers the importance of Joe Louis and Jackie Robinson. "What else in the world was there to be proud of?"11 Jefferson too could challenge the myth that African Americans were inferior. "White people believe they're better than anyone else on earth—and that's a myth. The last thing they ever want is to see a black man stand, and think, and show that common humanity that is in us all. It would destroy their myth. They would no longer have justification for having made us slaves and keeping us in the condition we are in. As long as none of us stand, they're safe."12 Thus it became Jefferson's role to stand, in both senses of the word, for his people. As he wrote in his tablet, "Man walk on two foots; hogs on four hoofs."13

Jefferson walks to the electric chair like a brave man and brings a sense of dignity to the ritual of his death. This is not an easy task, considering that he is executed in the storeroom on the bottom floor of the courthouse in a traveling electric chair. During the first half of the twentieth century, several Southern states sent the execution apparatus from county to county to carry out death sentences. Given the potential problems in administering the appropriate dose of electricity "painlessly," the casual way in which the chair was hooked up, turned on, and disassembled before going on to the next site suggest a certain callousness on the part of the state, a callousness probably related to the race of the executed man.

Although racism permeates *A Lesson Before Dying*, there is also hope for reconciliation in the character of the deputy Paul. Paul treats Jefferson like what the latter called a "youman," and Jefferson reciprocates by entrusting Paul with the delivery of his notebook to Grant. The deputy reaches across the racial divide when he suggests to Grant that they call each other by their given names. In the book's final scene, Paul reports that Jefferson was the bravest man in the room when he walked to his death. He offers his hand to Grant, "Allow me to be your friend, Grant Wiggins. I don't ever want to forget this day. I don't ever want to forget him."[14] It seems then that Jefferson's role as hero may extend beyond the black community and have an impact even on a white representative of the justice system. Critic Paul Auger claims that the transformation of Paul shows that the "white patriarchy is now being changed, not just penetrated." In his view, the old mythology of white power was not just rejected but was replaced with a new belief claiming that dignity transcends racial difference.[15] William Nash also notes the significance of ending the novel with the friendship of Grant and Paul. They could not save Jefferson, but their personal bond showed that it was possible to cross the racial barrier that led to Jefferson's suffering and death.[16]

Another critic places *A Lesson Before Dying* in the literary tradition where the execution of an innocent man is a "familiar trope to represent the broader repression of African Americans."[17] In other words, Jefferson, his trial, his sentence, and his death are a sort of metaphor for racial injustice in American history and particularly for the laws and policies that robbed the black community of positive male role models. One can certainly choose to read the novel to support any of these interpretations. A reader may also see it as a starting point for asking whether the system as it exists in the twenty-first century still reflects the conditions and attitudes that determined Jefferson's fate. How many of those on death row today were unable to assist in their own defense because they lacked the education or the intelligence to do so? How many were not articulate in explaining their movements at the time of the crime? How many have been provided with attorneys no more sensitive to the client's needs than Jefferson's? And how many prosecutors decide to seek the death penalty when the victim is white and someone black must pay the price?

A Lesson Before Dying was made into an HBO movie in 1999. The film is well cast with Don Cheadle as Grant, Mekhi Phifer as Jefferson, and wonderful performances from Cicely Tyson and Irma P. Hall as the aunt and godmother.[18] At one level, the film version is chiefly concerned with the transformation of the individuals Grant and Jefferson. The latter makes the journey from "hog" to man. Between the time of his trial and his last diary entry, "Tell the children I'm strong, tell them I'm a man," he comes to appreciate his own worth through the dialogue with the teacher. Even his appearance changes—from stupefied fear and shock at the time of the crime, to impassivity during the trial, to openness and sensitivity at the end of his life. Jefferson's eyes seem to come alive with a new level of understanding, a sure sign of humanity.

Grant begins the film believing there are only two choices for a black man in the South—he can either flee (Grant always raises the toast "To flight" before he takes a drink) or he can be dragged down to the level of a beast. He and Jefferson, at first, seem to represent the two options, the educated man who can escape and the hog. If those are indeed the only possibilities for African Americans, Grant's efforts with the children in the poor one-room school are destined to be futile. While he tells the children that he is giving them a chance to grow into responsible young men and ladies, he fears they will actually end up digging ditches for white men or working in their kitchens. He fears that nothing will ever change.

Thus Jefferson's role as a hero, a challenger of the white myths, becomes critical as it offers a third option. A black man can stay *and* challenge the status quo. That is what his girlfriend Vivian demands of Grant when she tells him, "If you run away, you run away from your people and you run away from me." He has made his decision to stay when, in the next scene, he asks her to marry him and introduces her to his aunt. From the dignity of Jefferson's death, Grant seems to gain the courage to stand as a man in his community, not to run away.

The character Paul, who represented the hope for racial reconciliation in the novel, is missing from the film. Instead, the scene that seems to prefigure the future is the long walk Grant and the children take from their poor segregated school to the courthouse. The camera catches their progress from every angle—through the cane fields and the "quarter," past the cemetery, into the town and past the white school, up the steps of the courthouse. On this trip they are going to visit Jefferson, but the scene suggests the walk that many of these young people would take a decade later as they join the civil rights movement. Then black people refused to make the choice between flight and dehumanization at the hands of the white power structure, but instead marched up to the seat of government and insisted on their rightful places there. With such a transformation, a fate like Jefferson's would not be a foregone conclusion for future generations.

The Senseless Slaughter of Songbirds[19]

To Kill a Mockingbird was published in 1960 during the modern civil rights era, but it is set in Maycomb, a small Alabama town, in 1936. One year after its publication, the novel had been translated into ten languages. It sold over a half million copies in fifteen years and was the third best selling novel of the twentieth century. According to the Library of Congress, *To Kill a Mockingbird* was second only to the Bible in being cited as making a difference in people's lives. In 2003, the American Film Institute voted Atticus Finch number one on the list of film heroes from the last one hundred years.[20] Undeniably, the novel and film are cultural icons in the United States. It is not unreasonable to argue that many Americans have derived some of their ideas about the justice system from the story.

One may read Harper Lee's novel from several perspectives. It can be seen as Scout's story—the narrative of a child meeting fear and injustice for the first time. Or it may be viewed as Atticus's story, one in which a man rises to the demands of his conscience even as his choices threaten those he loves most. For our purposes, it will be considered as a story about justice and its absence, one in which the death penalty figures as a significant element. Unlike *A Lesson Before Dying*, this book does not include a formal execution. Yet it does feature the trial of an innocent black man on capital charges—another trial with a preordained conclusion because the alleged offender was black and the alleged victim was white. In this case, the charge is rape rather than murder and although Tom, the defendant, is black and poor like Jefferson, Tom has one of the finest lawyers known to literature.

Atticus Finch seldom practices criminal law. He prefers writing ironclad wills and sorting out civil disputes. Indeed, his career at the criminal bar did not begin brilliantly, as his first two clients had been hanged at the Maycomb City Jail after refusing a reasonable plea bargain and insisting that "the s.o.b. had it coming to him" was a good defense. There was little Atticus could do in that case but "be present at their departure."[21] In contrast, when appointed by the judge to defend Tom Robinson, accused of the South's most heinous crime, raping a white woman, Atticus means to mount a real defense. He does so despite the disapproval of some neighbors, who claim that Finch "went against his raising," that he is "no better than the niggers and trash he works for."[22] Scout and her brother Jem feel the hostility toward their father when their classmates call him a "nigger lover." In the girl's eyes, the other kids make it sound like Atticus is running a still. Why, she wonders, were people criticizing her beloved father? She asks him, "Do you defend niggers?"

Thus Atticus has the opportunity—the teachable moment—to explain why he accepted the challenge of defending Tom. First, he admonishes Scout not to say "nigger," because such language is "common."[23] Tom is a clean-living, churchgoing, hard-working family man. If Atticus had refused to defend him because of his color he could not hold his head up in town, he would forfeit his authority over his children, he would not be fit to serve in the state legislature.

Every lawyer, Atticus claims, has one case in his lifetime that affects him personally—that goes to the essence of his conscience. "Before I can live with other folks, I've got to live with myself." Then, being the man he is, Atticus reminds Scout that most folks would disagree with him and that they are entitled to respect for their opinions. "Will we win?" Scout wants to know. "No," her father answers honestly, but "simply because we were licked a hundred years before we started is no reason not to try."[24]

Some folks in the community disagree so heartily with Atticus that a group of citizens form a lynch mob around the jail where Tom awaits trial. They arrive, "smelling of stale whiskey and pigpen," to find Atticus sitting at the door of the jail, reading, under the front light. Words are exchanged. "Get aside, you know what we want," the men threaten. "Go home," is the lawyer's advice. Perhaps the situation would have been defused or perhaps it would have heated up into violence if Scout, her brother Jem, and their friend Dill had not arrived to see what was going on. It is the little girl who, remembering her manners, steps up and asks one of the lynchers about his son, her classmate. "Tell him I said 'Hey,'" she says. Simply, decency returns to the scene. The mob stands down, Atticus is not injured, and Tom is not lynched. He will have his day in court.[25]

Of course, the jury comes from the same pool as the men outside the jail and shares the same prejudices. The more educated and tolerant townsfolk rarely serve on juries, but manage to be excused. Women are absent from the venire. Black citizens not only are not represented on the jury; they are confined to the "colored balcony." Justice is indeed a separate and unequal thing for those whose skin is not white.

The prosecution begins its case with the sheriff, who testifies that the victim had been beaten up but that no doctor was called to ascertain whether she was, in fact, raped. Thus Tom's trial for his life is based on the testimony of Mayella, the girl who had claimed rape, and her father, Bob Ewell. It was a case that no prosecutor would touch if the racial profile had been anything other than black defendant/white victim, especially given the reputation of the complaining parties. The Ewells "lived as guests of the county in prosperity as well as in the depths of the depression. No truant officer could keep their numerous offspring in school; no public health officer could free them from congenital defects, various worms, and the diseases indigenous to filthy surroundings." Their home is behind the garbage dump where the children scavenge. The only thing that makes Robert E. Lee Ewell "better" than his black neighbors is that "if scrubbed in lye soap with very hot water, his skin was white."[26]

There is no doubt that Mayella had been beaten, but as Atticus demonstrates, she had been struck by a left-handed person. Tom's left arm, 12 inches shorter than his right, is so useless it falls off the Bible when he is sworn in. But

Mayella knows what to do on the witness stand. "That nigger yonder took advantage of me an if you fine fancy gentlemen don't wanna do nothing about it then you're all yellow stinkin cowards, the lot of you." Real men would defend the honor of Southern womanhood and condemn a black man to death—despite the lack of evidence. In the balcony, Scout tries to understand what is going on. At first she thinks Mayella seems stealthy, like "a steady eyed cat with a twitchy tail." Later, she decides that Mayella must be the loneliest person in the world, for when Atticus asks her if she has many friends, she can think only that he is making fun of her. In Scout's view, Tom is probably the only person who ever treated the girl decently. "But when she said he took advantage of her and when she stood up she looked at him as if he were dirt beneath her."[27]

Atticus has no delusions that the structure holding white supremacy in place in Alabama is going to tumble down during this trial. Nonetheless, he tries to chip away at it in his summation. Arguing that the case should never have come to trial, he claims it is "as simple as black and white." There is no physical evidence of rape. What really happened was that Mayella violated the rigid Southern "code"; she tempted a Negro by trying to kiss Tom, the only person who had ever been nice to her. Tom himself is the evidence of her "crime," therefore Tom has to be put away. The Ewells had accused Tom in the cynical confidence that the jury would believe them, because the jury would accept the assumption that all Negroes lie and that all Negroes are basically immoral, and especially that "all Negro men were not to be trusted with our women." Those assumptions constitute "a lie as black as Tom's skin."

Atticus claims that skin color should not matter in court. There all men should enjoy equal treatment. "Our courts have their faults as does any human institution, but in this country our courts are the great levelers, and in our courts all men are created equal." Atticus is not naïve; he has spent enough hours in courtrooms to know of the vast disparities in treatment based on race. But perhaps, like Justice Thurgood Marshall, who said the American people would reject the death penalty if they knew how unfair it was, Finch hopes that pointing out the gap between American ideals and reality will move the jury to do justice.[28]

Not surprisingly, Atticus had been right when he told Scout earlier that there was no chance of winning. A jury in 1935 Alabama could not be expected to take Tom's word against the Ewells. That is obvious when the verdict of guilty and the sentence of death are returned. Even Reverend Sykes, the black minister, accepts the inevitable. "I ain't never seen any jury decide in favor of a colored man over a white man." But Atticus has raised enough questions in the jury's minds that they deliberate for five hours before rendering their verdict. And he has argued so eloquently for equal justice that the entire African

American audience in the courtroom rises when he leaves. "Miss Jean Louise, stand up. Your father's passin'," said the Reverend.[29]

Atticus promises that they will appeal the court's decision, and in fact, Tom does not go to the electric chair. But he is executed by the state of Alabama just the same. Not long after the trial, Tom is "shot trying to escape" from prison. His death is suspicious—the informal execution of an "escaping" prisoner happened often in the pre-civil-rights-era South, especially when the prisoner was black. The fact that Tom is shot seventeen times and that his alleged escape attempt involved running across a yard the size of a football field and trying, with his one good arm, to climb a security fence calls the official explanation into serious question.

A conversation immediately after the trial highlights other relevant issues. Jem asks his father why Tom has been sentenced to death when he didn't kill anyone. When Atticus replies that rape is a capital offense in Alabama, Jem argues that the jury was not required to give Tom death—they could have given him twenty years. Perhaps, his father suggests, the problem is with the standard of evidence. An evidentiary requirement that there be two eyewitnesses who actually saw the crime might save some innocent lives; otherwise there would always be a doubt. "The law says 'reasonable doubt,' but I think a defendant's entitled to the shadow of a doubt. There's always the possibility, no matter how improbable, that he's innocent."[30]

Thus Atticus and his children raise some of the fundamental issues surrounding the death penalty when the story was set (the 1930s), when it was written (1960s), and today. How can the system protect against punishing the innocent, especially when it is permeated with biases of race and class?

Several critics, writing about the themes in *To Kill a Mockingbird*, relate the story to actual events in the twentieth-century South. Christopher Metress finds parallels with the Scottsboro cases, where nine young black men were tried for rape in Alabama only a few years before Tom Robinson's trial. Their first attorneys provided so little representation that the U.S. Supreme Court reversed their convictions. By contrast, in the same time and place, Atticus "rose above racism and injustice to defend the principle that all men and women deserve their day in court, regardless of their ability to pay,"[31] and, one might add, their race. Patrick Chura finds links to the story of Emmett Till, who in 1955 was beaten, tied to a piece of heavy machinery, and thrown into a river after he flirted with a white woman. The two white men responsible for the crime were acquitted by a Mississippi jury. Chura claims that in the 1950s, after the Supreme Court ordered the desegregation of schools, Southerners, determined to protect white supremacy, revived the image of the "black rapist." Both Emmett Till and Tom Robinson were victims of this social trend. For Till and for Tom, accusations of violating the norms of interracial contact led to the death penalty.[32]

Whether inspired by Scottsboro or Emmett Till or any one of the countless other cases where black defendants were falsely accused and convicted in Southern courts, Harper Lee brilliantly captured the injustice that occurs when the law is used to enforce the dominance of one group over another.

The movie made from the novel in 1962 was immensely popular and successful.[33] Filmed in black and white with sets that, for the most part, look quite primitive by the standards of today's movies, it continues to provoke questions about law, justice, and power. As the words of the grown-up Scout provide a voice-over, the movie portrays the serious world of adults through the inquisitive eyes of children. The plot follows the book quite faithfully, with the story of Atticus's defense of Tom Robinson running parallel to the children's curious pursuit of their mysterious neighbor, Boo Radley. The two threads come together at the end when Boo saves Jem from the murderous intentions of Bob Ewell.

The authors of *Reel Justice: The Courtroom Goes to the Movies* claim that Atticus Finch embodies the lawyer's ideal, "to defend even the most hated and despised person in society, regardless of the consequences."[34] At first his children underestimate their father's abilities and contributions, noting that although he could explain anything, explaining was the only thing he was good at. One thing Atticus explains is that no one should ever judge a man until they walk around in his skin. Obviously, the willingness of the judicial system to judge Tom, along with the inability of the townspeople to walk around in his skin, is a central legal theme in the movie. From the moment the judge visits Atticus on his front porch and asks him to represent Tom, the case proceeds with a sense of doom. A drunken Ewell confronts Atticus several times outside the courtroom to assert that he should have killed "the nigger" himself and to threaten the lawyer and his family. The portrayal of Ewell is interesting. Although he is clearly meant to appear drunk, his overalls are clean and his teeth are excellent. In other words, he looks much less like a derelict than one would picture him in the book. Likewise, the "lynch mob" in the film consists of a quiet group of men in clean, pressed farm clothes and hats, who stand with guns in front of the jail where Atticus is protecting Tom. They look more diffident than ominous. The viewer can believe that the lynch mob and the people like them on the jury despise Tom, but one never feels their hatred. In fact, one feels a sort of tired resignation that Tom must be charged, tried, and convicted, and even threatened with lynching, because that is the way things are done.

Atticus defies those expectations by providing Tom with a vigorous defense, one that exposes the lies of the white witnesses and the sordid lives of Ewell and his family. So even though the prosecution "wins" in court, Ewell has to get even with Atticus for exposing him as both pathetic and vicious. For that reason, he spits in the lawyer's face and assaults Jem and Scout. It is not enough for the likes of Ewell that Tom is convicted and killed in the custody of the state. By really defending Tom, Atticus threatened the structure that allowed any white person to feel superior to any black person. Finch threatened to expose the flaws in a legal system in which race was more important than guilt or innocence, not because he rejected the system but because it failed to live up to its promise that all men were equal before the law.

The courtroom scenes, the dramatic center of the movie, are set in a realistic recreation of a segregated small-town Southern courthouse. There the white spectators crowd in on the ground floor and the blacks sit upstairs in the balcony. If the viewer looks closely, he or she will notice people drinking out of separate water fountains on the way into the building. The camera does not linger on the jury, but when they are in view they are notable for their lack of suits. The judge, however, wears a suit rather than a robe. Thus the great seriousness of a trial to determine whether a man will live or die contrasts with a fairly informal setting. It is both a defining event and a part of people's everyday reality. In this context, the cross-examination of Bob and Mayella Ewell, Tom's testimony, and Atticus's closing make it clear to everyone but the jury that the witnesses are lying and that Tom is innocent. Oddly enough there is no mention of a sentence, either by the lawyers or by the judge. It is unthinkable that a judge would hear a verdict of guilty in a capital case, dismiss the jury, and adjourn the court with not a word about what will happen to the defendant. Perhaps the filmmakers assume that everyone knows what Tom's fate will be. Atticus mentions that they have good grounds for an appeal, although as *Reel Justice* notes, it is hard to know what those grounds might be in 1935 when few criminal cases were reviewed on appeal.[35]

As in the novel, Tom is killed while allegedly trying to escape. In the film the incident happens on the very evening of the trial, when Tom is being moved to the prison. According to the deputy, who had intended only to wound him but killed him by mistake, Tom "ran like a crazy man." There is nothing in the dignified, stolid presence of the defendant in the courtroom that suggests he would ever run like a crazy man. The viewer must speculate about how he really met his death. In the movie's final sequence, after Boo Radley killed Ewell to save Jem and Scout, the sheriff summarizes the crimes and punishments. "A black man is dead for no reason. Now the man responsible is dead."

In *To Kill a Mockingbird* an innocent man is killed by the state just as in *A Lesson Before Dying*. In both stories, race is at the heart of the injustice. And although the major characters in both works despise the flaws in the system, the system prevails. But in neither does life return to the status quo ante. We are led to believe that Jefferson's death and the trial of Tom Robinson permanently altered their communities. The communities were changed, not—as proponents of the death penalty argue—because an evil person was removed, but because exposure of injustice in the criminal justice system is a prerequisite for reforming it.

Killing a Gift of God

While *A Lesson Before Dying* and *To Kill a Mockingbird* are revered for their literary merit, Stephen King's body of work consists largely of fantasy/horror thrillers that have appealed more to popular audiences than to critics. There are both fantasy and horror in *The Green Mile*, but there are also themes that reflect the reality of capital punishment in the United States.[36] That John Coffey, a black, indigent drifter with apparently limited intelligence, is condemned to death for the rape and murder of two little blond white girls is very plausible. That he is innocent of the crime but is provided with no defense is completely credible in Depression-era Louisiana. Fantasy becomes the necessary mechanism for demonstrating Coffey's innocence, but even fantasy does not extend far enough to allow innocence to save him from the electric chair.

Paul Edgecombe, a former prison guard, narrates the story from the nursing home where he resides at the age of 104. He recalls the events of 1932 when Coffey (and others) were executed at Cold Mountain Prison in Louisiana. Edgecombe was block superintendent over the "Green Mile," the area with green linoleum made up of six cells that comprised death row and extended to "Old Sparky," the electric chair. The novel offers interesting contrasts—the facilities are primitive and the justice system is rough, but the men who work with the inmates are, by and large, exceptionally decent. Even though the state had chosen a centralized place for executions, they took place in a sort of storage shed. Edgecombe describes it as a miserable room, without heat, where witnesses could see their breath in winter, and with a metal roof that was stifling in summer. There were no concessions to make the condemned man's last moments on earth physically comfortable, yet for the most part, the guards did what they could and treated the inmates with a basic respect.[37] They carried off each execution with dignity and meticulous attention to the solemnity of the occasion. Edgecombe explains that one of his major tasks was to keep the residents calm by talking with them and listening to their stories in the weeks before their death. As the execution neared, he would agree to virtually any request they wanted carried out posthumously. Like the sheriff in *A Lesson Before Dying*, Edgecombe did not wish to have any "aggravation" on death row. His fellow guards were generally humane, religious men, but ultimately, he recalled, "We were killers." Edgecombe had presided over seventy-eight deaths, far more than any of the murderers executed on the

Green Mile had done.[38] The irony does not escape him, at least in retrospect. Thus the story is told through the eyes of someone who worked day in and day out on death row, who came to know the condemned men as individuals, who carried out executions because it was his job and jobs were hard to come by during the Great Depression, but who came to question everything, especially when he had to preside over the killing of John Coffey.

Even before Coffey arrived on death row, Edgecombe reflected on the utility of capital punishment. Eduard Delacroix, a tiny Cajun, had raped and murdered a young girl and then, to hide her body, set fire to a house, killing six other people. Observing "Del" on the Green Mile, the guard saw just a mild-mannered man with a worried face. Whatever had been inside Delacroix that led to his crimes was gone. "Old Sparky never burned what was inside them, and the drugs they inject them with today don't put it to sleep. It vacates, jumps to someone else and leaves us to kill the husks that aren't really alive anyway."[39] Criminologists could follow Edgecombe's thought and ask what conditions—poverty, childhood abuse, brain injuries, substance abuse—create hospitable conditions for "whatever it is" to take root. But according to his reasoning, killing the "husk" served no social purpose.

Even so, capital punishment was the business of the Green Mile, and those who worked there did as the law required. They carried out a "good" execution when a Native American, inevitably called the Chief, was put to death. The Chief, believing that he would wake up in a place with cold, clear, beautiful water, walked with dignity to the chair. When the executioner pulled the switch, which someone had affixed with the label "Mabel's Hair Dryer," the cap hummed, and his body surged forward against the straps. There was a smell from the hot transformer, a second surge when the Chief's body twisted a little, then it was over. Edgecombe comments, "We had once again succeeded in destroying what we could not create." Witnesses mumbled among themselves; most had their heads down as if they were stunned or ashamed.[40] Although it was a "good" execution, the description is similar to Millard Farmer's in *Dead Man Walking*. It was shameful to take a man's life deep inside the prison in the dead of night.

There was nothing good about the second execution in *The Green Mile*. Percy, the sadistic guard, uses his political connections to be put in charge of Eduard Delacroix's death. Percy had developed an irrational hatred of Del. When combined with his fascination with killing, the worst was inevitable. Typically, the guards placed a sponge soaked in brine on the condemned man's head. The wet sponge "conducted the juice, channeling it, turning the charge into a kind of electric bullet to the brain."[41] This time Percy used a dry sponge, which had the effect of burning the man alive. Smoke curled out through the cap and the mask, Del's legs shot up and down like pistons, and he let out little howls of pain like "an animal caught and mangled in a hay baler." His body slammed back and forth in the chair and twisted from side to side. His shoulder broke with a crunching sound. Finally the mask burst into flames and those in the room could smell burning hair and flesh. After the fire was out, the dead man's skin peeled off. The whole episode took about two minutes, and it was likely that Delacroix was alive through most of it.[42] As the newspapers were not allowed to describe the execution, considering it too gruesome for a family audience, it is unlikely that it served as much of a deterrent. Rather it was a death by torture that served no purpose.

John Coffey's execution was, in many ways, even more of a travesty. Unlike Delacroix and the Chief, Coffey was a truly innocent man. He was a healer, not a killer. His miraculous powers allowed him to cure Edgecombe of a urinary tract infection, to restore Del's pet mouse to life, and to cure the warden's wife of a fatal brain tumor. It becomes clear that when Coffey was found with the two little girls, he had not raped and murdered them. Instead, he was trying to restore them to life. But no one in the "real world" would believe what Edgecombe gradually comes to understand as the novel unfolds.

John Coffey stood 6 feet 8 inches tall and weighed about 350 pounds. His eyes had a sort of "peaceful absence" in them. His body was covered with scars of unknown origin, but his demeanor was gentle and sad. Coffey had been arrested when a search party found him with the girls' bodies. "I couldn't help it. I tried to take it back but it was too late," he wept. Coffey's words sounded like a confession to the desperate father and the furious posse. The deputy who took him into custody spit in his face. Coffey might have been lynched, but he had the legal formality of a trial by jury. The twelve men who were not his peers took forty-five minutes to come back with a conviction and death sentence. The novel does not describe the trial, but when Edgecombe asked Coffey if his lawyer would be coming to visit, he replied, "I believe I've seen the back of him. He was given to me on loan," and wouldn't find his way up to the prison in the mountains. "Appeals weren't for the likes of John Coffey, not back then; they had their day in court and then the world forgot them until they saw a squib in the paper saying a certain fellow had taken a little electricity along about midnight."[43] In this case, the legal outcome seemed a foregone conclusion. The condemned man fit the stereotype of a black brute preying on innocent white girls. Coffey's lawyer was no Atticus Finch, looking for flaws in the state's evidence. Edgecombe himself finally found those flaws, but when he did it was far too late to stop the wheels of "justice" from moving ahead to the execution.

At first, Edgecombe had no doubts about Coffey's guilt. He was glad to see the condemned man suffer and cry because he had apparently committed a terrible crime and deserved to agonize over it. Paul fantasized that he could ask the governor for a stay of execution to prolong Coffey's misery. "Don't burn him yet. It's still hurting him, twisting in his gut like a nice sharp stick. Let him do to himself what we can't do to him."[44] Death in the electric chair might not be appropriate punishment for a rapist/murderer. Letting him drown in his own remorse would be more fitting.

But as Edgecombe came to know Coffey and to realize his gift for healing, doubts about his guilt developed. The prison officer used his days off to track down the condemned man's story, including a visit with the reporter who wrote the major news accounts. The journalist, a bitter man because of his own child's injuries, likened African Americans to dogs. He compared a Negro to a good mongrel dog—of no particular use to you, but you keep "it" around because you think it loves you. Dogs, he said, were also like Negroes, in that neither would help himself but expected to be cared for. The resemblance extended to attacking people for no reason. In the reporter's view, Coffey was there, he saw the girls, took them, raped them, and killed them. "A Negro will bite if he gets the chance, just like a mongrel dog will if he gets the chance and it crosses his mind."[45]

Such a "criminological theory" is chilling. Not only does the journalist dehumanize African Americans, comparing them to animals as Jefferson's lawyer had done in *A Lesson Before Dying,* but his analysis makes it futile to try to disprove Coffey's guilt by a rational approach. If black people are assumed to act irrationally, there is no point in looking for a reasonable motive or consistent behavior. A defense that such behavior is out of character would be meaningless.

But Edgecombe found other mitigating evidence to raise a reasonable doubt about Coffey's guilt. The state argued that he had removed some sausages from his lunch to feed the dog that should have protected the girls and then tied up his lunch again. A wrapped and knotted package of sandwiches was found in his pocket at the crime scene. Edgecombe discovered that Coffey could not tie his shoes—or presumably, the string around his lunch. Opening the package, taking out the sausages, and knotting the string again was beyond his capabilities. Likewise, the words that seemed to be a confession could be reinterpreted as the tragic statement of the healer who arrived too late to save their lives. "I couldn't help it. I tried to take it back but it was too late." If, like the prison guards, one had seen Coffey "take back" sickness and death, his statement was an admission of helplessness and despair, not of guilt. To the posse and to the prosecutor, what he said agreed with what they saw, and "what they were seeing was black." They thought he was confessing to a compulsion to rape and kill, and that after the compulsion worked itself out he came to his senses and tried to stop.[46] The police, prosecutor, judge and jury were completely wrong about Coffey, but their socialization made their version of events a foregone conclusion. Edgecombe and his fellow guards were able to understand things differently only because they knew John Coffey the man, not John Coffey the big black brute. After realizing that the condemned man was both innocent and blessed with the ability to heal the pain of others, one of the corrections officers (ironically named Brutus and called "Brutal") felt himself in danger of going to hell for assisting in Coffey's execution. They were "fixing to kill a gift of God" who never did harm to anyone. What would Brutus say when God asked him why? "That it was my job? My *job?*"[47] Yet many people in the criminal justice system and the courts have used precisely that defense, arguing that even if they had doubts about the death penalty, it was the law, their job, or the will of the people, and that killing a certain number of innocent people was an acceptable price.

Coffey's execution did take place. Stephen King presents him partly as a Christ figure, a blameless man who had to die for the sins of others, but also as a person too simple to communicate much in words and frustrated by his powerlessness. As he waited to approach the electric chair, Coffey told Edgecombe that he was ready to go. He was tired of being alone, tired of people "being ugly" to each other, "tired of bein in the dark. Mostly it's the pain. There's too much. If I could end it I would. But I can't."[48] But when the electricity was turned on and Coffey's death was imminent, his eyes were not at peace, but filled with fear, misery, and incomprehension.[49] Perhaps he was unable to understand a God who would give him some healing powers, but not enough to protect the innocent, a God who seemed to punish him for a life of service to others.

Edgecombe echoes the same questions when, at the end of his own life, he looks back on the execution of John Coffey. He wonders about a God who is supposed to be watching over all creation, "whose eye was on the sparrow," but who is willing to savagely sacrifice Coffey, "who only tried to do good in his blind way." If John Coffey was right and people were killed for love every day, "God lets it happen, and when we say 'I don't understand,' God replies, 'I don't care.'"[50]

The Green Mile poses the problem of evil in the context of the death penalty. How can a merciful deity not care when injustice is done? How can men have the presumption to judge each other and to take human life? "Old Sparky was a deadly bit of folly," in Edgecombe's view. People are "as fragile as blown glass, even under the best of conditions. To kill each other with gas and electricity, and in cold blood? The folly. The *horror*."[51]

When *The Green Mile* was released as a commercial film in 1999, many people talked about the horror it depicted, especially in showing the full two minutes of Del's intentionally botched execution.[52] Reviews were mixed concerning the movie's plot, its length (three hours), and its themes. Some critics found fault with the portrayal of John Coffey, regarding it as a racist caricature to portray a black man who "redeems" white people by taking on their pain.

On the other hand, Roger Ebert commends the film as "we are reminded of another execution 2,000 years ago."[53] Whatever one thinks of the movie artistically, its release did provide an opportunity for viewers to confront the death penalty with all its flaws, both as cruel and unusual punishment and as the possible destruction of the innocent.

Although the film, like the book, is set up as a flashback where the aged Paul remembers his days on the Green Mile, there are some crucial differences. The first thing the moviegoer sees is a group of men, obviously a posse, with rifles, dogs, and pitchforks crossing a cotton field. There is no sound. The scene is background for the crime John Coffey is accused of committing, and the rural white men in the search party could be interchangeable with those in the system that mistakenly finds him guilty. When the scene shifts to the elderly Paul at the nursing home, he unaccountably breaks into tears when a Fred Astaire and Ginger Rogers movie comes on TV. He explains that the musical takes him back to the year 1935 on the Green Mile.[54]

Most of the rest of the film takes place in the death row setting. A prison van drives through the grounds, where hundreds of inmates in striped suits, almost all of them black, work on chain gangs under the supervision of white men on horses. A giant, eight feet tall, barefoot and in overalls, emerges. Through camera tricks, the film makes Coffey appear at least two feet taller than the tallest guard. At first the consensus is that "the big dummy deserves to fry." The film then cuts back to the search party that found Coffey with the two little girls in his arms, patting their heads, and crying, "I couldn't help it. I tried to take it back but it was too late." As in the book, the deputy spits in his face.

As Coffey's gentleness, sadness, and power to heal emerge, Edgecombe cannot resist looking into the crime John allegedly committed. In the novel he meets with a journalist; in the movie, the character becomes the lawyer who "defended" Coffey. One can only imagine the vigorous defense provided by an attorney who compares African Americans to dogs who bite without cause. Significantly, when Paul asks about the condemned man's background, the lawyer knows nothing. "It's like he just dropped out of the sky," was the reply.

The film becomes quite creative in showing John Coffey's supernatural powers. Each time he accomplishes a healing—Edgecombe's infection, the dead mouse, the warden's wife—and each time he suffers vicariously, as when Del is killed, electricity fills the air and light bulbs shatter in their sockets. He seems able to read the minds of the guards and to anticipate events, even though his ability to express what he sees is childlike. (Some critics are offended that Coffey speaks in a sort of plantation dialect. Others argue that the portrayal by Michael Clarke Duncan shows him as dignified and sensitive and rescues him from the almost offensive racial caricature in the book.)[55] If one sees the role as a religious allegory, he might be viewed as one who knows things through faith rather than through reason. In any event, Coffey transfers some of his "gift of seeing" to Edgecombe, making it possible for the guard to visualize the killing of the girls and to realize for certain that John is innocent. The device works in the film, but it is logically less satisfactory than the evidence that Coffey could not tie his shoes, as Paul learned in the book.

At the conclusion of the film, it appears that the "gift" Edgecombe received from Coffey also became a curse. The former guard was "infected" with life that continued long beyond the lives of his friends and family. The man who was responsible for the deaths of scores of men, at least one of them innocent, cannot seem to die himself. Paul speaks the words that Brutus spoke in the novel—how could one stand before God and explain why he killed "one of his gifts"? But of course, the execution had to happen, the wheels of justice had turned too far. When the guards, filled with remorse, ask Coffey if he would like anything special before he is to die, he asks for a movie, a "flicker show." Somehow they come up with a print of *Top Hat* where Astaire and Rogers dance to "Cheek to Cheek." "Heaven, I'm in heaven," they sing. Coffey thinks he is seeing angels. As he is strapped into the electric chair, with tears running down his cheeks and the guards weeping openly, he repeats over and over, "Heaven, I'm in heaven."

The viewer does not watch the actual execution of John Coffey, but sees instead the reactions of those in the room. However, the camera does not look away during the Chief's and Delacroix's deaths. In presenting the contrast between the careful ritual of carrying out a legal process and the taking of a human life, the film makes its strongest statement. The Chief's execution, although clean and professional, is disturbing. Del's is simply horrifying. In the words of movie critic Andrew O'Hehir, the grueling executions "should do more to sour viewers on the death penalty than any number of earnest magazine articles."[56]

All the works studied in this chapter so far have dealt with death sentences for actually innocent persons. These men ended up on death row because they found themselves at the wrong place at the wrong time, both in the literal sense, that they were at the scene of the crime, and in the metaphorical sense, that they were black men accused of serious crimes by a racially biased society. The two remaining stories are set in the later twentieth century, when racism in America was less overt. Neither of the accused men in these stories is factually innocent. Nonetheless, race continues to play a crucial role.

What's a Father to Do?

At a glance, *A Time to Kill*,[57] the first—and some say the best—novel by lawyer John Grisham is strikingly similar to *To Kill a Mockingbird*. Both involve black men on trial for their lives in small Southern towns. Both focus on the defense lawyer, his moral choices, and the toll the case takes on his family. Both involve an interracial rape or alleged rape. However, significant differences aside from literary merit separate the two works. Between 1960, when Harper Lee published *Mockingbird*, and 1989, when Grisham's novel first appeared, the country experienced major developments in the social, legal, and even the ethical landscape. Whether those changes meant improvements in the racial environment portrayed in the two books is questionable.

In Clanton, Mississippi, in the early 1980s Tonya Hailey, a small African American girl, is brutally raped by two violent, drunken rednecks at the beginning of *A Time to Kill*. The men are arrested immediately and taken to jail by the black sheriff, where one of them confesses. The rapists are arraigned, the judge sets bail for one at $100,000 and the other at $200,000—more money than they are likely to see in their lives. The grand jury is scheduled to meet the following week. On the day of the arraignment, the little girl's father, Carl Lee Hailey, shoots and kills the two men in the courthouse lobby. In the process, he wounds Deputy Dwayne Looney. Hailey had planned the killing. He went to Memphis to buy the M-16 used in the crime and hid in the closet until the men passed. What possible defense could keep a black man from death row after he killed two white men in cold blood in the courthouse in full view of dozens of people?

Unlike Jefferson or John Coffey, Hailey does not have a court-appointed lawyer. He hires the cocky young attorney Jake Brigance. The story is really Jake's and, the author claims, it includes a great deal of autobiography. Before his writing career, Grisham was a small-town lawyer with a similar practice. He once saw a young girl testifying in court against her rapist. The author wondered what he would do if he were her father.[58]

Jake calls himself a "street lawyer" and describes his work as representing people, "living, breathing human souls, most with little money." He is in the trenches helping those in trouble, and proud of it. Brigance practices alone because he believes there is no other lawyer in the town of Clanton competent enough to be his partner. All the other good lawyers handle corporate accounts and wealthy clients. They had gone to Harvard and were pompous and arrogant.[59] Like many other Grisham protagonists, Jake is essentially a loner, and despite his professed interest in helping people, his empathy is limited. He can, however, identify with the father of a little girl who was wantonly raped and beaten. In addition, Brigance is thrilled at the publicity the Hailey case will generate. He imagines front page stories and magazine covers. One paper called it the most sensational murder in the South in twenty years. "He would have taken it for free, almost."[60] And Jake had some relevant experience. He had successfully represented a number of other black clients in intraracial murder trials. Their acquittals were possible with "an all white jury full of red-necks who could care less if all niggers stabbed each other."[61] How would a similar jury behave when the crime was interracial?

Grisham sets up the argument that becomes the justification for Hailey's act even before the shooting occurs. Carl Lee visits Jake at his office shortly after the rape. He asks the attorney what he would do if his little girl had been raped by two "niggers" and he got his hands on them? "Kill them," is Jake's response. Brigance argues further that he could get away with it because he is a white man in a white town who would be likely to have a sympathetic all-white jury. "This is not New York or California. A man's supposed to protect his family. A jury would eat it up."[62] Thus the basic legal question in *A Time to Kill* becomes whether a black man has the same right to take the law into his own hands as a white man or whether his act of revenge will be treated as a capital crime.

A number of characters express their support for the notion that fathers should not be held legally accountable for killing their daughters' rapists. Jake's wife Carla is of the opinion that it would be hard to convict in such a case.[63] The sheriff admits that "a man don't know what he'd do." Brigance points out that such a father could escape conviction if the "right folks" are on the jury. "People are tired of raping and robbing and killing. . . . There'd be a lot of sympathy for a father who took matters into his own hands. People don't trust our judicial system."[64] Some might argue that trust in the judicial system is further undermined when executions are placed in the hands of private citizens. Lucien Wilbanks, Jake's mentor, pursues the issue further. He explains that Carl Lee is a decent man with a good reason for killing, but the law says his reason is not good enough. His race and the bigotry in the area also work against him. "If he were white and he killed two blacks who raped his daughter, the jury would give him the courthouse."[65] Oddly enough, Lucien is presented as a longtime civil rights activist. Yet he fails to mention that letting white men operate outside the law to avenge alleged rapes accounted for the lynching of hundreds of black men.

Jake may be convinced that Carl Lee deserves to be found not guilty, but Lucien is required to teach him some fairly obvious points of law. For example, although the young lawyer is thrilled with all the media coverage of the case, Lucien needs to point out that because of the publicity it would be a good idea to file a motion for a change of venue. He also explains why an insanity defense is the only feasible strategy. It is necessary to give the jury a *legal* reason to acquit, because Carl Lee is as "guilty as hell." He took the law into his own hands and murdered two people. The act was carefully planned. "Our legal system does not permit vigilante justice." Yet Lucien considers the case a "trial lawyer's dream." The paradox is, "If you win, justice will prevail, but if you lose, justice will also prevail."[66] Apparently a win would mean that the rape of Carl Lee's daughter was a sufficiently mitigating circumstance for his crime. A loss would mean that the defendant had been afforded due process and that the law had been applied. Either was a version of justice.

Rufus Buckley, a politician ambitious to become governor, handles the state's case. He brags that he has sent more men to death row than any other prosecutor in Mississippi. Described as loud, abrasive, and sanctimonious, Buckley regards the people of Mississippi as his client. Not surprisingly, they and he hate crime. The prosecutor prides himself on his skill with juries of all sorts, white, black, or redneck. He "could inflame a jury to the point that it couldn't wait to get back to the jury room, have a prayer meeting, then vote and return with a rope to hang the defendant." In a press conference, he announces that he views the Hailey case as premeditated murder and believes the gas chamber is the appropriate sentence.[67]

When the case comes to trial, several questionable points of law arise. Jake's request for a change of venue has been denied, even though the Ku Klux Klan and crowds of black demonstrators outside the courthouse have to be separated by the National Guard. Despite this "circus," Judge Noose, under strong political pressure, holds that the trial would not be any fairer anywhere in Mississippi. Once they have made their way through the competing groups into the courthouse, potential jurors have to be death qualified. In other words, each member of the jury is required to express a willingness to sentence the defendant to death. The judge explains that if Carl Lee was convicted, "You will be called upon to sentence him to death." He notes that the death penalty is legal in Mississippi, and that he is required to excuse jurors who cannot not consider it. It would be unfair, he claims, to select jurors who could not follow the law.[68] The instructions seem to suggest that the death penalty is mandatory if Hailey is found guilty. At least, a potential juror unschooled in the law might interpret them that way, despite Supreme Court rulings against mandatory death sentences. These instructions may have led the jurors to think death or "not guilty" are the only options.

The jury finally seated in Hailey's case consists of ten women and two men. All are white. The defense, of course, hoped for a jury of fathers. Prior to the final jury selection, the novel describes attempts by both the prosecution and the defense to shape the panel, including a variety of improper contacts and crude attempts at intimidation. Before opening arguments begin, the process has been irreparably tainted.

Nonetheless, the trial provides some of the novel's dramatic high points. Although major legal arguments were supposed to center around Hailey's mental state, predictably the focus is actually on the justification for his actions. Deputy Looney, missing the leg he lost in the crossfire, is asked whether he believes Carl Lee should be punished. "I don't blame him for what he did.

Those boys raped his little girl. I gotta little girl. Somebody rapes her and he's a dead dog. . . . We oughta give [Carl Lee] a trophy."[69] The defense's closing also makes almost no mention of the *legal* defense of insanity. Instead, Jake devotes the bulk of the statement to describing his own daughter, explaining why rape is worse than murder, reiterating Looney's sentiments about Carl Lee's heroism, and describing how Tonya called for her daddy during the rape and abuse. "What would a *reasonable* father do? . . . Blow the bastard's head off. It was simple. It was justice."[70] Consistency would demand that the defense could not argue both that Carl Lee was insane and that he acted reasonably. But such niceties do not prevent the summation from bringing tears to the eyes of many in the courtroom.

The foreman polls the panel immediately after they retire into the jury room and finds five guiltys, five undecideds, one pass, and one not guilty. After a debate about the use of the word "nigger" during deliberations (surprising because up until that moment, no one in the novel seemed to object to the N-word), it appears that several jurors want to convict based on the evidence of premeditation. They would have acquitted had Carl Lee caught the men in the act and killed them on the spot, but they believe his prior planning of the time and place of the shooting constitutes guilt.

By the second day of deliberations, the jurors "felt like hostages." Klansmen and black demonstrators (apparently no white people demonstrated for Carl Lee) yell outside. The National Guard remain on duty. Several fear "the mob" will storm the courthouse if Carl Lee is convicted. In that atmosphere, one of the women jurors asks her colleagues to close their eyes and imagine a blue-eyed, blond little girl raped and tortured by two black men. They should imagine she was their daughter. Would they kill the "black bastards?" All twelve say they would. How then, she asks, can they convict Carl Lee?[71] The argument for color-blind vigilantism wins the day.

Hailey is found "not guilty by reason of insanity." The judge smiles at the verdict and set the defendant free, as there had been no expert testimony that he was dangerous or in need of further psychiatric treatment.[72] Everyone in the courtroom knows the insanity defense was a legal fiction.

The reader's first reaction is probably relief. Grisham skillfully developed sympathy for the defense and animus toward the prosecutor. But a closer look raises some serious questions. Although superficially *A Time to Kill* deals with equal justice regardless of race, the treatment of the black characters and racial issues belies that theme. For example, an account of a service at the African American church sounds like a minstrel show. It describes the congregation's "glorified frenzy." The choir shrieked, the minister "hopped around," yelling and perspiring. There was "bedlam," then the reverend "jigged to the pulpit."[73] The NAACP, often the only organization to represent black defendants in capital cases, also comes in for abuse. They are portrayed as self-interested public-ity seekers, "dedicated to rescuing black murderers from various gas chambers and electric chairs in the South. . . . Their goal was to martyr the defendant be-fore the trial and hopefully hang the jury."[74] A clergyman and veteran civil rights activist tells Carl Lee, "Your acquittal by an all white jury will do more for the black folk of Mississippi than any event since we integrated the schools. And it's not just Mississippi, it's black folk everywhere."[75] Has the civil rights movement come to this? Even after being found not guilty, Hailey and his fam-ily would go back to a community where they lived in poverty and where every-one—the judge, the district attorney, the police, even his own lawyer—referred to people like him, unapologetically, as "niggers." Atticus Finch had told his daughter not to use the word because it was "common." In this story, set fifty years later, the term was still common. Even little Tonya, the rape victim in whose name everything was done, was not treated with respect. Although legal etiquette usually forbade revealing the name of a rape victim, Tonya was differ-ent. Her identity was known because of "her daddy." Jake wanted the little girl "to be seen and photographed in her best white Sunday dress sitting on her daddy's knee."[76] Had she been a middle-class white child, would her privacy have been so invaded? Whatever equal justice was being offered to Carl Lee, it did not include being treated with dignity by white people.

Given the state of the law in the late twentieth century, Carl Lee Hailey should not have received the death penalty. To execute him would have re-quired ignoring the serious mitigating circumstances of his crime. On the other hand, by making him into a hero, *A Time to Kill* makes a mockery of the judicial process and sets a frightening precedent. Since Reconstruction, blacks had suffered at the hands of whites who believed that interracial rape was a crime requiring retribution, who evaded the legal process, taking the law into their own hands and punishing the alleged rapists as they saw fit. Their justifi-cation was the same as Carl Lee's—the system was too slow and too unreliable.

Thousands of people who have never read the novel have seen the very en-tertaining 1996 film starring Matthew McConaughey as Jake and Samuel L. Jackson as Carl Lee.[77] The story line follows the book quite closely, although a few differences are of interest. The movie opens with two drunken, disrepu-table young men, sporting a Confederate flag in the back of their pick-up truck. For fun, they throw cans of beer at black people, and eventually they ab-duct and rape Tonya Hailey. Although no details of the rape are shown on screen, throughout the montage the little girl's voice calls for her daddy. In the film, her father does not wait for the rapists to be arraigned, much less tried. He shoots them on the way into court for their bail hearing. As in the book, Carl Lee visits Jake before the murders and lays the foundation for their jus-tification. He mentions that four white boys who raped a black girl in the

Delta got off. Are there reasons to assume that the men who attacked his daughter will also be set free? No one ever finds out because they are dead before entering the courtroom. The arguments are the same as in the novel. As Carl Lee says, people are tired of raping and killing. They should sympathize with a man who takes the law into his own hands, even if he is black. Others, including Deputy Looney on the witness stand, agree that fathers must protect their daughters. Apparently even the police lack faith that the criminal justice system will convict the guilty and free the innocent.

Justice in this film seems as arbitrary as being struck by lightning. Jake claims that he wants to "save the world one case at a time" and that he believes in safety and justice, but not forgiveness or rehabilitation. He argues that the death penalty is not used often enough, but when his law clerk asks who deserves the death penalty, he can only answer by saying that Carl Lee does not but drug dealers do. When she questions who is entitled to make those decisions, no answer is forthcoming. The justices who decided *Furman* would have no trouble finding Jake's system "arbitrary and capricious."

During the trial, the obnoxious district attorney played by Kevin Spacey clearly has the law on his side. He argues that Hailey confessed to the murders, that even though a terrible wrong had been done to his family, Carl Lee did not have the right to kill. But if the state had the better legal argument, the defense had the emotional appeal. Rather than have one of the jurors ask the panel to envision the rape and the "imagine that she is white," that device became part of Jake's closing argument. To one watching the movie for the first time, the speech is very effective indeed. On second thought, however, proving that black victims deserve justice as much as white victims by playing to the jury's prejudices seems to undermine the racial reasoning of the case. The jury is being asked to pretend that the rape victim is white so they can understand how her father felt. Are they supposed to also pretend that the rapists were black? Is that the truth Jake has asked them to seek with their eyes closed?

The closing argument obviously has a powerful impact on the jury. Earlier when, contrary to the judge's orders, they took a number of straw polls, the majority had believed Hailey guilty. In the film's next scene after the summation, a young boy runs out of the courthouse shouting "He's innocent. He's innocent." Unlike the defendants in the other films examined here, Carl Lee was not unjustly convicted. He was found not guilty, even though he was poor and black and accused of an interracial crime. One is left to wonder if the difference is that his attorney was able to fit his offense into the community's prejudices. In that case, setting Carl Lee free did not really threaten the race, class, and gender power structure in the community at all. It simply affirmed that white folks sometimes chose to let blacks share in the exercise of patriarchal power. How effective would Jake's closing argument have been if the rapists had been two college boys from Ole Miss instead of two "rednecks?" Would the jury have imagined a different picture?

A review by Wilda White argues that no one in the film believes in justice, but that everyone either circumvents or distorts it. She cites the prosecutor's removal of blacks from the jury and the judge's deal with the appeals court to ensure that his ruling on change of venue will not be reversed. The police ignore the law when the sheriff clubs a Klansman about to bomb Jake's house and watches as Jake finishes beating him up. A deputy joins the Klan. The law clerk breaks into the state psychiatrist's office through a window.[78] It all makes an interesting plot, but hardly qualifies as justice.

The title of the book and movie suggest that there is an appropriate "time to kill"—not necessarily at the hands of the state in the gas chamber, the electric chair, or with lethal injection, but with a gun wielded by an outraged citizen. The final section of this chapter will return to the question of the legitimacy of the state-administered death penalty, even when the condemned man is a bigot who kills out of hatred for those he deems inferior.

Capital Punishment, Not Capital Torture

The Chamber, John Grisham's fifth novel, was published five years after *A Time to Kill.*[79] During that time the author published best-sellers at a prolific rate. Apparently, he also gave thought to the arguments surrounding the death penalty, as the later book may be read as an extended argument against capital punishment. On the one hand, plot and characters seem to suffer in the service of its message. On the other hand, millions of people read the book and were exposed to its arguments.

As is usual in a Grisham novel, the hero is a young, independent-minded lawyer. In this case, Adam Hall leaves his successful practice with a major Chicago firm to work the last month of appeals for his estranged grandfather, who sits on Mississippi's death row. Sam Cayhall, the grandfather, was sentenced for his involvement in a Ku Klux Klan bombing that killed two little boys in 1967. (Adam's father had changed his name after the incident. Thus Sam does not know immediately that his new lawyer is his grandson.) Before leaving for the South, Adam learns from Sam's recently fired attorney that his grandfather is intelligent, though not educated, that he is well-read and articulate, a good jailhouse lawyer, and a "horrible racist and bigot" who shows no remorse for his crimes.[80]

In the late 1960s, Sam was involved with the Mississippi Klan (he was a third-generation member) when they devised a strategy to intimidate whites who worked for civil rights, as well as their usual black victims. One such target was Marvin Kramer, a Jewish lawyer who registered African Americans to vote and bailed Freedom Riders out of jail. Unfortunately for all concerned, on the morning that Sam and a mysterious confederate rigged a bomb in Kramer's office, the lawyer's five-year old twins had gone to work with their father. The two children were the victims of the deadly explosion, although their father, who later took his own life, was certainly a casualty too.

Sam was the only one arrested for the bombing, and he took his Klan oath of secrecy seriously. He was tried three times in all. The first two trials in the late 1960s, which took place before juries of "patriots" with Klan rallies on the courthouse lawn, resulted in mistrials when no verdict was reached. By the third trial in 1981, however, the climate has changed in Mississippi. African Americans vote and serve on juries. Aware of the political realities, an ambitious district attorney (who later became governor) refiles the case against Sam Cayhall and charges him with two counts of murder. He is found guilty and sentenced to death.

Sam had a good lawyer for his third trial. Appeals argued that Cayhall had been denied his right to a speedy trial, as he was convicted of a crime fourteen years after it happened, and that he had been subjected to double jeopardy. Although the Supreme Court heard the appeal, the justices ultimately denied both claims. A second round of appeals charged that gory pictures of the dead boys should not have been admitted into evidence, that the trial should have been moved, and that the district attorney improperly selected too many blacks for the jury. When those appeals were denied, Sam fired his lawyers. Thus Adam comes to the prison in Parchman, Mississippi, twenty-eight days before the scheduled execution to handle his grandfather's last legal efforts.

Sam provides Adam with a description of life at Parchman prison. He paints a detailed and grim picture. The state apparently built its prison in the hottest place it could find and designed the maximum security area to operate like an oven. The only windows are small and useless, and the planners of the "little branch of hell" decided not to provide any ventilation and of course, no air conditioning. The facility would sit "proudly beside soybeans and cotton and absorb the same heat and moisture from the ground. And when the ground was dry, the Row would simply bake along with the crops." Residents of death row sleep on a piece of foam, six feet by two feet and four inches thick, set on a metal frame fastened to the floor and wall. They are given two sheets and sometimes blankets in the winter. Back pain is common, but eventually the body adjusts. Little relief is available, as prison doctors are not friends to death row inmates. And if the physical conditions are not miserable enough, Sam explains that "the horror of death row is that you die a little each day. You live in a cage and when you wake up, you mark off another day and tell yourself you're one day closer to death."[81] The novel does not exaggerate the misery of Mississippi's death row. In 2002, a federal court found that conditions in the facility violated the constitution's prohibition on cruel and unusual punishment.

One of Adam's grounds for appeal is that the gas chamber itself is cruel and unusual punishment and, implicitly, that its use violates the evolving standards of decency of the 1990s. His grandfather provides him with the stories of botched and gruesome executions during his time on death row. The first execution after the death penalty was reinstated was a child murderer called "Meeks." Drunk and out of practice after years of not using the gas chamber, the executioner mixed the first batch of lethal gas incorrectly. Although the condemned man was strapped in the chair and the witnesses watched, no deathly poison filtered through the chamber. The participants waited ten minutes while the executioner brewed another mixture. This time he followed the correct recipe. Meeks held his breath as long as he could. When he inhaled, he started shaking and jerking. His head beat furiously on a metal pole behind the chair, his eyes rolled back, he foamed at the mouth. He thrust his head against the pole for several minutes until it split open. The death took at least five minutes. It was officially pronounced "instant and painless."[82] The fictional Meeks execution is virtually identical to the actual execution of Jimmy Lee Gray, the first man gassed in Mississippi after the death penalty was reinstated.[83] After another similar "instant and painless" execution, the authorities at Parchman devised a way to strap down the convict's head so it would not hit the pole, making it easier for the witnesses and guards to watch.

By the time Sam's execution approached, the Mississippi legislature had voted to change from gas to lethal injection—but only for those convicted after the law was passed. Adam's appeal is meant to challenge their reasoning, which seemed to be that the gas chamber was cruel if your trial occurred after 1989 but not if it occurred before that date. Sam's comment gets to the heart of the issue: "This is capital punishment, right? Not capital torture."[84]

It is to be expected that the condemned man and his attorney would make arguments against the death penalty. In *The Chamber*, however, as in real life, a number of prison officials also express reservations about capital punishment. The warden hates the death penalty. He understands society's "yearning" for it and has "memorized all the sterile reasons" for it—deterrence, removing killers from the community, biblical arguments, the need for retribution, relief to the victim's family. He even believes a few of the arguments. But he despises the actual killing, the walk to the chamber, strapping the man into the chair, asking for his last words, nodding to the executioner, looking at the witnesses, removing the body. He had once testified to the legislature in favor of life without parole as an alternative and almost lost his job.[85] The prison attorney claims that "Every time we kill someone here I think the whole world's gone crazy." But, in his view, the prison staff was just doing its job. "If society wants to kill criminals, then someone has to do it."[86]

Sam's daughter Lee, a Memphis socialite who had cut herself off from her family and created a new life for herself, offers her unique perspective. She is probably the only fifty-five-year-old white woman in the country with a father on death row. She finds the death penalty "barbaric, immoral, discriminatory, cruel, [and] uncivilized." But she also believes victims have a right to want retribution.[87] Adam seems to have arrived at a strong moral conviction against capital punishment independent of his grandfather's case. He announces himself as well educated and well read on Eighth Amendment issues. His position is, at first, intellectual. It gradually becomes more impassioned. Sam provides another part of Adam's education on the subject. He puts the young lawyer to the test, quizzing him about cases and arguing that the Supreme Court changes its mind whenever it wants to. The death penalty was constitutional for hundreds of years, unconstitutional with *Furman*, then four years later it was acceptable again. Such inconsistency came from the "same bunch of turkeys wearing the same black robes." Because he believes that the Court is motivated by politics and self-interest, Cayhall thinks any Supreme Court ruling in his favor was improbable. He rightly notes the Court's impatience with death row cases. "The Reagan boys are tired of reading too many appeals, so they declare certain avenues closed."[88]

Aside from moral and constitutional issues, politics always plays a role in the capital punishment debate. Sam explains to his grandson that Mississippi needs to use its gas chamber. Texas, Florida, and Louisiana were "killing them like flies." Mississippians beg for an execution; it would make them feel better to eliminate a murderer.[89] The smooth, media-wise, ambitious Governor David McAllister (almost a clone of the district attorney in *A Time to Kill*) knows that Sam's execution would be great for his polling numbers. In fact, McAllister had successfully prosecuted Cayhall in his third trial and had used that publicity to run for governor on a platform of more jails, longer sentences, and "an unwavering affinity for the death penalty."[90] He toys with the possibility of clemency, hoping that Sam will point a finger at an accomplice. But despite a creative effort by the defense to bombard the governor's office with calls asking for a pardon, to no one's surprise he refuses—and makes a statement to the press. "Justice may be slow, but it still works. . . . I cannot overrule the wisdom of the jury that sentenced him, nor can I impose my judgment upon that of our distinguished courts. Nor am I willing to go against the wishes of my friends the Kramers. It is my fervent hope that the execution of Sam Cayhall will help erase a painful chapter in our state's tortured history. I call upon all Mississippians to come together from this sad night forward, and work for equality. May God have mercy on his soul."[91] It is a brilliant political statement, in which the governor denies personal responsibility for Sam's death, invokes the memory of the victims, and places himself on the side of justice and equality, leaving the matter of mercy in the hands of the Almighty.

Many things Sam has done in his life would require mercy and forgiveness. At one point he asks whether it is fair to confront a condemned man with his ancient sins. But the literature of capital punishment seems to require just such a confrontation, and Sam Cayhall has plenty of sins to consider.

Leading up to his role in the bombing that killed the Kramer twins, Sam had a great deal of experience with the sort of violence that Southern whites used to keep black people "in their place." As a boy of fifteen, he was involved in a lynching where a mob took a young black man from the jail, dragged him to the woods, beat and hanged him. Why? The alleged rape of a white woman. Later, in front of both men's children, Sam shot his black farm hand Joe Lincoln. Why? Joe had defended his son when Sam accused him of stealing. In that case, cold-blooded murder, Cayhall was not arrested. Rather, he and the sheriff had a good laugh.[92] It could be argued that there are ample crimes for which to sentence Sam to death. He has several intentional killings to his credit, and even if he had an accomplice at the bombing, he is still guilty of the capital crime of felony-murder. In many ways, Sam Cayhall is the perfect character to highlight arguments about the death penalty. He is not innocent like Jefferson, Tom Robinson, or John Coffey. He was not even provoked, like Carl Lee Hailey. He is instead an angry, hate-filled man, carrying out the prejudices he has learned in a white supremacist society. Is capital punishment cruel and unusual, even for someone like Sam? Is it wrong for society to take a life, even if much of it was spent doing damage to others?

Grisham forces the reader to consider the reality of execution by describing the procedure in minute and objective detail. The day before he was scheduled to die, the inmate would be moved to the Observation Cell, where he could visit with his lawyer and minister and watch "his own private drama on television." Death row was locked down and "deathly quiet." In this case, the prison staff use the time to practice the execution, much as the guards did in *The Green Mile*. At Parchman, the staff actually tested the gas, using a rabbit they called "Sam." "The poisonous gas was released slowly and a faint mist of vapors rose from under the chair and drifted upward. At first, the rabbit didn't react to the steam that permeated his little cell, but it hit him soon enough. He stiffened, then hopped a few times, banging into the sides of his cage, then he went into violent convulsions, jumping, and jerking, and twisting frantically. In less than a minute, he was still."[93]

An hour before the execution, the condemned man moved to the Isolation Room, next to the chamber. At this point, the executioner mixed the chemicals; the warden and his staff made last-minute preparations and saw the witnesses take their seats. Twenty minutes before midnight, the doctor strapped a stethoscope to the convict's chest and the inmate went with the warden to visit the chamber, apparently so he would not be shocked when ushered in for the real execution. On the one hand, Grisham notes the ghoulishness of the observers' fascination. The chamber was "always filled with people, all about to watch a man die. They would back him into the chamber, strap him in, close the door, and kill him."[94] On the other hand, the Mississippi procedure was comparatively "humane and thoughtful," allowing the inmate to remain in familiar surroundings. In Louisiana, "they were removed from the Row and placed in a small building called the Death House" for three days under constant observation. Condemned prisoners in Virginia were moved to another city.[95]

Sam does have the opportunity to repent and to take responsibility for his crimes. When the time arrives for the execution, his words echo Gary Gilmore's "Let's do it." Adam does not stay to watch the actual gassing, so the reader does not see the end through his eyes. Before he leaves, he notices that the chamber room is filled with people who stare at Sam, then look away. Adam thinks they are "ashamed to be here taking part in this nasty little deed."[96] The shame of those who take the condemned man's life and of those who watch is a remarkably consistent theme in the death penalty literature. As Sister Helen commented, if the death penalty is so noble, why is it carried out deep in an isolated prison in the dead of night?

Like many other films, *The Chamber* begins with the crime.[97] The explosion at Marvin Kramer's office follows immediately upon a scene where the twins call to each other from windows placed side by side. As the building goes up in flames, a shadowy figure watches from across the street close to a statue of a Confederate soldier. For the most part, the movie featuring Gene Hackman as Sam and Chris O'Donnell as Adam reiterates the plot of the book. Sam spouts racist and anti-Semitic sentiments, but eloquently describes the flaws of the capital punishment system. By the time Adam arrives at Parchman, with only twenty eight days until the execution, there are few legal strategies available to spare his grandfather. He attempts to argue that the gas chamber is cruel and unusual, providing an opportunity to describe the horrors of asphyxiation with lethal vapors and the botched executions using that method. He also makes the claim that Sam suffers from diminished capacity due to years of Klan indoctrination and uses a related argument that Sam's racist perspective renders him mentally incompetent to be executed. Although both claims are clearly the product of desperation, they do raise the interesting issue of whether racist hatred is a mental defect and therefore whether it might be a mitigating factor. In another variation on the question of racism and responsibility, the film explores rather unsatisfactorily the notion that the rich and powerful use "violent redneck assholes" like Sam to do their dirty work—and to take the consequences. But Adam is not able to prove such manipulation and therefore that part of the film seems like a road going nowhere. Likewise, Adam's search for Cayhall's accomplice would not save Sam from execution. He would still be guilty of felony-murder, as his death warrant specified. The film fails, not in raising these issues, but in leaving them unfinished.

As critic Barbara Shulgasser notes, the film "puts the death penalty into its seedy political context."[98] Crowds demonstrate and scream outside the prison in an odd juxtaposition. On the one side, Klansmen in full regalia call for Sam to be freed. The other side seems to comprise a number of African Americans and lots of white people waving American flags, all yelling and cheering for blood. Into this mayhem comes the smarmy governor with his handlers to proclaim that although many want Sam to be spared, he is not wiser than the courts and therefore cannot grant clemency. He speaks firmly of guilt and responsibility and meeting one's maker. The crowd, with the exception of the Klan, goes wild.

The last few minutes of the film illustrate the confusion over whether it is a story of the death penalty or a story of family healing. As in the novel, Adam does not stay for the actual execution. But the audience goes into the gas chamber with Sam and watches the entire process, including his last gasping for air and foaming at the mouth. Meanwhile Adam runs out of the prison, across the yard, and ultimately into the arms of his Aunt Lee. In the final frame, they express the hope that their family's ghosts have been exorcised. After all the arguments against capital punishment, it appears that the movie Cayhall family may live happily ever after. Conversely, in the last pages of the book, Adam signs up to work as an anti-death-penalty litigator. There the experience of Sam's execution seems to have given meaning to his life beyond the personal.

All of the novels and films discussed in this chapter are about power, about the use of the criminal justice system and the ultimate penalty to maintain or to unseat power. The three executions, Jefferson, John Coffey, and Sam Cayhall, and the death of Tom Robinson actually accomplished little or nothing to preserve public safety or to act as a deterrent. In the short run they work to maintain the status quo of race and class. All reveal deeply ingrained biases in the criminal justice system. In every case, the victims were white. In four of five cases in this chapter, the accused was black. All of the defendants were either poor or working class; all of the victims enjoyed a higher status. In each instance, actual guilt or innocence took second place to the belief that taking one more life would put the social framework back into balance.

The executions may have offered a moment of retribution to the victims' families and to those with power in the community. More importantly, they had the unintended consequence of transforming individuals. Grant Wiggins and his pupils, Scout and Jem, Paul Edgecombe, and Adam Hall would never again look at the justice system in the same way. In that sense, the killings provided a long-term challenge to the status quo.

The next chapter will examine a number of films that are not derived from books but that offer additional perspectives on the subject of capital punishment.

· 5 ·

KILLING TO SHOW THAT KILLING IS WRONG: THE DEATH PENALTY IN THE MOVIES

During the last decades of the twentieth century and the first years of the twenty-first, filmmakers have repeatedly visited the subject of capital punishment. In addition to *Dead Man Walking*, *The Green Mile*, and *The Chamber*—discussed in the previous chapter—the 1990s saw the release of *Last Dance* and *Last Light*. *Monster's Ball*, *The Widow of St. Pierre*, and *The Life of David Gale* appeared shortly after the turn of the century. During a time when the United States was executing approximately one hundred people per year, none of the films demonstrates that the death penalty has redeeming social value. In fact, each casts a critical eye on the system. David Dow states that the potential issues surrounding the death penalty are better represented in Hollywood movies than in documentaries.[1] As this book argues, it is through such cinematic, often fictional, representations that most Americans form their opinions of what capital punishment is really like. They may be forced to confront the flaws in the system that can result in the conviction of the innocent, and to realize that even the guilty are human beings. That realization forces consideration of the question raised in *Dead Man Walking* and numerous other films—why does the state kill someone to show that killing is wrong?

This chapter will look at death penalty films from the last decade, but it will also review several older but very powerful examples of the genre: the classic *I Want to Live* (1958), *Dance with a Stranger* (1985), and *The Thin Blue Line* (1988). The movies are grouped according to topic—death row workers, women sentenced to die, the question of innocence, and the universal issues.

Some of the films actually lead up to an execution and focus on the accused. In some the killing is the catalyst for developing the lives of other characters. Some are excellent movies with fine acting performances. Susan Hayward won an Oscar for *I Want to Live*, as did Halle Berry for *Monster's Ball*. A few are not very good at all. One might wonder why a group of talented actors got involved in *The Life of David Gale*. Nonetheless, all are provocative and provide an audience with opportunities to analyze the operation of the death penalty.

Just Doing Their Job

Both *Last Light*[2] and *Monster's Ball*[3] center on men who work as corrections officers on death row. The former was made for TV, with Kiefer Sutherland directing and playing the condemned man, Denver Bayliss. In a twist on the usual racial pattern, Forrest Whittaker plays the guard who struggles with his role on death row. The film embodies what Robert Jay Lifton has described as a common experience of guards and wardens—the feeling of "excruciating guilt" based on a perception of the "essential wrongness" of killing another human being, regardless of the circumstances.[4] He refers to a psychological process called "doubling," where one has two selves—the execution self who does the dirty work that is normal within a "killing institution," and the everyday self. The latter would never kill another person and is morally at odds with the execution self. He is forced to develop a distancing mechanism, to keep from seeing the condemned person as a fellow human being and to focus instead on the crime for which he is being punished. Thinking about the horrible things the inmate did allows the guard to fend off feelings of his own guilt and to overcome the qualms of his everyday self.[5]

Of course, not all corrections workers share those attitudes, but Lifton's description perfectly fits the character of Fred Whitmore, played by Whittaker. He is disturbed by what he sees at the prison, beginning his first day on the job when he brings Bayliss up from "the hole." The troublesome inmate had been kept naked in a four-by-ten-foot cell, in total darkness, for five weeks. "I saw someone who wasn't a man anymore," Fred tells his wife that night. His supervisor at the prison, a sadistic lieutenant, tries to initiate Fred into the ways of the row. If you realize that the condemned men are "not like you," you can just do the job. A guard cannot see anything in common with the inmates or he would not be able to eat or sleep, the lieutenant explains. He contends that Bayliss deserves everything he gets—the hole, beating with a baton, stomping—because he was convicted of killing a correctional officer, "*my* officer." Fred Whitmore tries to take on the "us versus them" attitude, but like Bayliss, he is not able to conform to the institution's expectations. For interfering with the gratuitous brutality in the prison, Fred gets suspended. His difficulties at work lead to conflict with his wife and son. He is not doing well at reconciling his execution self with his everyday self.

Ultimately, and somewhat improbably, Fred and Bayliss develop a friendship that allows each man to tell about his life. Fred describes his abusive father and the ambivalence he felt when his father died. In a story very reminiscent of Gary Gilmore's, Bayliss talks about growing up in institutions. Although he admits to the killing of the prison guard that landed him on death row, Bayliss, who may or may not be an excellent con man, claims that the murder was set up by the guards, including the lieutenant.

The day before the execution Fred tells his young son that he will be working all night, that he needs to "finish the job" and stay with Bayliss until the end because "he's got nobody else." The boy gets to ask the questions: Why do they kill people if killing is wrong? Why do they care if he commits suicide if they are going to kill him anyway?

"To show they got the power," his father answers.

As a prison spokesman later states to the press, the execution went smoothly. Bayliss thanks Fred for being his friend as the two walk toward the electric chair. Anonymous hands strap him in, the hood is placed over his head, and the current is turned on by invisible men. No one is "responsible" for the death. Bayliss's body jerks a few times in a rather rhythmic motion and he seems to die peacefully. In the next scene, Fred mops up the chamber, while the music "Please Call Home" plays in the background. In the final frames, he arrives at his house, picks up his son, and hugs him. A graphic giving the number of people executed in the United States during the previous decade then appears on the screen.

What are we to make of the ending? The movie seems to lose its focus. For Bayliss, as for Gilmore, one could argue that death was a relief after the misery of prison. For Fred, having "his" inmate gone will probably mean fewer conflicts at home and at work. He has reported the lieutenant's abuses to the warden, and perhaps his conscience will be less troubled. Given its enigmatic conclusion, it seems that *Last Light* stands as a more successful comment on prison violence and brutality than on capital punishment.

In many ways, the execution of Lawrence Musgrove is the focal event of *Monster's Ball*. Without the execution, nothing would have happened as it did. Many people, in addition to the man who sat in the electric chair, find their lives inexorably changed. We know nothing of Lawrence himself or his crime except that he tells his son Tyrell, "I'm a bad man. You've got the best of me." The best, apparently, is his ability to draw portraits that capture a person's character. He explains, "It takes a human being to see a human being." A human being who is at that very moment living through his last night on earth, his "monster's ball."

Lawrence's execution is "unblinkingly filmed."[6] The camera follows as the guards shave him, as he puts on a large disposable diaper, as he is strapped into the chair, and as the cap is affixed to his head. The condemned man's last words are "push the button." The button is pushed, his body jerks convulsively, and smoke comes out of his head. Lawrence's death ends his story, but his execution ripples out from death row into the lives of the guards and the lives of his wife and son.

Billy Bob Thornton plays Hank Grotowski, a member of the "death team," a profession shared with his father and his son, called Sonny. The racist father is retired, but he still dominates the family home where the three men live a life that seems sustained by hatred—for African Americans, for women (both Hank and his son must resort to cold, anal intercourse with the same prostitute), and even for each other. Because Sonny does not seem to share fully in what critic A. O. Scott calls their "brutal code of masculine behavior,"[7] he discovers that he is in the wrong line of work.

As former Mississippi prison warden Don Cabana wrote, being part of an execution team is the "ultimate male bonding. Breaking those strong, silent ranks is something you're strongly conditioned not to do, even when you're opposed to the penalty."[8] Lawrence's execution is Sonny's first, and he breaks the strong, silent ranks. Having seen the condemned man as a human being, Sonny fails to play his role in carrying out the execution. Instead he vomits during the walk to the chair. Hank cannot tolerate his son's failure. He believes it reflects badly on him. Hank attacks and beats the boy, calling him everything from "a piece of shit" to "woman," "pussy," and "nigger." The demeaning terms seem interchangeable. Sonny ends his loveless life the next day by shooting himself in front of his father and grandfather. The suicide changes Hank's life and brings him into contact with Leticia, the ex-wife of the executed man, played by Halle Berry. The remainder of the film is their story, which begins with another tragedy, the death of her son, Tyrell.

The movie is not "about" capital punishment, nor is it "about" racism. It does, however, portray the multiple effects of both. At the end of the film, Hank and Leticia can see three graves from where they sit outside Hank's back door. Literally, the graves probably belong to Hank's mother, wife, and son, but they could also be those of Lawrence, Sonny, and Tyrell. As columnist Rick Groen notes, "The state-sanctioned death is compounded by others . . . white and black alike have despoiled their future, killing the best of what they are."[9]

Both films can be seen as examples of the brutalizing effects of the death penalty system. The killings on death row are not insulated from the outside world. In both *Last Light* and *Monster's Ball*, as in *The Green Mile*, what Lifton called their excruciating guilt spills over from the execution site to the "real" lives of the men who administer the punishment.

No Chivalry for Bad Girls

Although women make up only a small percentage of those subjected to the death penalty in the United States (about 2.8 percent of executions since 1632), they are not totally absent from death row. Women facing capital punishment in the early twenty-first century are both similar and different from the men who make up about 98 percent of those sentenced to death. The numbers show the same sort of geographical distribution. Since *Gregg v. Georgia*, all executions of women have taken place in the South. Minority groups and the poor are overrepresented, regardless of sex. Women, however, are much more likely to be condemned for murders of family members or intimate partners, while men more often get the death penalty for killing strangers, and seldom for killing spouses. Some scholars have argued that women who kill are more disposed to do so after a history of abuse or under coercion by an accomplice, although such information does not always come out at trial.[10]

This chapter will look at three films in which women are sentenced to death for murder: *I Want to Live*,[11] *Dance with a Stranger*,[12] and *Last Dance*.[13] The first two are based on actual cases. Barbara Graham was executed for a murder committed in the course of a robbery in California in 1955. Her story became *I Want to Live*, for which Susan Hayward won a best actress Oscar in 1959. *Dance with a Stranger* (1984) follows the events that led Ruth Ellis, the last woman executed in England, to shoot her faithless boyfriend. Although *Last Dance* (1996) is apparently a work of fiction, the crime it depicts and the major character bear a remarkable resemblance to Karla Faye Tucker, who was on death row in Texas when the film was made and who was executed in 1998 amid great controversy.

I Want to Live begins and ends with a statement on the screen describing it as a "factual story" based on articles, letters, and interviews conducted by journalist Ed Montgomery. Nonetheless, the film takes some liberties with events. It clearly supports the position that Graham was innocent of murder, although other contemporaries believe she was guilty as charged. At one level, the story of Barbara Graham is a study in how a woman who violates gender role expectations can find the public, and the jury chosen from that public, willing to believe her capable of anything. There is no doubt from the opening scene of the film—a night club with jazz, booze, sugar daddies, marijuana, and men wearing sunglasses at night—that Barbara inhabits a world outside the respectable mainstream. The audience first sees Graham upstairs above the club in bed with a client sharing a postcoital cigarette. Yet even then, she is a "good time girl" with a heart. After seeing a photo of the customer's family in his wallet, she saves him from arrest and humiliation by claiming to have paid for the room. She takes the blame for an encounter that would have snared her client in a federal violation of the Mann Act.

No one saves Barbara, who besides being a "party girl" or a "hipster chick," lives by her wits writing bad checks, driving getaway cars, and luring men into gambling scams. She has followed in her mother's footsteps, with a juvenile record and arrests for vagrancy and soliciting. Her "friends" persuade her to provide them with a false alibi for a robbery, which leads to her first felony conviction and a prison sentence for perjury. As Barbara is released from that sentence, the matron reminds her that she still has choices. In what seems foolish optimism, she makes some bad ones, especially marrying an apparently abusive heroin addict who refuses to provide for her and their son. Thus, despite her best intentions, Barbara returns to the old gang—just in time to get arrested along with them for the robbery and murder of Mabel Monahan. The movie makes it clear that the crime took place before Graham arrived to rejoin the men. Thus the audience does not doubt her innocence. But everyone who counts in the film—the press, the public, and ultimately the judge and jury—concludes that if she can be a loose woman, she can be a killer.

From the time of Barbara's arrest, a modern viewer recognizes procedures that were common before the 1960s Supreme Court spelled out the rights of the accused. The police "grill" the suspect all night without revealing the charges against her. Her requests for a lawyer and for a chance to use the bathroom are ignored. One officer calls her a "lousy hop-headed slut" while another refers to her as a "hard cookie." Reporters realize immediately that playing up her racy past will sell papers. As Barbara herself describes the situation, charging her with capital murder means votes for the district attorney, circulation for the newspapers, and promotions for the cops. It doesn't help that she has no way to verify her alibi for the night of the crime, but on the other hand, no one ever produces a shred of physical evidence that she was involved at the scene. According to the movie, the only evidence against her is the testimony of her fellow suspects—all of whom have something to gain by incriminating her. The gang members apparently believe that the state will not execute a woman. If they claim Barbara did the killing and she is not put to death, surely their lives will be spared, as they admit only to being her accomplices.

But neither Graham nor her lawyer focuses on the state's responsibility to prove her guilt beyond a reasonable doubt. Instead, they harp on her need to have an alibi. In desperation, she agrees to a fellow inmate's suggestion that her friend "Ben" claim he was with Barbara in a motel. Ben turns out to be an undercover police officer, and the inmate proves to be a jailhouse snitch who gets her sentence reduced for betraying Graham. Against the advice of her court-appointed attorney, Barbara takes the stand at her trial. She loses any semblance of credibility with the jury when the prosecutor asks about her previous conviction. "Perjury," she admits, and her fate is sealed.

The remainder of the movie proceeds to Graham's execution with a sense of inevitability. One after another, her appeals—ineffective counsel, entrapment by the police—are denied. A psychiatrist retained by her attorney is convinced that although Barbara is "totally amoral" and "a compulsive liar," she has an aversion to violence and would not have beaten someone to death. He also notices what, up until now, no one has seen. Barbara is left-handed and the killing blows were inflicted by a right-handed person. (Atticus Finch would have made that the heart of his case.) But the psychiatrist's evidence cannot be used in court, and to make matters worse, he dies during the appeals process, leaving no notes behind.

As Graham moves toward her execution date, she realizes that she does want to live, mainly out of love for her son. While she waits for the legal process to correct the injustice against her, the executioners prepare the lethal gas as if they were doing a science project. Critic Bosley Crowther calls the last portion of the film "a harrowing synthesis of drama and cold documentary detail."[14] At the end, the strong, sassy, resilient woman is terrified and, as in other successful death row films, the audience feels her terror. Barbara goes to the gas chamber stylishly dressed and groomed, but wearing a mask so she will not have to see the witnesses lurking like vultures to watch her die. At that point, her reactions are far more decent and humane than those of the morbidly curious all-male observers.

Although *I Want to Live* was filmed almost five decades ago, and the acting seems overdone by contemporary standards, it remains a powerful portrayal of death penalty issues. One critic calls it a "condemnation of the American judicial system" and a "damning condemnation of the media, who latch onto her case with sensationalizing vigor [that] still feels relevant today."[15] Other works considered in this book have looked at men who were judged guilty because of their race. Barbara Graham was judged guilty at least in part because her lifestyle violated the gender roles and moral code of the time.

Lawrence Russell notes that at exactly the same time that Graham's case was unfolding in California, Ruth Ellis was hanged in England for shooting her boyfriend. The two women shared a number of qualities—the very features that placed them outside the circle of respectable society. Both were divorced single mothers, "quasi-prostitutes, barflies pursued by brutish, substance-abusing males, victims of passion and personal histories from which they [were] unable to escape."[16] *Dance with a Stranger* follows Ellis's story from her meeting with David Blakely until, in the last scene, she murders him. The film refers to Ellis's trial and execution only in the final credits. But even without the trial, prison, and hanging scenes, it is of interest as it portrays what led such a woman—amoral and deceitful, but nonviolent like Barbara Graham—to kill the man she loved. One must also speculate about why, when the death penalty was seldom used, the British government found it necessary to put her to death. In fact, the film may be seen as an extended brief that might have been written by the defense to argue the mitigating evidence in Ruth Ellis's favor.

With hindsight, it is difficult to understand why Ellis, played by Miranda Richardson, became fixated on Blakely. A woman of her experience had certainly met other handsome, upper-class men. But like Barbara Graham, she had no gift for choosing the right one. The film chronicles the mutually destructive relationship between the two. Although it ultimately costs Blakely his life, the affair cost Ellis her job, her home, a pregnancy, her self-respect, and, some might argue, her mental health. It is clear that Blakely abused Ruth both physically and psychologically. When she kills him, it appears to be an act of deranged jealousy. But it might also be called self-defense.

The film implies that, given the history of the relationship, the balance of Ellis's mind was disturbed when she pulled the trigger. In several scenes preceding the shooting, as her behavior becomes more obsessive and irrational, she says things like "How did I get here?" Under the British capital statutes in 1955 when Ellis was executed, the insanity defense was frequently interpreted generously to spare a defendant's life. It may be, as Vincent Canby suggests, that Ruth Ellis was hanged "less for her crime than for her way of life at a time when women were expected to remain squeaky clean."[17] Her trial lasted only a day and a half. The jury obviously had no empathy for Ellis. They found her guilty after deliberating a mere fourteen minutes. She was executed twenty-four days later despite a petition with fifty thousand signatures asking for clemency. Ellis may well have been caught in a political tug-of-war. The Conservative Party, in power at the time, was firmly committed to capital punishment. They could not be seen to give in to public pressure to commute her sentence or they would risk appearing "soft on crime."[18]

In the late 1990s, Ruth's sister attempted to have her conviction reduced to manslaughter on the grounds that the jury had not heard that Blakely abused Ellis and that he had caused her to miscarry by beating her.[19] Perhaps if Ruth Ellis had had a lawyer who described the violence against her, or perhaps if she had been tried at a time when domestic abuse was better understood, her fate would have been different. Had she been convicted of manslaughter, she would have served a prison term of several years and been released.

Cindy Liggett, the condemned woman in *Last Dance*, is played by a very drab Sharon Stone. Not a glamorous call girl like Barbara Graham and Ruth Ellis, Cindy is a working-class woman who commits a brutal murder while high on cocaine. Her male accomplice makes a deal with the prosecutor to provide evidence against Cindy in return for a prison sentence. He testifies falsely that they were using only alcohol and marijuana, thus denying Cindy the potential mitigation that acknowledging a two-day cocaine high might have provided. Her original lawyer fails to mount any real defense, so Cindy, in the midst of a vengeful political atmosphere, is sentenced to die. The audience meets her when she is on Texas death row, where four other female inmates—two African Americans, one Hispanic, and one older white woman—also await execution.

Critics have commented on the unfortunate coincidence that *Last Dance* was released shortly after *Dead Man Walking*. Despite some plot similarities, the former clearly suffers by comparison with Sister Helen Prejean's story. Yet at least in part because it involves a woman rather than a condemned man, *Last Dance* raises several compelling issues.

A young lawyer appointed to the state Clemency Board through his political connections is assigned to prepare an obligatory report on Cindy's case. From the outset there is no real expectation that the governor, who has never granted clemency to anyone, will commute her sentence. The attorney Rick Hayes, played by Rob Morrow, uncovers the failings of Cindy's legal representation and wonders why she should die just because her lawyer was terrible and her victim was rich. Students of the death penalty know there is nothing surprising about those characteristics of the case. As he tries to raise issues for an appeal, Rick also finds an intractable prosecutor who had used this trial to build his career and has no intention of appearing soft on crime. "The public is behind us," he claimed. Meanwhile, to illustrate just how political calculations influence the justice process, the hard-line governor decides he can make one offer of clemency. Of course, he chooses not Cindy, but a black inmate who has written a book, appeared on television, and gathered letters from professors at Yale Law School. The erstwhile condemned man asks, "How can you kill a man who's on the *New York Times* bestseller list?"

Apparently the state of Texas had no problem with killing a woman. Early in Rick's tenure at the Clemency Board his supervisor says with a wink-wink, nudge-nudge, "If women want equal treatment, more of them will be executed." Both men get a good laugh from that one. Likewise, the governor expresses what is sometimes called "equality with a vengeance" when he explains that he is not considering clemency for Cindy. The sex of the murderer made no difference to the victim, he remarks, and her sex makes no difference to him.

Without clemency, Cindy's only hope is that the courts will agree to reopen the appeals process to hear Rick's arguments about her drug-induced state and the ineffectiveness of her first counsel. The strategy does not work, although her execution is delayed at the last minute while the court decides whether to hear her appeal. As in most of the other death penalty movies, the preparation of the chemicals for her lethal injection and the practice testing of the straps that will hold her on the gurney remind the viewer that when the state kills, it does so with careful premeditation and intention. But if there is stark realism in the official pre-execution ritual, the narrative scenes just before Cindy's death seem totally unreal. Rick is allowed to spend the night in Cindy's cell with her and although they sleep in opposite bunks, such contact seems the figment of a misplaced romantic imagination injected into a most inappropriate place. The romance on death row is not the only thing that reminds us that we are watching a Hollywood film. During virtually the entire movie, it seems that only three people work in the state capitol building—Rick, his boss, and his brother. Halls are empty, galleries are devoid of legislators and tourists. Nothing but this story is going on in Austin.

Practically every critic finds *Last Dance* a mediocre film—both in comparison with *Dead Man Walking* and on its own terms. Richard Alleva complains that the audience never knows who Cindy is, that the interviews with Rick do not "adduce even an interesting enigma." The film offers fascinating details that are not developed—a suggestion of class warfare in the crimes and the possibility that Cindy was avenging the sexual exploitation of her mother. Alleva concludes that the only things one learns about the justice system are things we already know—"that politicians value votes over individual lives, that lawyers groan under their case loads, that parents of murdered children are often in favor of capital punishment, that accomplices to crimes may shift the burden of guilt onto their partners."[20] Barbara Shulgasser calls *Last Dance* "simplistic, puerile rubbish" because it concerns "stuff we see every night on TV—corruption in high places, an inhumane system and selfishness."[21] *Maclean's* calls it "just another case of justice denied."[22] Without a doubt the story is quite flawed and the criticisms of the system it portrays are not revelations, but if most of us already know those things, why do they persist? That virtually every capital punishment film features those same issues may not be so much a weakness of the movies as a failure of the larger political system.

An actual case working its way through the court system when *Last Dance* was released involves some extraordinary similarities with the film. Like Cindy, Karla Faye Tucker was convicted of a brutal robbery-murder in Texas. According to testimony, on a high that involved virtually every drug known to man or woman, she and a male companion used a pickax to kill a couple where they found them in bed. Tucker was the child of a prostitute who gave her drugs and taught her to "turn tricks" when she was a young teenager. In prison, Tucker underwent a religious conversion, ministered to her fellow inmates, and fell in love with and married her chaplain. As her execution approached, a national outcry arose urging that her life be spared. Much of the support for clemency came from the Christian right, usually supporters of capital punishment. Despite pressures from many of his political supporters, Governor George W. Bush ordered that Tucker's execution proceed. She became only the second woman executed in the United States since the death penalty was reinstated in *Gregg v. Georgia*. Some people claim that Bush's refusal to consider Tucker's gender in evaluating her case was a victory for formal equality. Like the governor in *Last Dance*, he argued that it was just a routine execution and that the sex of the person put to death was irrelevant.

The parallels between Tucker's case and the fictional Cindy Liggett are strong. They may not be completely coincidental, although Karla Faye Tucker was not executed until two years after the film's release. Critic Jack Sommersby noted that *Last Dance* "explor[ed] whether convicted murderers are capable of growing into more emotionally caring, moral people while in prison, . . . whether this constituted an eventual pardon, and, if not, then what is the purpose of correctional institutions?"[23] The same point was a common argument against executing Tucker. She had become a good Christian woman who wanted to serve others. What was the point of killing her, other than simple vengeance?

Both Karla Faye Tucker's and Cindy's stories, along with the life and death of Barbara Graham and Ruth Ellis, raise questions about the workings of the judicial system in a patriarchal society. People are never judged without some consciousness of their sex as well as their race. As long as inequities persist in the society as a whole, it is to be expected that the justice system, including the application of the death penalty, will reflect those biases.

Actual Innocence

Unlike many of the other films in this chapter, *The Life of David Gale*[24] seems to have been developed intentionally to convey an anti-death-penalty message. Unfortunately, the plot undermines and even contradicts that position. Because the film is so contrived, the audience neither realizes the horror of Gale's situation nor cares about the real-life implications of the story.

David Gale, played by Kevin Spacey, is a most atypical resident of Texas death row. He has a Harvard degree and had a brilliant career as a philosophy professor. (Lest the viewer forget his pedigree and how far Gale has fallen, he wears a sweatshirt from his alma mater through most of the movie.) During a lecture to a rapt auditorium of students, Gale explains that while desire is transient, the value of integrity is lasting. His devotion to this formulation is soon tested. While his role as a dedicated opponent of capital punishment and one of the leading lights in an abolitionist group called DeathWatch reveals his integrity, he easily succumbs to the momentary pleasures, the "transient desire" of alcohol and sex with a graduate student. The latter encounter costs him his job when the young woman accuses him of rape. Even though the student drops the charges, Gale's wife divorces him, takes their son, and moves to Spain. The former professor becomes a full-time alcoholic and, with the exception of his former colleague Constance, his DeathWatch associates don't want him around tainting the group's reputation. Although Gale manages to get on the wagon, his previous excesses make him the number one suspect when Constance is found dead, apparently the victim of a brutal murder and rape. She was suffocated by a bag taped over her head, handcuffed, and forced to swallow the key to the cuffs. Gale had once written an article describing how the Romanian police used that technique to destroy their political rivals. In addition, his semen is found inside the victim. A tripod at the crime scene suggested that the murder had been videotaped, but no tape surfaces. Gale is convicted and sentenced to death.

Although there are suggestions that his lawyer behaved incompetently, Gale sticks with the same attorney throughout the appeals process. In fact, the lawyer serves as the go-between for the arrangement that frames the film's plot. In the last three days before his execution, Gale agrees to tell his *real* story to reporter Bitsey Bloom (Kate Winslet) if her magazine pays $500,000 to his son. Through the interviews between the condemned man and the journalist, the audience learns most of the events leading up to the murder. The final twist—that Constance committed suicide while Gale filmed her death and that the whole thing was meant to prove that the state of Texas could and would execute an innocent man—is revealed only after Gale is put to death.

That the machinery of capital punishment is so faulty that the innocent really do get killed by the state is probably the most effective argument made by opponents of the death penalty. Yet this film cheapens that powerful and troubling reality by making the abolitionists the ones who manipulate the system for their own political ends. As Mark Steyn writes in the *Spectator*, the movie creates "the impression that the anti-death penalty movement is a bunch of weirdsville death cultists."[25] The characters, particularly Gale and Constance, have brought out all of the standard rational arguments against capital punishment, including the likelihood of convicting the wrong person. In a televised debate between Gale and the governor of Texas (who looks remarkably like George W. Bush and is described as being "in touch with his inner frat boy"), the governor promises that if the professor can name just one innocent person executed in Texas, he will declare a moratorium. One might argue then that Gale gave his life to save others. Was that the integrity he preached to his students? Or was it a wild stunt that made the anti-death-penalty group look like a crazy bunch of zealots? Is the movie, as Roger Ebert states, "corrupt, intellectually bankrupt, and morally dishonest?"[26]

One may credit *The Life of David Gale* with attempting to place the issue of capital punishment in the center of a commercial film with a first-rate cast. Unfortunately, the story was marred not only by the moral ambiguity of a man orchestrating his own execution; it also had some remarkably stupid plot elements. Bitsey Bloom, crack reporter, was unable either to turn in a faulty rental car for a working replacement or to use a cell phone. Gale, a full professor with tenure, was fired by his university without an opportunity to present his side of the case. His accuser was a graduate student who was expelled in the middle of a semester even before grades had been turned in. Ultimately though, it is the total contrast between the supposedly brilliant and privileged David Gale on death row to achieve a political mission and the actually innocent men who have faced execution that is disturbing. The convicts wrongly sentenced to death are much more likely to resemble the uneducated, mentally handicapped, poverty-stricken African American Earl Washington—almost executed for rape and murder in Virginia—than a Harvard Ph.D.

Randall Adams, convicted of killing a Dallas police officer and the subject of the 1988 "hybrid docudrama,"[27] *The Thin Blue Line,*[28] is far closer to the death row norm than David Gale. Adams, who is usually described as a drifter, protested his innocence through his trial, death sentence, appeals, and the commutation of his sentence to life in prison. He stuck by his story that on his way back from looking for a job he ran out of gas and was picked up by 16-year-old David Harris in what would turn out to be a stolen car. Both men agreed that they had done some drinking, smoked some marijuana, and gone to a drive-in movie. Adams claimed that Harris had dropped him off at his motel where Adams's brother was asleep in their room about 9:30 p.m. Harris asked to stay but Adams refused, claiming that his brother would object to a stranger moving in with them.

At about 12:30 that night police officer Robert Wood was shot when he stopped a blue car for driving without lights. Although the next day Harris bragged to his friends that he had killed the officer, he later blamed Adams. When the film was shot, Harris, on death row for another murder, seems to admit in the final sequence that he killed Officer Wood and that Adams was just unlucky. Perhaps, Harris suggested, he accused Adams because the latter had refused him a place to stay. The year after the film was released, Adams was retried and acquitted. Harris was convicted of the murder and sentenced to another life term.

At the time of the movie's opening, critic Hal Hinson wrote in the *Washington Post* that director Errol Morris had at least created a reasonable doubt of Adams's guilt. That response made Hinson feel uncomfortable, because if Morris was correct "there's the chance they [the story's conclusions] were come to unfairly."[29] Since then, dozens of studies of the death penalty support the conclusion that the process that determined Adams's guilt was indeed unfair. The case is all too typical in that the police desperately wanted to solve the murder of a law enforcement officer in the line of duty. Adams, a rather marginal citizen with no roots in the community, made a good suspect. On the other hand, the film reveals that although Harris already had an extensive record as a juvenile, people in his hometown gave him every benefit of the doubt. They didn't want to "ruin a boy's life" by connecting him with the crime. Instead of looking carefully at David Harris, the police used him as an informant. He testified against Adams in exchange for his (temporary) freedom. The defense attorney also believed that the state charged Adams rather than Harris because the latter was a juvenile when the crime was committed and thus ineligible for the death penalty. They could charge Adams, but not Harris, with a capital offense.

The case put on by the state of Texas relied on a number of questionable witnesses in addition to Harris. The infamous "Dr. Death," a psychiatrist who testified that every defendant he interviewed was likely to commit future violence, interpreted Adams's lack of remorse as proof that he was a sociopath. Of course if Adams was innocent (as he was), he would be unable to show remorse. Other witnesses included a couple who "positively identified" Adams but later admitted to lying in exchange for money and a promise not to prosecute their daughter for an unrelated robbery. The judge was an unapologetic admirer of law enforcement and seized on the term "thin blue line" to describe the tenuous barrier between law and chaos maintained by the police. His comments in the film include an amazing calculus. He argued that the Texas Court of Appeals upheld the guilty verdict 9–0. Although the United States Supreme Court reversed 8–1, the judge claimed he was "endorsed" by a score of 10–8!

The story of Randall Adams is typical of many death penalty cases on film and in real life. The police used questionable tactics in trying to extract a confession. Major testimony against him came from an informant who stood to gain by lying. Eyewitness testimony and "expert" witnesses were at best unreliable and at worst knowingly false. The victim was sympathetic; the defendant a "nobody." The major factor that set Adams's trial apart from many others that led to death sentences was the quality of his defense attorneys—one an experienced capital attorney, the other dedicated to her client and the truth. Nonetheless, without Errol Morris and *The Thin Blue Line*, Randall Adams would, at the very least, have spent his life in prison.

While *The Life of David Gale* was a fictional tale of a man trying to prove what was wrong with the "machinery of death," *The Thin Blue Line* demonstrates those failings in a real man's life.

Set in 1849–50 on a remote French-administered island off the coast of Canada, *The Widow of St. Pierre* would at first seem to have little to do with the death penalty in the United States in the twenty-first century.[30] But in fact it offers a timeless view of the issues surrounding capital punishment. The exotic setting and the oddities of the legal system only serve to clarify the universality of the questions raised when the state takes a life.

The island is frigidly cold, mostly barren, and, not surprisingly, the majority of those who live there are poor. The ruling class is composed of the top administrative appointees and military men, all of whom serve at the pleasure of the government in Paris. The elite fraternize only with each other and have little contact with the islanders. The exceptions are the Captain, whose duties include looking after prisoners, and his wife, called Madame La (for Madame La Capitaine). One thread in the story concerns the deep and passionate love between the husband and wife. That thread becomes intertwined with the story of the murderer, Neel Auguste.

Auguste and his friend Olivier, after coming in from a grueling fishing expedition, get drunk and argue foolishly about whether their wealthy neighbor is fat or large. One stupid drunken thing leads to another, and before the night is over the two men have murdered the subject of their dispute. Sober, abashed, frightened, and repentant at their trial, they are unable to give a coherent reason for the killing. Olivier dies in a cart accident immediately after the trial, but Auguste is sentenced to death by guillotine, as French law required. (Presumably in the interest of using the most humane method of death, the French Republic provided that no other form of execution was permissible for civilians.) St. Pierre, however, has no guillotine, and one has to be shipped from the Caribbean island of Martinique, a journey of several months. In addition, no ship's captain will allow an executioner on board—even if they would transport a killing device—so someone willing to kill Auguste has to be found in St. Pierre.

While waiting for the guillotine (called a "widow" in French slang), Neel Auguste is housed in a cell in the Captain's courtyard. There Madame La, with her husband's blessing, sets upon her scheme of rehabilitation. At first she offers Neel extra food and comforts, such as a lamp, for helping with her greenhouse. Before long, the prisoner is not only growing plants but also working on projects around the town, mending roofs, shoveling snow, and other "community service" by way of restitution for his crime. "Show them who you really are," Madame La urges. "Show them that people can change." After he single-handedly saves the pub and its owner from death and disaster, Neel's rehabilitation back into the community seems complete. He is the local hero—except that his death sentence still looms. Repeatedly the film implies that the state's plan to put Neel to death will be thwarted. Posters advertising for an executioner are torn down in disgust by the townspeople. Even though many are desperate for money, no one will earn it by killing Auguste. Finally a poor immigrant has to be tricked into taking the job. The ship carrying the "widow" then runs aground some distance off the island. If further proof of his humanity is needed, Neel himself helps to bring the ship, its crew, and the cargo safely ashore. He even refuses an opportunity to escape rather than cause problems for the Captain.

Meanwhile the provincial officials grumble about their dilemma. Auguste's popularity is "alarming," and one of the political leaders acknowledges that although the court had condemned a criminal, they will execute a good person. But, they ultimately decide, French law requires it. As a local woman scoffs, the officials "just want to look good to Paris." The social and economic gap between Auguste and those who get to decide his fate is vast. Unlike the people whose life is on the island and who have restored Neel to their community based on his repeated demonstrations of decency, the leaders have their fingers firmly fixed on the political pulse of Paris. Like contemporary politicians who depend on the polls for guidance in clemency decisions, these men also read the political tea leaves. In other words, even though it has become clear that Neel's death would "redress nothing and solve nothing," no one in power except the Captain will address the irrationality of taking his life and run the risk of displeasing Paris. Rather they can deflect their responsibility by arguing that they were just doing what the law required.

The Captain follows his conscience as well as the wishes of his wife. He refuses to order his soldiers to participate in the execution. His punishment is a charge of mutiny and a return to France, where he will face a firing squad. Thus Neel is killed to show that killing people is wrong. The Captain is killed to show that refusing to kill people is also wrong.

Virtually every death penalty theme, except perhaps racial injustice, plays itself out in this film—class bias, the abuse of power, the deflecting of responsibility, the effects on those who prepare the condemned man for death, and of course, the futility of killing a man who would make a positive contribution to the community. The murdered man had no family, so Neel's death offered retribution to no one. It would be difficult to argue that executing Neel Auguste would deter future drunks from getting into foolish arguments that lead to tragic consequences. Two women became widows and two children were orphaned. But presumably the governor and his friends "looked good to Paris."

It may be easier to see the futility, indeed the stupidity, of Neel's execution by removing the story into a remote time and place. It is, however, almost impossible to avoid making pointed comparisons with the contemporary world.

Whether intentional or not, the films discussed in this chapter all share a perspective critical of the death penalty. Whatever the method—guillotine, hanging, electric chair, gas chamber, or lethal injection—in every instance the state carefully and intentionally takes a life. Often it is the life of a man or woman who lived on the margin of society and who therefore seems expendable. There is no doubt that those who were executed were found legally guilty of a terrible crime. In several cases, however, their actual guilt is not as clear. Not one of the films showed a community that was improved by carrying out an execution. Not one provides evidence to show why it is sensible to kill someone to show that killing is wrong.

Some people inside and outside the film industry believe that movies can spark social changes, that they can affect people's principles because they reach large segments of the population and because of "their capacity for getting under people's skin." Although not everyone reacts in the same way, "people are moved when they are confronted with real stories about real people, not just reports from a human rights organization."[31] The films in this chapter were sometimes based on actual cases, sometimes fictional. All, however, put a human face on the death penalty.

The novels considered in the next chapter also provide portraits, rather than statistics, about the process of capital punishment.

·6·

IF WORDS COULD KILL: CRIME FICTION AND THE DEATH PENALTY

The separate genre of fiction dealing with the detection of crime dates back at least to the late nineteenth century, when Arthur Conan Doyle developed the immensely popular Sherlock Holmes stories. Today there are a number of subgroups within the general category that most bookstores label "mystery." Some novels fall into the "whodunit" designation, where the reader, along with most of the characters, tries to determine who committed the crime. Others, called "police procedurals," center on an investigation in which law enforcement types and readers know the identity of the guilty party but where the plot follows the attempt to bring the offender to justice. Both whodunits and police procedurals generally end before the criminal is tried and sentenced. Legal thrillers, on the other hand, often include extensive courtroom scenes. The working out of the prosecution and defense cases is typically at the center of the plot.

Like any other fiction genre, crime novels run the gamut from good to awful. The four books considered in this chapter, *Suspicion of Vengeance* by Barbara Parker, *The Red Scream* by Mary Willis Walker, *Time's Witness* by Michael Malone, and *Reversible Errors* by Scott Turow, are all well-written, intelligent explorations of the issue of capital punishment within the context of crime fiction.[1] Surprisingly, they are virtually the only recent examples of mysteries dealing with the topic. Both Parker and Turow are lawyers, and both feature attorneys as major characters in their fiction. Parker has developed a series of six books featuring solo practitioner Gail Conner and her fiancé, criminal defense lawyer Anthony Quintana. Turow's attorney characters vary from novel to novel, although some reappear in peripheral roles. Not surprisingly, both of their books considered in this chapter include extensive legal arguments and critical courtroom scenes. Mary Willis Walker is a journalist, and her protagonist, Molly Cates, shares that profession. In *The Red Scream*, Molly's job leads her to investigate an apparent serial killer. The novel focuses on questions about his guilt for one of the crimes and the reporter's efforts to find the truth before the execution occurs. *Time's Witness* is told through the eyes of Cuddy Magnum, chief of police in Hillston, North Carolina. It combines the elements of a police procedural, as Cuddy tries to solve several current murders, with the court proceedings involved in attempting to remove an innocent man from death row. What the four novels have in common, besides their generally good literary quality, is the ability to illuminate the flaws in the capital system. In each one, a man innocent of the crime for which he was sentenced sits on death row. In every case, the convicted man is poor and uneducated. All were pressured by the police. Two are arguably mentally ill. None had a decent attorney at his first trial. All exist within a political system that values following opinion polls and pleasing powerful constituents more than doing justice. Three of the stories take place in the South—in Florida, Texas, and North Carolina. The other is set in Illinois (before the moratorium). Given that these novels are fiction, not reality, the themes developed in them bear a remarkable resemblance to issues raised by critics of the real death penalty.

"Them without the Capital Gets the Punishment"[2]

In *Suspicion of Vengeance*, by Barbara Parker, Kenny Ray Clark sits on Florida's death row for the brutal murder of a young woman during an apparent home robbery. Her baby, left unattended for hours, choked and died in his crib. Although the baby's death is ruled an accident and Clark is not held responsible for it, the tragedy certainly adds to the public outrage surrounding the crime. Clark's grandmother, who had worked for attorney Gail Conner's parents, prevails on her to take Kenny Ray's case. Although Conner usually handles civil matters, she cannot resist the call to help an old family connection and eventually persuades her fiancé Anthony Quintana, a noted criminal lawyer, to get involved as well.

Although the plot has its share of the coincidences and red herrings that make crime fiction fun to read, it also reflects some careful research on death penalty law, as the author mentions in her acknowledgments. Parker consulted practicing members of the criminal justice system and scholars, including Michael Mello, who has defended clients on death row and written about the issue in law journals.[3] Thus Parker has the information to provide a realistic portrayal of the process that sentenced Kenny Ray Clark to death row. Most of the evidence against him comes from a single respectable but unreliable eyewitness and a jailhouse snitch. His original lawyer, appointed by the court, is a "practicing alcoholic" who had not tried a capital case in years.[4] During the penalty phase, Clark's history of abuse might have been seen as a mitigating factor. He had been beaten by his stepfather with brooms, belts, and extension cords, and sexually assaulted by another of his mother's boyfriends. The jury learns little of these events. But the attorney is not totally to blame for the lack of full disclosure. The client himself is embarrassed to have his history of sexual abuse made public. Although Clark's sister tells about their difficult childhood and the grandmother takes the stand to say that her grandson was a good boy and that killing is always wrong, those statements have little impact on the jury. The state produces family members who provide victim impact statements and a psychiatrist who testifies to Clark's future dangerousness. The prosecutor ends with pleas to value the victim's life and calls for retribution. He argues that "the penalty of death is the appropriate response of a civilized society."[5] The assertion that civilization is synonymous with vengeance apparently convinces the jury. Kenny Ray is convicted and sentenced on the flimsiest of evidence, aided by the prosecutor's emotional references to the heinousness and atrocity of the crime.[6]

When Clark claims inadequate assistance of counsel in his first appeal, the same judge who had originally appointed the alcoholic attorney hears the case. He finds that the failure to put on any real defense was a professional judgment within the lawyer's discretion.[7] However, as a death row inmate in Florida, Clark had an advantage over those similarly sentenced in other states. Florida requires that those who receive capital sentences must be provided with lawyers throughout the appellate process. Many other death penalty states leave it up to the condemned person to find a lawyer after the initial appeal. Until Gail Conner came on the scene, Kenny Ray was represented by the Capital Collateral Representatives (CCR), a group of attorneys—overworked and underpaid—who specialize in death penalty appeals. Overwhelmed with clients as CCR is, they are happy to hand over the Clark case, even to an attorney inexperienced in criminal law.

In a capsule summary of death penalty law, a CCR associate explains her workload to Conner, noting that she is fighting the state for her clients' lives. "Who do you think they are? A bunch of Ted Bundys? . . . Most of them are from poor and violent homes. They can hardly read and write. They're addicts and alcoholics. A few were juveniles at the time of the crime and the Supreme Court says it's okay if we execute them. Half of the people sentenced to death are black, and the Supreme Court sees no problem with that." She continues, noting that the Court has "no problem rejecting a claim of innocence as long as the prisoner got a fair trial, but would someone tell me what that is? I've seen cops lie, witnesses make mistakes, and defense lawyers fall asleep. Killing people to prevent killing doesn't work, hasn't worked, and never will, but damn, it feels good."[8] One thing that capital punishment seems to accomplish is to transform the lawyers who take on capital appeals to fulfill a pro bono requirement. They study the case and learn about the client and wonder "how the next man with similar facts and a better trial lawyer got life or an acquittal." They come to ask the question, "What are we going to gain, killing this man? A lawyer who takes a capital appeal gets inside the system, really inside. And sometimes, not very often, he finds a man who shouldn't be there at all. . . . You don't know joy until you see that man walk into the light." Whatever the outcome, none of these attorneys see their work on the death penalty as a waste of time. "Maybe they do only that one case, but they all say thank you. Now I see how it is. I understand."[9]

Over and over, literature and films tell the same story. Many people who are exposed to the workings of the capital punishment system—especially those who work on the defense side—are never the same. They are unable to find the benefits in state-sponsored killing. In *Suspicion of Vengeance*, her family and friends fear that Gail Conner has become so obsessed with the Clark case that she will lose her health and her practice. On several occasions she does lose control while arguing for her client. Gail is outraged when the attorney for the state makes a standard argument for the necessity of capital punishment. "Life without the possibility of parole is a lie because legislators can change their minds and let these people out. There are no recidivists with the death penalty. If we save one innocent life, it's worth it."[10] The DA does not explain whether it is "worth it" if no innocent lives are saved or if an innocent life is taken.

As the plot unfolds and the appeals fail (partly because, as the novel demonstrates, the Antiterrorism and Effective Death Penalty Act of 1996 truncates the process), one last hope is that a corrupt wealthy developer will use his influence to ask the governor for clemency. Self-interest and arrogance stand in the way. Likewise, the sheriff who becomes aware of Clark's innocence will not come forward. He will not be in the position of disclosing that "the men and women who did their best on this and a thousand other cases can't be trusted to get it right. That's how the press would see it. The defense lawyers would love me. I would create mistrust and disrespect for my office and everyone in it. What's at stake here is the rule of law, and how that public regards that law, with respect and confidence."[11] He seems to be arguing that it is necessary to conceal the mistakes in the system, even to the extent of executing an innocent man, in order to retain public trust in the (failed) system.

The novel does not have a happy ending; in that sense that Clark's innocence does not keep him from being killed. Gail Conner fails to save her client's life and takes little consolation from his grandmother's belief that Kenny Ray's soul will enjoy a better fate. The lawyer joins the crowd outside the prison during the execution, noting the protesters on both sides with all the usual placards. She hears the governor's sanctimonious statement on the radio, extolling due process and closure, listens to the death penalty advocates cheering and the nuns singing hymns. The reader does not witness the lethal injection that kills Clark, only the resignation Gail experiences. Yet it is really unnecessary to observe the death to know that the system has failed. On the other hand, as this is fiction and not life, before the book ends Anthony Quintana manages to see that the guilty are punished and that romance triumphs.

Robert Croen in the *Pittsburgh Post-Gazette* points out that any first-year law student could have told Gail at the outset that "procedure is more important than justice . . . that guilt or innocence may have nothing to do with the outcome of the trial."[12] *Publishers Weekly* also notes that if Parker "has an ax to grind, it is the legal system's determination to put judicial procedure and the public's thirst for vengeance ahead of the sanctity of human life."[13] Of course the audience demographic for Parker's work is probably not first-year law students, but a wider public, less acquainted with the legal system. To such readers, the message that legal procedure that meets the necessary standard for "due process" may still lead to the conviction of the innocent might come as something of a surprise.

One may argue that crime novels reach different people than nonfiction or commercial films. Members of the reading public often choose detective fiction because it typically involves a tidy ending where good triumphs over evil and justice is restored. The troubling issues raised by a defective death penalty system do not allow for such neat resolutions and may remain with readers after they have closed the book.

Certainly Mary Willis Walker's *The Red Scream* forces similar questions about procedures and about actual guilt and innocence.

One More Texas Execution

Just as Barbara Parker developed a heroine who mirrored her own legal profession, Walker, a journalist, created Molly Cates, who writes about crime for a monthly magazine. Molly has just published her first hardcover book, a "true crime" work about the serial killer Louie Bronk, currently on death row and only days away from his execution by lethal injection. There seems little doubt that Bronk committed a series of brutal murders along Texas highways. He earned the nickname "The Texas Scalper" for his signature treatment of his female victims. And, as if shaving their heads were not sufficient degradation,

Bronk sexually molested the dead bodies. But the crime that sent him to death row—the murder of wealthy socialite Tiny McFarland—is a slight variation on his typical modus operandi. Tiny had been killed and scalped at her own home, far from the interstate highways. Her murder is a capital offense because it was combined with a robbery, making it murder in the commission of a felony. The other victims had been killed and sodomized after death, but in Texas "desecration of a corpse" combined with murder is not death-eligible. The social and financial status of Tiny McFarland and the media attention to her death make zealous prosecution of the crime and the ultimate punishment virtually inevitable. Louie has confessed to killing her and the other "scalper" victims. Thus when the book opens not only is his execution imminent, to a great many people it seems an excellent example of justice.

Molly Cates is an opponent of the death penalty, but even she expresses the view that she will not be sorry to see the end of Louie Bronk. Her interviews with him have been a test of her determination. Bronk writs abysmal "poetry," illiterate rhyming couplets describing his crimes. In exchange for talking with the journalist, the inmate insists that Molly try to get his poetry published. In addition, Bronk is physically repulsive. He is in his thirties, short and wiry, "with an unpleasant-looking hard paunch asserting itself against his belt." He has dark greasy hair and stringy arms covered in tattoos done in prison. He sweats profusely, a "prolific sweater. Even in cold weather, and even fresh from the shower, he smelled like a man who had never had a bath." When Bronk opens his mouth, "the man's lower jaw was crowded with jumbled, crooked teeth. If looked as if he had twice as many as was intended." Molly compares it to catching a normal-looking fish, opening its mouth, and finding that you had caught a live piranha.[14] Her book, called *Sweating Blood*, describes Bronk and his crimes. It makes the argument that in this case the state of Texas has done its job by convicting him.

A few days before Bronk's scheduled execution, a series of events raises doubts. Molly receives some new "poems," not written by Bronk but claiming to admire his murderous work. The second Mrs. McFarland is murdered. A witness who testified at Bronk's trial whom the condemned man invited to the execution is also found dead. Louie suddenly claims that although he killed the women along the highway, Tiny McFarland was not one of his victims. Molly's life is threatened. Most of the novel is occupied with Molly's attempt to find out who really killed Tiny and to keep that person from killing anyone else.

Several issues raised in *The Red Scream* are worthwhile in discussions of the death penalty. There is the matter of legal guilt and actual guilt. It is one thing to draw a death row portrait of an actually innocent man who evokes sympathy for the injustice he suffered—Jefferson in *A Lesson Before Dying*, John Coffey in *The Green Mile*, Kenny Ray Clark in *Suspicion of Vengeance*—and another to create a disgusting character like Louie Bronk who nonetheless does not deserve execution if he did not commit the specific crime for which he was sentenced. The argument against capital punishment is no less valid, but much less appealing, if the condemned man is responsible for other grisly killings. But despite the district attorney's claim that innocent persons are never sent to the death chamber because "we don't prosecute innocent people,"[15] cases in fiction and in the real world prove otherwise. It seems beyond the scope of human competence to claim that the criminal justice system is infallible. Killing a man for the wrong crime, no matter how repulsive he is, does not vindicate the system.

Walker takes the reader through a familiar Texas saga. Before Bronk was picked up, the police set their sights on the McFarland's live-in babysitter, mainly because he was Hispanic. The authorities then apparently took advantage of Bronk's narcissistic personality and his craving for attention. They provided him with enough information about Tiny McFarland's murder so that, once he had started confessing to the other crimes, he admitted to that one too. Witnesses lied about seeing Bronk's car at the scene.

Molly herself and her issues of intellectual honesty serve as a sort of metaphor for the criminal justice system. Like the authorities, she has determined that Bronk killed Tiny McFarland. She never looked for evidence that might contradict that hypothesis. Similarly, the police often decide on a suspect early in an investigation and stop considering any information that might bring their conclusion into doubt. Such a rush to judgment is even more likely when the victim is a prominent member of the community and the defendant is "an empty excuse for a man" with no redeeming traits.[16] Bronk had been physically and sexually abused as a child. He drank excessively and used drugs. Those facts, however, rather than mitigating his responsibility seemed to make him more of an outsider.

As a journalist, Walker introduces an unusual angle on the role of the media. Charlie McFarland, the husband of two murder victims, argues with Molly Cates that coverage of violent crimes encourages others to copy them. "I blame everybody who keeps this animal in the public attention by writing about him, making him into some sort of a celebrity." He agrees that people have the right to know the bare facts, "but when you write this long book that goes into his childhood and past and what the shrinks say and, Christ, even his poetry, it just makes me sick." When Molly claims that serial killers do not read books, that the only printed material they are likely to look at is pornography, Charlie counters, "How do you know they don't get off on stuff like you write?" Even though 80 percent of Americans believe, wrongly, that the high level of homicide in the United States is the fault of the media,[17] few would be specific enough to blame true crime literature for giving killers inspiration and instruction.

Once Molly believes that she has evidence that Louie Bronk is innocent of the McFarland murder, she races frantically to see that he gets a stay of execution. His lawyer is pessimistic. She reminds Cates that the Supreme Court seems ambivalent on the question of innocence. The Court has not declared whether it is unconstitutional to execute someone who might be innocent. In addition, the state of Texas has a thirty-day limit for filing new evidence. The courts are free to ignore anything brought forward more than a month after a man is sentenced. Thus, bogus claims such as "lost witnesses, newly uncovered alibis, confessions that were given by people now dead" can be disregarded, along with any real proof that the condemned person did not commit the crime. For the truly innocent, the only hope is executive clemency. In a state where only the politically appointed Board of Pardons and Parole has the power to recommend clemency to the governor and where they never make that recommendation, the chances of the innocent escaping execution are very slim indeed. Louie's lawyer notes that the Board would surely not recommend commutation for him. Even if he could raise some legal questions, "it wouldn't matter—they are out for blood."[18]

In desperation, Molly gets an appointment to meet with the governor, a woman who appears to be modeled on former Texas governor Ann Richards. She was "tough on law and order. She's got to be, and politically she has to support the death penalty."[19] As expected, the governor refuses to delay the execution, even though Molly asks what harm it could do to wait until the recent murders were solved. "What harm?" the governor asked. "My opponents in the legislature would say I was soft on mass murderers and every attorney with a death row client would be beating on my door."[20] Even though most Texas governors attended the occasional execution, this one did not. "Executions would be a waste of my time," she said. "I *delegate* executions."[21] It is a political necessity for Texas governors to favor capital punishment, although direct knowledge of what they actually favor does not seem so necessary.

Readers of *The Red Scream*, on the other hand, get quite a detailed picture of the execution process. As an invited witness, Molly observes "a neat and well-maintained death." She describes the excitement among the witnesses using the familiar metaphor of "vultures gathering for the kill. . . . She was one of them."[22] Some among the crowd were required to attend, some were invited by the condemned man, and others "just like coming." The director of public information commented, "We could solve our cash flow problems by selling tickets to these damn things if they'd let us."[23] As most who write of executions, Molly senses that so many people were present "because that way no one is responsible. Safety in numbers. This is all an exercise in passing the buck." Before entering the death row area, men leave their sidearms and women leave their handbags outside, but wearing a Stetson inside seemed acceptable. Molly is hit with "the dank odor of ancient dungeons. . . . this killing place had absorbed into its walls and floors and bars all the terror and death that had passed through." The air itself is "corrupted." She has a sense of unreality. The world in 1993 is supposed to be enlightened, "not an age when people were put to death in cold damp prisons. But this was real. They were here, a group of people gathered behind brick walls at midnight to enact an ancient ritual. *To try to cure the tidal wave of crime by making one blood sacrifice.*"[24] Walker's account of the execution is notable more for her attempt to understand and describe the meaning of what goes on as the state takes a life rather than for its description of the last hours or minutes of the condemned man. In fact, Louie's death appears to be an easy one. He takes a breath, "eyes wide open in surprise, he coughed twice and was still. If she blinked she would have missed it." Molly observes no last minute resistance, no "red scream." Rather, "the line between being alive and being dead was so narrow it was almost imperceptible."[25] The apparent peace of Bronk's death, however, does not excuse the state's action. "I think that in all my years of reporting on crime I have never seen a more premeditated homicide," Molly comments when she thinks of the execution.[26]

Throughout the novel, after Molly notes that Texas leads the world in executions, Walker has various characters express justifications for capital punishment. Some are rebutted within the text, others fail because of their own illogic, some may be convincing. Charlie McFarland, the husband of two victims, argues that death is the only way to incapacitate the offender. "Every time I pick up the goddamned newspaper, I read about a new murder committed by some Louie Bronk clone who's out on parole. We're letting these guys out to prey on our families." Many people probably agree with McFarland that the criminal justice system is not to be trusted and the only way to really "get tough" is through the death penalty. The district attorney concurs that the "moronic incompetents we've got on the parole board will read the file upside down and let him walk. And do you have any doubt that he'd kill again as soon as he got out?"[27] Later Walker opines that those who read in the paper that Bronk's execution has taken place will say, "Good. That's one animal that won't be back out on the streets. We ought to do more of that."[28] The author presents the argument that much of the support for capital punishment grows out of a need for specific deterrence—a need to assure that *this* offender will not kill again. Although Texas did not have life in prison without parole in 1993 when the novel was set, that policy has since become widespread. It provides the specific deterrence without the death penalty.

A more philosophical pro-capital punishment argument in Walker's text involves the death penalty's symbolic and cathartic purpose. The quotation above (". . . to enact an ancient ritual. *To try to cure the tidal wave of violent crime by making one blood sacrifice.*") refers to the "blood sacrifice" of execution perceived as a cure for widespread social violence. At another point in the novel, Molly realizes that it is "comforting to pretend that all the random violence in the world was concentrated in one evil man, a criminal locked up in a nine-by-twelve foot cell in East Texas." Once he is disposed of, "the world would be restored to sanity."[29] That belief more than any other—the notion that executing someone will cleanse families and communities and restore them to wholeness—seems to account for the persistent approval of capital punishment despite evidence of its flaws and failures.

Money Walks, Rich Folks Never Do No Time[30]

Jill Baumgaertner, who reviewed *Time's Witness* by Michael Malone for *The Christian Century*, calls it "moral fiction . . . not weighed down by stale pieties but fresh and fun and finally even redemptive."[31] At one level, the novel is concerned with large philosophical questions such as the problem of evil and the meaning of justice. At least the narrator of the story, Hillston Police Chief Cuddy Magnum, wrestles with those issues. In a more focused way, Malone stated that in writing the book, he wanted to talk about a death row case tied in with "all sorts of political secrets—not the least of which is that there is a relationship between racism and capital punishment."[32] Some argue that all mysteries involve a search for truth that is ultimately a moral quest. Others would note that it is impossible to talk about the death penalty in the United States without talking about racism. But Malone is especially successful in telling a good story at the same time he makes the reader think about rights and wrongs.

The capital case at the heart of the novel involves an African American Vietnam War veteran, George Hall, who shot Bobby Pym, a white police officer, outside a seedy bar in the black section of Hillston, North Carolina. Malone has set several of his novels there. Hillston is a community stratified by race and class well into the final decades of the twentieth century. In Hall's trial, the state claims that the shooting was cold-blooded murder by a man who had a "problem with authority." Hall maintains that he killed the officer in self-defense and refuses a plea bargain, although his not-very-bright public defender tries to talk him into pleading to a lesser charge. The insufferable, self-righteous prosecutor, going for the national record for capital convictions, tells the jury that shooting the policeman in the back as he "ran for his life" was "premeditated, intentional malice aforethought" and asks for the death penalty. He persuades the jury, who "didn't even stay out long enough to order dinner."[33] In fact, the whole first trial takes two days. "There were no pretrial motions, there were no challenges, there was no striking of jurors, there were no requests for directed verdicts against the state for not proving its case, no exceptions to overrulings, there was no wasting time on behalf of a stubborn man without friends or money."[34]

The original trial is really the back-story of the novel, which opens on the day before Hall's scheduled execution. At the last minute, the governor grants a four week stay, ostensibly because a very prominent citizen has died and Hall's death would distract attention from the funeral. Hall now has a first-rate defense attorney, Isaac Rosethorn, who was also Magnum's mentor. He can use the stay of execution to attempt to get George a new trial. The search for the truth about the shooting of Officer Pym not only determines whether Hall will live or die but leads as well to the unveiling of a whole web of political, business, and police corruption that puts the events into an entirely different light.

Rosethorn argues that the way to win an appeal is not by "great legal leaps in enlightenment. You get them by little procedural screw-ups. The law's an anal compulsive. That's its virtue and its vice both."[35] In a theme raised in several of the books and movies examined here, Rosethorn points to the apparent tension between procedural correctness and truth. Sometimes the law's concern for the former can reveal the truth, sometimes it works to obfuscate it. In Hall's case, his attorney finds that one of the original jurors had been "deaf as a post."[36] For that reason, the State Supreme Court sets aside the first verdict and orders a new trial. "[I]t was not because his Fourteenth Amendment rights to equal protection under the law had been violated by a biased judge and an all-white jury; nor because his Eighth Amendment rights against cruel and unusual punishment had been violated by his receiving a death penalty conviction for a homicide that was not of an 'unusually heinous nature,' that it was devoid of 'malice aforethought' or 'cool deliberation,' and that resulted from a situation of mutual combat."[37] The situations quoted above are those that would be considered aggravating or mitigating circumstances and would influence a jury's decision about both guilt and sentencing. Hall's lawyer finds cases similar to his where both victim and assailant were black and the charge was likely to be manslaughter; cases in which both victim and assailant were white and the defendant was found not guilty by reason of self-defense; and two in which charges were dropped. In the latter cases, the victim was black, the assailant white. The only situation that led to capital charges involved a white victim and a black assailant—the very argument made in *McCleskey v. Kemp.* At one level, then, Malone is arguing that institutional racism in the criminal justice system is responsible for Hall's original death sentence and that it was a serendipitous procedural matter that saved the life of an innocent man. Few individuals outside of fiction could count on an Isaac Rosethorn to rescue them from the malfunctioning machinery of death.

The State Superior Court where Hall's retrial takes place is a beautiful space where "it was easy to sit in that room believing Justice was on her throne and blind as a bat to anything but the bright light of Truth." In fact, as Chief Magnum knew, "Justice has got a real eye for color (she prefers white), and for class (she likes upper and middle); . . . she always was, and still is, a bitch on the poor, and a pushover for power." The class structure in the courtroom is clear. "[T]he lower class gets to be the criminals, the middle class gets to be the jury, and the upper class gets to be the judge." The law defines the deeds done by the poor as crime—"when you shoot up, take a knife to a spouse, write a bad check, bop someone on the head and snatch a purse, or steal $162.54 from a gas station." White collar crime is a different story. Justice "doesn't mess much with big time corporate shenanigans and government slip ups."[38]

But just such shenanigans, helped along by some corrupt police officers, are what Magnum and his force uncover behind the shooting that had put George Hall on death row. That investigation, along with Rosethorn's brilliant defense, wins a verdict of not guilty in Hall's retrial. But saving the life of one innocent man does not suffice to constitute a happy ending for *Time's Witness*. The reader cannot miss the message that a single vindication does not repair a broken system. Several characters address that theme. Among the most effective is the warden of the state prison that houses death row. He has supervised many executions. After he learns that the governor manipulated the date of Hall's scheduled execution to embarrass his political rival, and that the lieutenant governor has ties to corruption, he reflects on his job escorting condemned men to their death. "Some I took that walk with, they went singing hymns. Even whistling, one fellow, sure the governor's call was coming. Some we dragged sobbing through the door. Some said they were guilty as sin, some died swearing their innocence, and some, well, we'll never know." But guilt or innocence, even faith makes no difference "after that door clangs shut. They all shit their pants the same, all drool the same color blood, fists grab at the chair just the same. And watching, there's always some witness who pukes and runs off." But, the warden said, "My business was, carry out the execution for the State. . . . But if there's no such thing as the 'State' that's better than you and me and [the governor], then what in God's heaven am I killing [them] for?"[39] And although George Hall is a free man for the first time in decades, the reader last sees him standing outside the prison participating in a vigil the night of the next execution. Joe Bonder, the condemned man, had allegedly killed a clerk in a convenience store holdup. His accomplice blamed Joe for pulling the trigger and got a four-year sentence. Bonder had an IQ of 75. When the warden told him the date set for his death, he said, "Yes sir, I understand." The next day, "he's asking me when he can go home and see his mama."[40] Only a small crowd protests Bonder's execution. "There weren't as many as there were for George, or the time before George, or the time before that." But if the public is taking capital punishment more as a matter of course, one of the protesters notes that historically "other irritating little groups of cranks" had called for an end to slavery and war and genocide. A reporter objects that an execution is not genocide because the man had been given a fair trial. Then the protester "gave her some figures about the race, income level, education, and IQs of those scheduled for executions across the country, and where in the country and why. But the reporter didn't write it down and she left a few minutes later."[41]

Even if it is no longer news, critics of the death penalty continue to remind Americans of the disparity and discrimination in its application. Some repeat the statistics in news stories and reports; others, like Michael Malone, illustrate patterns of injustice in the form of a story. Scott Turow raises many of the same issues in *Reversible Errors*.

There's Just No Point in Giving Up on a Human Being

For two years, while working on *Reversible Errors*, author Scott Turow served on Illinois Governor George Ryan's commission to examine capital punishment. Ryan had declared a moratorium on executions and appointed the panel after several factually innocent men were found on the state's death row. Turow, as a former prosecutor, a practicing criminal lawyer, and a prominent author of legal fiction, came to the commission calling himself a "death penalty agnostic."[42] He later told an interviewer that writing *Reversible Errors* had even more impact than the study in making him into an opponent.[43] The novel underscores human fallibility and the consequent fallibility of the justice system. If individuals are flawed and prone to error, how can they construct a machinery of death that never goes awry?

Arthur Raven, former prosecutor, currently successful in a lucrative private practice, is appointed by the court to represent death row inmate Romeo (Rommy) Gandolph in a federal habeas appeal. At the outset, Raven is not enthusiastic about reentering criminal law. Working with defendants made him feel "assigned each day to clean out a flooded basement where coli form bacteria and sewer stink rotted almost everything. Someone had said that power corrupted. But the saying applied equally to evil. Evil corrupted. . . . The backflow from such acts polluted everyone who came near."[44]

At this point, the only thing that can save Rommy, the only "reversible error," would be proof of his innocence. According to Arthur, his client seemed to be both desperate and crazy. "Craziness just seemed to have eaten the center out of him." As his eyes "darted about like frenzied bugs," Arthur understood why Gandolph's previous lawyers had tried to raise an insanity defense. "As people commonly use the word 'crazy," Rommy Gandolph without question was. Yet not crazy enough. Sociopathic. Borderline personality disorder, maybe even flat-out schizoid. But not thoroughly lost in the wilderness, not so entirely without a compass that he did not know wrong from right, which was what the law required for a defense."[45] Despite a signed confession, a conviction, and a death sentence handed down by a judge, Rommy claims to Arthur that he did not commit the triple murder and sodomy for which he is scheduled to die.

The defense attorneys have nothing to go on until coincidentally, another inmate in the same prison who happens to be terminally ill, comes forward to confess to Gandolph's crime. If that confession is true, Arthur then faces an awesome responsibility. His job changes from ensuring that Rommy has exhausted all legal options that due process afforded to trying to save an innocent life. Now, "justice, indeed the whole principle of law—that it would make fairer the few elements of existence within human control—depended on him. He was the main variable; his work, his wits, his ability to wage and win civil society's most momentous battle."[46]

It is one of Turow's strengths as a writer that he portrays Arthur (and indeed all of the characters) as fully nuanced individuals, with flaws and fears and hang-ups and with virtues as well. The "other side" of the Gandolph case, the prosecutor Muriel Wynn and the police officer who solved the case, Larry Starczek, believe firmly in Rommy's guilt.

Starczek considers himself a "good cop," one who does his job, even though the original evidence against Gandolph had required cutting a few corners. He did not actually find the victim's cameo necklace on Rommy. Also, the most damning evidence, Gandolph's confession, involved pressure that a suspect with an IQ of 75 was unlikely to resist. As long as Rommy protested his innocence, Starczek refused him access to a bathroom. When the suspect soiled his pants, it was considered evidence of guilt. After that humiliation, Gandolph attempted to ingratiate himself with the officer by admitting to virtually everything he was asked. He even "wrote" a confession, although in the last part of the novel, it becomes clear that Rommy is illiterate. Starczek's motives are complex. He pursues the case out of anger at the brutality of the murders but also as a sort of gift to the ambitious Muriel, his sometime girlfriend. The Gandolph conviction puts her career on a trajectory likely to lead to the office of district attorney. She cannot take the political risk of reopening the case and argues vehemently against it, even though someone else now claims to have committed the crimes.

It falls to the Federal District Court to determine the credibility of Erno Erdai, the man who has confessed. The judge, a "renowned constitutional scholar" with a history of civil rights litigation, has "faith in the law as the flower of humanism." He resents the legislation that limits habeas corpus proceedings in death penalty cases and through a sort of legal loophole, he allows the testimony that could reopen Rommy's case. In court, Erdai admits to killing the three victims and to framing Gandolph. In the judge's view, "to bring this kind of evidence forward on the eve of execution—that . . . was the epitome of what the legal profession stood for."[47] The Federal Court of Appeals disagreed, reversed, dismissed Gandolph's habeas petition, and lifted the stay on his execution. It finds Erdai's testimony unconvincing and uncorroborated by forensic evidence (although there was no forensic evidence against Rommy either). It also notes that Erdai is a convicted felon with a motive for "punishing" law enforcement authorities and that his current statements contradict his version of events at the time of the murders. The court concludes, "We agree with the state that the direct evidence of Mr. Gandolph's guilt [the cameo and the confession], on which the trier of fact long ago relied, has gone unquestioned." Arthur is full of regret, for Rommy and for himself. He has learned that he is a person of passion and "that those passions had a place in the law. The light had gone forth, and now, by court order, it would be shuttered again."[48] Death penalty cases usually evoke passion, and as Turow argues in a *New Yorker* article, it is because of their intense emotional resonance that capital cases so often involve error.[49]

It is actually the police and the prosecutor's office who track down the truth in the Gandolph case. They find the gun, fingerprints, another suspect, stolen property, and an alternative explanation. Even so, Muriel has to persuade Starczek that Gandolph should get a new trial and that Starczek will have to tell the truth about the victim's cameo. Starczek "hated this stuff about the law," especially if it means that Gandolph might be found not guilty. "I don't want to have to look at this guy on the street. I'd rather take my chances in court, lose my pension, obstruction. Whatever." Ultimately, as their case unravels, Muriel decides to dismiss the charges. "He confessed," Starczek says, clinging to the only shred of evidence against Rommy and refusing to admit that his entire case had been built on a lie.[50]

Critic Sam Lieth has noted that *Reversible Errors* is really concerned with discovery, "the sifting of interested accounts; the emergence of hidden connections; the sudden coup in cross-examination; the painstaking unraveling of the truth."[51] In the legal sense, "discovery" means disclosure of evidence. In its more conventional senses, it involves the acquisition of knowledge or even the experience of revelation. At one level, the reader of *Reversible Errors* discovers how the criminal justice system has convicted and almost executed the wrong man. At another level, the novel unfolds the stories of the major characters entwined with the Gandolph case. But perhaps the most important discovery is that the law is only an imperfect instrument, especially when it comes to taking a life. Muriel muses over several such realizations. She has come to understand "the freight of pain carried inside every courthouse." In her youth, she had sensed the anger among victims and defendants and "her own righteous need to smite evil. But now what stayed with her was the legacy of hurt" for victims, even for criminals, and "certainly for [the defendants'] families, who were usually as innocent as the other bystanders, their sole mistake loving someone who'd come to no good."[52] At another point, she wonders why "inflicting more harm would make life on earth better for anyone." She was convinced that most survivors of murder victims "in some remote segment of their consciousness—the primeval part that was scared of the dark and loud noises—assumed that when the right person died, the one who deserved to be removed from the planet, when that occurred their loved one would come back to life. That was the pathetic logic of revenge, learned in the playpen, and on the sacrificial altar, where we attempted to trade life for life."[53] An elderly black lawyer offers another discovery, making a simple but elegant argument against the death penalty. "Hoodlum or not, you can't ever give up on a human being. . . . You know why? Because there is just no point in that. Can't be any reason to what we're doing here, if we're going to give up on people."[54] Finally, Arthur shares his revelation that if the law could be an instrument of injustice, it was also the best instrument for restoring justice. When his client is released from prison, "the utter monstrousness of what happened to Rommy Gandolph stormed over Arthur—that and the supreme satisfaction of knowing that . . . he had commanded the power of the law for Rommy's benefit, that the law had made right what it first had made wrong."[55]

Some might argue that Arthur's statement could be read as support for capital punishment if adequate guarantees against error were incorporated into the law. On the other hand, perhaps the power of the law might be more efficiently and effectively employed if it were not used to make things wrong in the first place. Turow's comments in an interview are instructive. He noted that the corruption that often accompanies capital cases is inextricably bound with their high profile nature. Participants in a death penalty case may allow their appetite for attention or for advancement to lead to unethical decisions. The temptation is likely to be less in a non-capital case; thus there will be fewer errors to reverse. He argues further that death cases involve emotional turmoil for persons on all sides of the issue, as *Reversible Errors* portrays so successfully. The legal system cannot assuage those emotions or restore the world. "To the extent that we expect that of capital punishment, it fails."[56]

In all the novels studied in this chapter, the system of capital punishment failed and an innocent man was sent to death row because of flaws and biases in the legal structure. Every one of the defendants was poor and poorly educated. Not one of them had adequate assistance of counsel in his original trial. Each was subject to what was arguably improper questioning. In several cases, the interrogation led to a false confession that became the major evidence against the accused. All of the victims were respectable members of the community, while the offenders were marginal, expendable men. Every prosecutor enjoyed political gains as a result of getting a capital conviction. All four men were innocent of the crimes for which they were sentenced to death. Two were saved, two were executed. Those who were exonerated were spared only by a series of unforeseen circumstances. According to contemporary crime fiction, the death penalty error rate is 50 percent.

·7·

THE POWER OF STORIES

Popular culture entertains, but it can also enlighten. Those who watch a film or read a book and reflect on what they have experienced may afterward look at the world in a slightly different way. The audiences who involve themselves with the books and movies examined in this work will encounter fascinating characters—some admirable, some repulsive, some tragic. Through their stories, the system of capital punishment—what Justice Blackmun called the "machinery of death"—is revealed not as a finely tuned, perfectly functioning instrument but as an unreliable, glitch-riddled device, always subject to human error.

At present, one can see signs of progress and also signs of regression in the way Americans are addressing the issue of capital punishment, in the way the standards of decency are evolving. A play called *The Exonerated* ran for most of 2003 on Broadway and in other cities. It is a documentary based on the stories of six actually innocent people released after spending years on death row. Famous actors and in some cases the "condemned" men and women themselves have made up the cast. As a pro-death-penalty prosecutor commented after watching a performance, "If you're going to be abstract about it, you may have one result in your thinking. If you have to face another human being, you may have another." The play's producer intended that very result, "to move the debate about the death penalty into the realm of individual lives," in the process exposing the "bias, error, tricks, lies, cruelty and institutionalized blood lust" in the system.[1]

In another dramatic effort to draw attention to the death penalty, congregations nationwide participate in a movement called "For Whom the Bells Toll." Each time a state executes someone, the churches toll their bells once for each year of the life of the person being put to death or, symbolically, thirty-three times in memory of Christ's age at the time of his execution. They believe their witness makes people aware of "the steady drumbeat of executions, averaging more than one a week," most of them in Texas, Oklahoma, and Virginia.[2]

Meanwhile the issue of capital punishment remains, if not at the forefront, at least on the agenda of the courts and legislatures. During the Supreme Court term that ended in July 2003, the justices handed down several relevant rulings. They allowed the appeal of a Texas death row inmate, Thomas Miller-El, who claimed that his jury had been tainted by racial bias. They also overturned a Maryland case on the grounds that the defendant, Kevin Wiggins, had had ineffective assistance of counsel. His court-appointed attorneys had failed to carry out any investigation into his history of childhood abuse, evidence the Court believed might have mitigated the jury's sentencing decision. The decisions suggest that the Court majority is becoming more concerned that the lower courts may not be sufficiently vigilant in monitoring the quality of justice in capital cases.[3]

The Supreme Court continued to deal with capital punishment issues in the 2003–2004 term. On the one hand, they let stand a lower court ruling that Arkansas could force an inmate to take the medication that would make him "sane" enough to execute and a South Carolina case that upheld a murder conviction for a woman who used crack cocaine during pregnancy and whose baby was stillborn.[4] The justices agreed to rule on whether the 2002 decision *Ring v. Arizona*, which required that juries, not judges, make all factual determinations in death cases, was retroactive. Inmates in five states—Arizona, Idaho, Montana, Colorado, and Nebraska—would have been effectively removed from death row, or at least resentenced, if the Court had decided that *Ring* should be applied retroactively.[5]

Perhaps the most dramatic story before the Court comes from Texas and concerns Delma Banks. During Banks's trial in 1979, several witnesses for the state lied, apparently with the prosecution's knowledge. The state then argued that the defense attorneys had not uncovered and exposed their malfeasance in a timely manner. The Court of Appeals for the Fifth Circuit, which oversees Texas, did not grant Banks's habeas petition. But only ten minutes before his scheduled death, with Banks strapped to a gurney, the Supreme Court stayed his execution. A group of retired state and federal judges, including a number of prominent Republicans, joined Banks's appeal.[6] It may be that the pace and quality of the machinery of death in Texas has come to trouble the high court's standards of decency.

News from other states indicates that the evolution of standards of decency is not a one-way process. Although the Supreme Court held in *Coker v. Georgia* in 1977 that capital punishment for the rape of an adult woman violated those standards, Louisiana has maintained a law that makes the rape of a child a capital offense. Although no one has been executed for any crime other than murder since 1964, in August 2003, a Louisiana man received a death sentence for raping an eight-year-old girl.[7] And, although DNA evidence has been widely heralded as an important tool in vindicating innocent defendants, prosecutors in Florida and several other states have supported legislation to limit its use in old cases.[8]

Governor Mitt Romney of Massachusetts supports the death penalty and wants to see it reenacted there. He has appointed a commission to draft legislation that would be foolproof, that would require the "highest evidentiary standard" for a death sentence. Some would argue that Romney is trying to have it both ways—to play to his Republican supporters by endorsing capital punishment, but to position himself as opposed to any system that might execute an innocent person. It remains to be seen whether Romney can "save the death penalty by circumscribing it."[9] However, he is following a time-honored strategy where supporters of the death penalty make just enough reforms to satisfy their critics and to keep the punishment alive.

The development of more "humane" methods has been an effective way to deflect criticism that executions are cruel and unusual. Many people believe that lethal injections have made the death itself painless—for the criminal and for the witnesses who observe his last minutes. However, a number of scientific studies have shown that one of the chemicals typically injected, pancuronium bromide, could cause an extremely painful death. The drug "paralyzes the skeletal muscles but does not affect the brain or nerves." A person could be conscious but unable to move or speak, suffering a paralysis that masked intense distress. The American Veterinary Medical Association condemns the use of pancuronium bromide for euthanizing pets.

In addition, the lethal drugs are typically administered by persons without medical training because doctors do not take part in executions, as their code of medical ethics forbids it. It would seem that the possibility is great that a prisoner is conscious, paralyzed, and suffocating—a painful death prohibited for cats and dogs, but permitted in 37 states and the federal system. A death row inmate in Tennessee has challenged the constitutionality of the state's process of lethal injection as cruel and unusual punishment.[10]

Congress and several state legislatures are mindful of public concerns about the death penalty, especially about the possibility of executing innocent persons. Legislation supported by a bipartisan coalition in the House of Representatives includes provisions to require the preservation of physical evidence in federal criminal cases, to expand the availability of post-conviction DNA testing, and to stimulate states to provide a more adequate level of legal representation for death cases by providing them with financial incentives.[11] Although one might argue that the proposal before Congress would only apply a Band-Aid to a cancer patient, at least the provision dealing with court-appointed attorneys is a tacit recognition of the deep class biases in the capital system.

One of the most highly publicized assessments of the death penalty came from the commission appointed by Illinois Governor George Ryan after he declared that state's moratorium on executions in 2000. The commission was made up of persons with diverse backgrounds and qualifications and included supporters, opponents, and some like Scott Turow who at the outset were "death penalty agnostics." After twenty-four months of deliberations, the commission members were unanimous in recommending that if the death penalty were to be continued in Illinois, a number of procedural reforms would be absolutely necessary. Their proposals included:

- videotaping of all questioning of capital suspects
- prohibiting capital sentences on the testimony of a single eyewitness, an "in-custody informant" (jailhouse snitch), or an uncorroborated accomplice
- barring capital sentences for mentally retarded persons
- review of individual prosecutors' decisions to seek the death penalty conducted by a statewide commission
- limiting capital punishment to crimes where two or more persons were murdered; where the victim was a police officer, a firefighter, or an officer or inmate in a corrections institution; where the murder was an attempt to obstruct justice; or where torture was involved
- requiring judges to concur with any capital sentence voted by a jury
- mandating that the State Supreme Court review every capital sentence to insure that it was proportionate compared to other death sentences in the state.[12]

While the Illinois state legislature approved several of those proposals in May 2003, the moratorium remained in place at the end of that year. Meanwhile, one of the best tactics for spreading the concerns of the Illinois commission has been through a small book (about 125 pages of text) by Scott Turow called *Ultimate Punishment: A Lawyer's Reflections on Dealing with the Death Penalty*.[13] Turow's reputation as the author of six best-selling legal thrillers gives him access to an audience who might not pay attention to the actual commission report but who will consider his analysis because they like his novels. Thus, once again, popular culture has provided an avenue for bringing complex legal matters to light.

Turow lays out facts about the unreliability of the current capital system in the United States, using Illinois as an example, and argues that the prospect of error is the "leading cause for reduced support for the death penalty." Because most people would agree that executing innocent persons "stands justice on its head,"[14] the debate over whether to maintain a system known to be prone to mistakes involves a "struggle for the national soul."[15] Turow respects the point that victims' families are often the strongest advocates of the death penalty. He notes that they believe the execution will bring their grief to a conclusion. They often feel that the offender should not be better off (i.e., alive) than his victim. In response, however, he claims that allowing life or death to "hinge on the emotional needs of the survivors" violates a fundamental notion in law that like crimes should be punished alike. Putting the victims first and measuring a crime by the survivors' response offers "no meaningful way to distinguish among murders." He ultimately argues that survivors' wishes must be subordinated to other elements in the "calculus of justice." The criterion for evaluating the death penalty must be the larger one of "what's best for all of us."[16]

What is not best for all of us is a flawed system for doling out decisions about life and death. Turow advances the point that if killing an offender is ever to be justified, one must assume extreme precision, "a fine-tuned sense of what ultimate evil is and an unerring judgment regarding the identity of the guilty person."[17] As this book has repeatedly demonstrated through the use of popular representations of the death penalty, the system is more like a blunt instrument than a fine-tuned one, more riddled with flaws than unerring, more haphazard and random than precise. In at least eleven of the works studied here, the person on death row was either clearly not guilty or there were serious doubts about his or her guilt. The very problems that the Supreme Court in *Furman* identified in declaring the death penalty unconstitutional as applied are almost identical to the concerns raised by the Illinois Governor's Commission. Not only is the system unreliable in deciding who is actually guilty, it sentences the poor, members of minority groups, and those with unconventional lifestyles disproportionately.

In 2003 *Broken Justice: The Death Penalty in Virginia*, an unofficial report produced by a broad coalition of groups, found that "the criminal justice system is crippled by procedures that fail to ensure a reliable determination of guilt or innocence."[18] Through the stories of a number of innocent men sent to death row, the text illustrates that Virginia's low rate of reversal in death cases occurs not because the state is less fallible than others but because the procedures that might reveal and reverse wrongful convictions are severely truncated. The most egregious example is the twenty-one-day rule prohibiting a defendant from raising any new evidence more than three weeks after the conclusion of his first trial. Almost as detrimental to discovering the truth is the state's pathetic funding for indigent defense counsel, its procedural default rule that penalizes a defendant when his (incompetent) attorney fails to raise objections even if the failure to object is a "plain error," and its failure to provide any legal assistance to indigents after conviction. The report also found numerous examples of prosecutorial misconduct as well as conspicuous geographical and racial disparities in the application of the death penalty. Many of the fictional stories of abuses in the capital system considered in this book could have been plucked from the pages of Virginia court records.

What can we summarize from the popular works studied here? The books and films about Gary Gilmore, Dick Hickock, and Perry Smith raise questions about how the states proceed against expendable men convicted of high profile crimes. No one doubts the guilt of these three men, nor of Robert Lee Willie, discussed in *Dead Man Walking*, but one can certainly have doubts about the process that led to their executions. All four of them, along with Denver Bayliss in *Last Light*, owe at least some of their motivation to murder to lessons learned while growing up in state institutions. In *Time's Witness*, Malone describes the condemned George Hall as a man without (powerful) friends or money. Except for the early portrayal of David Gale, there is not a single example among the stories in this book where the individual on death row enjoyed a position of consequence in the community. All were marginal in some way. Their race, their class, their mental deficiencies or illness, their gender, or their lifestyle placed them on the periphery of society.

One cannot avoid facing the deep biases in the capital punishment system. In some of the stories—*A Lesson Before Dying, To Kill a Mockingbird, The Green Mile, A Time to Kill, Monster's Ball,* and *Time's Witness*—the racial bias was overt. In *Dead Man Walking* and *Reversible Errors* it was more subtle. *I Want to Live* and *Dance with a Stranger* exemplify societal assumptions about women who violate gendered expectations. Bias and economic marginality work hand in hand to disadvantage a defendant, not least because he or she is likely to be represented at trial by an inadequate attorney, as was the case for Gilmore, Hickock, Smith, Pat Sonnier, Robert Lee Willie, Jefferson, John Coffey, Sam Cayhall, Cindy Liggitt, Kenny Ray Clark, Louie Bronk, George Hall, and Rommy Gandolph—the vast majority of the characters examined here. The notable exceptions are Tom Robinson, who had the good fortune to have the paragon of lawyers, Atticus Finch, as his attorney, and Carl Lee Hailey, lucky enough to hire the ambitious Jake Brigance. Even for those who had better representation in the appeals process, the system usually thwarted their ability to raise questions about their initial conviction. Only George Hall and Rommy Gandolph were able, through the efforts of skilled appellate attorneys, to be vindicated before it was too late. Even in those cases, as with Randall Adams in *The Thin Blue Line*, it required a fortuitous stroke of luck, as well as the truth, to save innocent men from execution. Supporters of capital punishment will claim that releasing an innocent man from death row proves that the system works. But in fiction and in real life, exonerating a person wrongly convicted far too often depends on a happy accident or an unforeseen discovery.

None of the books or movies can be used to claim that the death penalty is a deterrent. In fact, a number of them argue, and most demonstrate, that executions carried out in the dead of night in dark quarters deep within a prison suggest that the state is ashamed of its role in killing, not that it is sending a positive moral message. Virtually all the stories that feature an execution show how it destroyed other lives beyond that of the convicted man or woman. For example, Gary Gilmore's death damaged his mother and brothers, Pat Sonnier's brought tremendous sadness to his family, Jefferson's and Tom Robinson's led both to grief and to a greater understanding of injustice. The execution of Lawrence Musgrove in *Monster's Ball* was responsible for the deaths of Sonny and Tyrell. Because the French government killed Neel Auguste, the honest, moral Captain was also executed and two innocent women were widowed.

The counterargument to the position that capital punishment harms more than the person executed is that it provides solace to the victim's family and restores the community. Yet not a single example of this healing and "closure" shows up in these books and films. Angry survivors, such as Vernon Harvey in *Dead Man Walking* or the parents of the little girls in *The Green Mile* or Bob Ewell in *To Kill a Mockingbird,* do not wake up to a better world after their nemesis is removed from it. Only Truman Capote's *In Cold Blood* carries a postscript implying unconvincingly that one person's death may restore life to harmony.

One of the state's attorneys in *Dead Man Walking* argues that putting the condemned man to death is a matter of "simple justice." These stories have shown neither simplicity nor justice in the application of the death penalty. They have often shown death at the hands of the state to be premeditated and carefully orchestrated—a choreographed ritual that bears little resemblance to the messy, impulsive crimes that usually led to the sentence of death. The films were particularly effective in showing prison officials preparing deadly gas (as in *I Want to Live* and *The Chamber*), the electric chair (*The Green Mile, Last Light, Monster's Ball*) and lethal injection (*Dead Man Walking* and *Last Dance*). Even if the people involved were "just doing their job," their work clearly involved the conscious, careful extinction of a human life. And, as *Dead Man Walking* asserts, this task is being carried out in our name.

It has been a principal argument in these chapters that stories—fiction, biography, film—have the power to move our understanding of the death penalty from an abstraction to a deeper appreciation of the human beings on all sides of the process. Not only do the victim and the offender share a common humanity, the representatives of the state operate as mere men and women within the context of a legal system with all the flaws and failings inherent in any human undertaking. One final example from popular culture may illustrate the point.

In an episode of the television drama *The West Wing*, the president of the United States, played by Martin Sheen, must decide whether to allow the first execution of a federal prisoner since *Furman*.[19] President Bartlet had expected the Supreme Court to grant a stay. When they fail to do so, the life or death decision falls to him. Members of the White House staff discuss familiar arguments against capital punishment, the racial and class bias in the system, the failure of the death penalty as a deterrent, the rejection of the penalty by all other democratic countries. They also consider how the president's political enemies would attack him if he were to commute the sentence.

At another level, characters confront the morality of capital punishment. The president, a devout Catholic, calls the Pope, who apparently encourages him not to allow the execution. A staff member hears a sermon at his synagogue explaining that the Old Testament "eye for an eye" was meant to be a rejection of excessive vengeance. A political consultant who happens to be a Quaker urges morality over political expediency. Finally, after deciding not to grant clemency, the president meets with the priest who has been his longtime spiritual advisor. Both are unhappy. "Only God gets to kill people," the clergyman argues. In response the president claims that he prayed for wisdom, but that none came. Now he's "pissed" at God for not helping him through the crisis.

The priest tells a story. A man who lived near a river saw the water rising all around him. A newscaster on the radio announced, "The town is flooding. Everyone should evacuate." But the man said, "I have faith. God will protect me." Next, two men in a rowboat came near his house. "The town is flooding, come with us." But the man refused. "I have faith. God will protect me." Later a helicopter flew over his house and let down a rope. "Climb up. The town is flooding," the pilot said. "I have faith. God will protect me," the man insisted. Later when the man, who had drowned, presented himself in heaven, he asked, "God, why didn't you protect me? I had faith in you." The Lord replied, "I sent you a newscaster, a rowboat, and a helicopter. What more did you want me to do?"

In case he missed the point, the priest translated for President Bartlet. "He sent you a pope, a rabbi, and a Quaker and the words of his Son. What more did you want?"

. . . .

If we pay attention, American citizens can hear powerful stories that force us to confront the moral, legal, and practical questions surrounding the issue of capital punishment. Standards of decency—the practices that we believe reflect the values of our society—evolve from the way we choose to turn those stories into political reality.

NOTES

Introduction

1. Stephen B. Bright, "Sleeping on the Job," *National Law Journal*, December 4, 2000.
2. Gary Young, "When Jurors, Judges, and Lawyers Snooze, Do Clients Have Recourse?" *New Jersey Law Journal* 169 (August 26, 2002), 10.
3. Paul Schiff Berman, "Review Essay: The Cultural Life of Capital Punishment: Surveying the Benefits of a Cultural Analysis of Law: When the State Kills: Capital Punishment and the American Condition," *Columbia Law Review* 102 (May 2002), 1167.
4. Ibid., 1140.
5. Gary M. Stern, "Courtroom Life Imitates Art," *National Law Journal*, July 22, 2002.
6. See for example, Stuart Banner, *The Death Penalty: An American History* (Cambridge, MA: Harvard University Press, 2002), 239–245.
7. Penny J. White, "Errors and Ethics: Dilemmas in Death," *Hofstra Law Review* 29 (Summer 2001), 1269–70.
8. Ibid., 1275.
9. *Furman v. Georgia*, 408 U.S. 238 (1972).

Chapter 1

1. Jesse L. Jackson, Sr., Jesse L. Jackson, Jr., and Bruce Shapiro, *Legal Lynching: The Death Penalty and America's Future* (New York: The New Press, 2001), 23.
2. Hugh Bedau, quoted in Michael L. Radelet and Marian J. Borg, "The Changing Nature of the Death Penalty Debate," *Annual Review of Sociology* 26 (2000), 55.
3. Adam Liptak, "Death Row Numbers Decline as Challenges to the System Rise," *New York Times*, January 11, 2003.
4. Stuart Banner, *The Death Penalty: An American History* (Cambridge, MA: Harvard University Press, 2002), Chapter 1.

5. Louis Masur, *Rites of Execution: Capital Punishment and the Transformation of American Culture* (New York: Oxford University Press, 1989), Chapter 2.

6. Banner, *Death Penalty*, 100–110; Masur, *Rites of Execution*, 60, 76.

7. Banner, *Death Penalty*, 98–99.

8. Masur, *Rites of Execution*, 5.

9. *Ibid.*, 48–52. See also Banner, *Death Penalty*, Chapter 2; Robert Jay Lifton and Greg Mitchell, *Who Owns Death? Capital Punishment, the American Conscience, and the End of Executions* (New York: Perennial, 2002), 31–32.

10. Masur, *Rites of Execution*, 120–124.

11. Ivan Solotaroff, *The Last Face You'll Ever See: The Private Life of the American Death Penalty* (New York: HarperCollins, 2001), 3.

12. Banner, *Death Penalty*, 9–10.

13. Lifton and Mitchell, *Who Owns Death*, 34.

14. Banner, *Death Penalty*, Chapter 6; Masur, *Rites of Execution*, 116.

15. See Solotaroff, *Last Face*, 3.

16. Jackson, *Legal Lynching*, 17.

17. *In re Kemmler,* 136 U.S. 436 (1890).

18. Lifton and Mitchell, *Who Owns Death*, 47–48.

19. Paul Schiff Berman, "Review Essay: The Cultural Life of Capital Punishment: Surveying the Benefits of a Cultural Analysis of Law: When the State Kills: Capital Punishment and the American Condition," *Columbia Law Review* 102 (May 2002), 1152.

20. Nine states (Arizona, Oregon, Washington, Missouri, Kansas, South Dakota, Tennessee, Minnesota, and North Dakota) abolished the death penalty for murder in the early twentieth century. The ban was permanent only in Minnesota and North Dakota.

21. Banner, *Death Penalty*, Chapter 8.

22. *Furman v. Georgia*, 408 U.S. 238 (1972).

23. Deborah W. Denno, "Execution and the Forgotten Eighth Amendment," in *America's Experiment with Capital Punishment: Reflections on the Past, Present, and Future of the Ultimate Penal Solution*, ed. James R. Acker, Robert M. Bohm, and Charles S. Lanier (Durham, NC: Carolina Academic Press, 1998), 567; Solotaroff, *Last Face*, 7–9.

24. Ibid., 10.

25. Lifton and Mitchell, *Who Owns Death*, 63.

26. Despite two executions during the 1990s when inmates caught fire from the malfunctioning electric chair, officials in Florida defended its use. "A painless death is not punishment," according to the state's attorney general. See Lane Nelson, "A Killer Year," in *Death Watch: A Death Penalty Anthology*, ed. Lane Nelson and Burke Foster (Upper Saddle River, NJ: Prentice Hall, 2001), 252–53.

27. Denno, "Execution and the Forgotten Eighth Amendment," 569.

28. Lifton and Mitchell, *Who Owns Death*, 64.

29. Gary N. Howells, Kelly A. Flanagan, and Vivian Hagan, "Does Viewing a Televised Execution Affect Attitudes Toward Capital Punishment?" *Criminal Justice and Behavior* 22. (December 1995).

30. Francis T. Cullen, Bonnie S. Fisher, and Brandon K. Applegate, "Public Opinion about Punishment and Corrections," *Crime and Justice* 27 (2000), 13–14.

31. Stephen B. Bright, "The Politics of Capital Punishment: The Sacrifice of Fairness for Executions," in *America's Experiment with Capital Punishment*, ed. Acker, Bohm, and Lanier, 117–120.

32. Daniel T. Kobil, "The Evolving Role of Clemency in Capital Cases," in *America's Experiment with Capital Punishment*, ed. Acker, Bohm, and Lanier, 531–46.

33. Robert M. Bohm, "America's Death Penalty Opinion: Past, Present, and Future," in *America's Experiment with Capital Punishment*, ed. Acker, Bohm, and Lanier, 44.

34. Lifton and Mitchell, *Who Owns Death*, 213.

35. *Ibid.*, 225.

36. Radelet and Borg, "The Changing Nature of the Death Penalty Debate," 53–54.

37. Ibid., 44–45.

38. Ibid., 48–49.

39. Solotaroff, *Last Face*, xii.

40. Cullen, Fisher, and Applegate, "Public Opinion," 11.

41. Ibid., 22–23.

42. Ibid., 22–23.

43. Edmund F. McGarrell and Marla Sandys, "The Misperception of Public Opinion Toward Capital Punishment: Examining the Spuriousness Explanation of Death Penalty Support," *American Behavioral Scientist* 39 (February 1994), 500–14.

44. John T. Whitehead and Michael B. Blankenship, "The Gender Gap in Capital Punishment Attitudes: An Analysis of Support and Opposition," *American Journal of Criminal Justice* 25 (2000), 1–13.

45. Christopher Dennis, Marshall H. Medoff, and Michelle N. Gagnier, "The Impact of Racially Disproportionate Outcomes on Public Policy: The U.S. Senate and the Death Penalty," *The Social Science Journal* 35 (April 1998), 169–74.

46. Mark Hansen, "More for Moratorium," *American Bar Association Journal* (December 2000), 92.

47. Liptak, "Death Row Numbers Decline."

48. Bohm, "American Death Penalty Opinion," 25–26.

49. Cullen, Fisher, and Applegate, "Public Opinion," 9.

50. Lifton and Mitchell, *Who Owns Death*, 249.

51. Wendy Kaminer, "The Switch," *New York Times*, July 7, 2002.

52. Jeffrey L. Kirchmeier, "Another Place Beyond Here: The Death Penalty Moratorium Movement in the United States," *Colorado Law Review* 73 (Winter 2002), 23.

53. Radelet and Borg, "The Changing Nature of the Death Penalty Debate," 54.

54. Austin Sarat, *When the State Kills: Capital Punishment and the American Condition* (Princeton, NJ: Princeton University Press, 2001), 255–56; Rhonda McMillion, "Pulling the Plug on Executions," *American Bar Association Journal* (November 2000), 99; Hansen, "More for Moratorium."

55. Barry Scheck, Peter Neufield, and Jim Dwyer, *Actual Innocence: When Justice Goes Wrong and How to Make It Right* (New York: Signet, 2001), 281–83.

56. Ibid., 340.

57. David E. Rovella, "Fixing the Penalty," *National Law Journal*, June 19, 2000.

58. Stephen Semararo, "Time for Reform of Death Penalty," *National Law Journal*, July 24, 2000.

59. Jackson, *Legal Lynching*, 3–5.

60. Jodi Wilgoren, "Governor Assails System's Errors as He Empties Illinois Death Row," *New York Times*, January 12, 2003.
61. Kirchmeier, "Another Place," 45–48.
62. Bob Burtman, "Innocence Lost," in *Machinery of Death: The Reality of America's Death Penalty Regime*, ed. David R. Dow and Mark Dow (New York: Routledge, 2002), 155.
63. Kirchmeier, "Another Place," 56.
64. Larry O'Dell, "Conservative Republican Leads Anti-Death Penalty Push," Associated Press, January 20, 2001.
65. Marcia Coyle, "Trimming Death Sentence Errors," *National Law Journal*, February 11, 2002.
66. Kirchmeier, "Another Place," 69.
67. "Dead Man Walking Out," *The Economist*, June 10, 2000.
68. Jim Yardley, "Texas Death Row Appeals Lawyers Criticized," *New York Times*, December 3, 2002.
69. Jim Yardley, "Texas Retooling Criminal Justice in Wake of Furor," *New York Times*, June 1, 2001.
70. "Dead Man Walking Out."
71. Raymond Bonner, "Sentence Thrown Out in Pennsylvania Over Withheld Evidence," *New York Times*, August 30, 2001.
72. Michael Graczyk, "Man Executed Despite Mexico's Pleas," at Findlaw.com, August 15, 2002.
73. Bob Herbert, "Tainted Justice," *New York Times*, August 6, 2001.
74. David R. Dow, "Fictional Documentaries and Truthful Fictions: The Death Penalty in Recent American Film," *Constitutional Commentary* 17 (Winter 2000), 511.
75. Barbara Norrander, "The Multi-Layered Impact of Public Opinion on Capital Punishment Implementation in the American States," *Political Research Quarterly* 53 (December 2000), 773.
76. Ibid.
77. Lifton and Mitchell, *Who Owns Death*, 4.
78. Banner, *Death Penalty*, 311.
79. Ibid., 305.
80. "Dead Man Walking Out."

Chapter 2

1. Stuart Banner, *The Death Penalty: An American History* (Cambridge, MA: Harvard University Press, 2002), 232–33.
2. Since the mid-twentieth century, in many cases the Court has held that the Fourteenth Amendment "incorporates" provisions of the Bill of Rights. The language that no state may deny life, liberty, or property without due process of law is interpreted to mean that, for the most part, the states must subscribe to the rights of the accused listed in the Fifth, Sixth, and Eighth Amendments.
3. *Trop v. Dulles*, 356 U.S. 86 (1958).
4. *Rudolph v. Alabama* 375 U.S. 889 (1963).

5. This chapter includes discussion of several other cases where members of the Court expressed important ideas by dissenting from a denial of certiorari, for example, in *Callins v. Collins* and in the 2002 case of Toronto Patterson, executed in Texas for a crime he committed at 17.

6. *Furman v. Georgia*, 408 U.S. 238 (1972).

7. Jeffrey L. Kirchmeier, "Another Place Beyond Here: The Death Penalty Moratorium Movement in the United States," *Colorado Law Review* 73 (Winter 2002), 14.

8. *Furman v. Georgia*.

9. Banner, *Death Penalty*, 264–65.

10. Ibid., 284.

11. Kirchmeier, "Another Place Beyond Here," 18–19.

12. *Woodson v. North Carolina*, 428 U.S. 280 (1976).

13. *Gregg v. Georgia*, 428 U.S. 153 (1976).

14. *Coker v. Georgia*, 433 U.S. 584 (1977).

15. *Enmund v. Florida*, 458 U.S. 782 (1982).

16. *Tison v. Arizona*, 481 U.S. 137 (1987).

17. *Payne v. Tennessee*, 501 U.S. 808 (1991).

18. Austin Sarat, *When the State Kills: Capital Punishment and the American Condition* (Princeton, NJ: Princeton University Press, 2001), 41.

19. *Payne v. Tennessee*.

20. *McCleskey v. Kemp*, 481 U.S. 279 (1987).

21. For more discussion of *McCleskey*, see for example David Cole, *No Equal Justice: Race and Class in the American Criminal Justice System* (New York: The New Press, 1999); David VonDrehle, *Among the Lowest of the Dead: The Culture of the Condemned* (New York: Random House, 1994), 266; David C. Baldus and George Woodworth, "Race Discrimination and the Death Penalty: An Empirical Overview," in *America's Experiment with Capital Punishment: Reflections on the Past, Present, and Future of the Ultimate Penal Sanction*, ed. James R. Acker, Robert M. Bohm, and Charles S. Lanier (Durham, NC: Carolina Academic Press, 1998).

22. John C. Jeffries Jr., *Justice Lewis F. Powell, Jr.: A Biography* (New York: Charles Scribner's Sons, 1994), 451.

23. See, e.g., U.S. General Accounting Office, "Death Penalty Sentencing: Research Indicates Pattern of Racial Disparities," in *The Death Penalty in America: Current Controversies*, ed. Hugo Adam Bedau (New York: Oxford University, 1997), 268–272.

24. *Strickland v. Washington*, 466 U.S. 668 (1984).

25. *Burger v. Kemp*, 483 U.S. 776 (1987).

26. *Murray v. Giaratanno*, 492 U.S. 1 (1989).

27. David E. Rovella, "Pryor Defends Death Row Policies," *National Law Journal*, February 11, 2002.

28. *Mickens v. Taylor*, 535 U.S. 162 (2002).

29. Marcia Coyle, "A Bizarre Murder Case Sharply Divides High Court," *National Law Journal*, April 1, 2002.

30. Michael Mello and Paul J. Perkins, "Closing the Circle: The Illusion of Lawyers for People Litigating for their Lives at the Fin de Siecle," in *America's Experiment with Capital Punishment*, ed. Acker, Bohm, and Lanier.

31. Penny J. White, "Errors and Ethics: Dilemmas in Death," *Hofstra Law Review* 29 (Summer 2001), 1276–1284.
32. *Simmons v. South Carolina*, 512 U.S. 154 (1994).
33. *Weeks v. Angelone*, 000 U.S. 99–5746 (2000).
34. *Ford v. Wainwright*, 477 U.S. 399 (1986).
35. *Adkins v. Virginia*, 00–8452 (2002).
36. *Penry v. Lynaugh*, 492 U.S. 302 (1989).
37. *Adkins v. Virginia*.
38. *Stanford v. Kentucky*, 492 U.S. 361 (1989).
39. Michael C. Dorf, "The Story Behind the Supreme Court's Refusal to Hear a Recent Death Penalty Case," *Findlaw's Writ*, September 4, 2002.
40. *Herrera v. Collins*, 506 U.S. 390 (1993).
41. See, for example, Jesse L. Jackson, Sr., Jesse L. Jackson, Jr., and Bruce Shapiro, *Legal Lynching: The Death Penalty and America's Future* (New York: The New Press, 2001), 62.
42. David R. Dow, "How the Death Penalty Really Works," in *Machinery of Death: The Reality of America's Death Penalty Regime*, ed. David R. Dow and Mark Dow (New York: Routledge, 2002), 28–29.
43. Stephen B. Bright, "The Politics of Capital Punishment: The Sacrifice of Fairness for Executions," in *America's Experiment with Capital Punishment*, ed. Acker, Bohm, and Lanier.
44. *United States v. Quinones* 196 F.Supp.2nd 416, 420 (S.D.N.Y.).
45. Dow and Dow, *Machinery of Death*, 5–6.
46. Mandy Welch and Richard Burr, "The Politics of Finality and the Execution of the Innocent: The Case of Gary Graham," in *Machinery of Death*, ed. Dow and Dow, 128– 29.
47. *Callins v. Collins*, 510 U.S. 1141 (1994).
48. Edward Lazarus, "A Basic Death Penalty Paradox That is Tearing the Supreme Court Apart," *Findlaw's Writ*, October 31, 2002.
49. Ibid.
50. "Court Reviews Death Penalty Case," Associated Press, November 5, 2001.
51. Victoria Ashley, "Death Penalty Redux: Justice Sandra Day O'Connor's Role on the Rehnquist Court and the Future of the Death Penalty in America," *Baylor Law Review* 54 (Spring 2002), 408.
52. Ibid., 419–425.
53. Hugh Adam Bedau, "Habeas Corpus and Other Constitutional Controversies," in *The Death Penalty in America: Current Controversies*, ed. Bedau, 241.
54. Carol S. Steiker and Jordan M. Steiker, "Judicial Development in Capital Punishment Law," in *America's Experiment with Capital Punishment*, ed. Acker, Bohm, and Lanier, 47–48.
55. Bedau, "Habeas Corpus," 242.
56. Steiker and Steiker, "Judicial Development," 68–69.

Chapter 3

1. Norman Mailer, *The Executioner's Song* (Boston: Little, Brown, 1979; New York: Vintage International, 1998); Truman Capote, *In Cold Blood* (New York: Random

House, 1965; New York: Vintage, 1994); Sister Helen Prejean, *Dead Man Walking* (New York: Vintage, 1994); Mikal Gilmore, *Shot in the Heart* (New York: Random House, 1994).

2. Harper Lee, *To Kill a Mockingbird* (New York: Warner Books, 1960); Ernest J. Gaines, *A Lesson Before Dying* (New York: Vintage, 1993); John Grisham, *A Time to Kill* (New York: Wynwood, 1989; New York: Dell, 2003); John Grisham, *The Chamber* (New York: Doubleday, 1994).

3. Stephen King, *The Green Mile* (New York: Pocket Books, 1999).

4. Stanford Pinsker, "Imagining American Reality," *The Southern Review* 29 (Autumn 1993), 767.

5. Jonathan Dee, review of *The Executioner's Song* by Norman Mailer, *Harper's Magazine* (June 1999), 76.

6. Joan Didion, "Let's Do It," review of *The Executioner's Song* by Norman Mailer, *New York Times*, October 6, 1996.

7. Ibid.

8. Ibid.

9. Gilmore, *Shot in the Heart*, 397–98.

10. Quoted in Elizabeth Glieck, "Seeing Ghosts: Gary's Brother Explains the Bleak Gilmore Past," *People Weekly*, June 13, 1994, 51–54.

11. *Shot in the Heart*, dir. Agnieszka Holland, 98 min., 2001.

12. *New York Times*, March 27, 2002.

13. Gilmore, *Shot in the Heart*, 69–70.

14. Ibid., 341.

15. Mailer, *Executioner's Song*, 796.

16. Gilmore, *Shot in the Heart*, 159.

17. Ibid., 171.

18. *Shot in the Heart* (2001).

19. Gilmore, *Shot in the Heart*, 86.

20. Ibid., 243.

21. Diane Turbide, review of *Shot in the Heart* by Mikal Gilmore, *Maclean's*, July 18, 1994, 52.

22. Review of *Shot in the Heart* by Mikal Gilmore, *The Economist*, July 9, 1994, 90.

23. Glieck, "Seeing Ghosts," 51–54.

24. *The Executioner's Song*, dir. Lawrence Schilller, 136 min., 1982.

25. Ibid.

26. Mailer, *Executioner's Song*, 288–92.

27. Ibid., 415–445.

28. Ibid., 489, 639, 873, 955.

29. *The Executioner's Song* (1982).

30. Gilmore, *Shot in the Heart*, 329.

31. Mailer, *Executioner's Song*, 828–31.

32. Gilmore, *Shot in the Heart*, 378.

33. Don DeLuca, "Mikal Gilmore Delves into a Past that Gave Birth to a Murderer," and Mike Duffy, "HBO Film Does Justice to the Brothers Gilmore," Knight-Ridder-Tribune News Service, October 12, 2001.

34. Mailer, *Executioner's Song*, 305–06.

35. Gilmore, *Shot in the Heart*, i.

36. Ibid., 345.

37. Roz Kaveney, review of *Shot in the Heart* by Mikal Gilmore, *New Statesman*, July 22, 1994, 46–47.
38. Mailer, *Executioner's Song*, 980–81.
39. Gilmore, *Shot in the Heart*, 351.
40. Marcelle Clements, "Still Living with a Story of Death," *New York Times*, October 7, 2001.
41. George Plimpton, *Truman Capote* (New York: Doubleday, 1997), 214–15.
42. Brian Conniff, "Psychological Accidents: *In Cold Blood* and Ritual Sacrifice," *The Midwest Quarterly* 35 (Autumn 1993), 77–95.
43. Capote, *In Cold Blood*, 88.
44. Ibid., 66.
45. Conniff, "Psychological Accidents."
46. Capote, *In Cold Blood*, 247–48.
47. Conniff, "Psychological Accidents."
48. Capote, *In Cold Blood*, 190.
49. Ibid., 31.
50. Ibid., 166–69.
51. Ibid., 200–01.
52. Ibid., 55.
53. Ibid., 201.
54. Ibid., 278–79.
55. Ibid., 132–34.
56. William J. Nance, *The Worlds of Truman Capote* (New York: Stein and Day, 1970), 204.
57. Capote, *In Cold Blood*, 55.
58. Ibid., 240.
59. Ibid., 290.
60. Nance, *Worlds of Truman Capote*, 181.
61. Capote, *In Cold Blood*, 257.
62. Ibid., 283.
63. Ibid., 257–58.
64. Ibid., 217.
65. Ibid., 273.
66. Arthur Koestler, *Reflections on Hanging* (New York: Macmillan, 1957), 73–74.
67. Capote, *In Cold Blood*, 294–97.
68. Ibid., 299–300.
69. Ibid., 303–05.
70. Ibid., 307.
71. Ibid., 329–30, 336–37.
72. Plimpton, *Truman Capote*, 185–86.
73. Capote, *In Cold Blood*, 337–38.
74. Ibid., 340–41.
75. Conniff, "Psychological Accidents."
76. See Nance, *Worlds of Truman Capote*, 212.
77. Plimpton, *Truman Capote*, 174–75.
78. Nance, *Worlds of Truman Capote*, 174–76.
79. Quoted in Plimpton, *Truman Capote*, 215.
80. *In Cold Blood*, dir. Richard Brooks, 134 min., 1967.

81. Roger Ebert, Review of *In Cold Blood* (June 9, 2002) [online at www.suntimes. com/ebert reviews].

82. *In Cold Blood*, dir. Jonathan Kaplan, 178 min., 1996.

83. Jeffrey L. Kirchmeier, "Another Place Beyond Here: The Death Penalty Moratorium Movement in the United States," *Colorado Law Review* 73 (Winter 2002), 25–26.

84. Ibid.

85. Jason Berry, "Dead Man Walking: Eyewitness Account," *National Catholic Reporter* 29 (July 2, 1993), 9.

86. Raymond A. Schroth, review of *Dead Man Walking* by Sister Helen Prejean, *America* 169 (September 18, 1993), 20–21.

87. Prejean, *Dead Man Walking*, 5–7.

88. Ibid., 32.

89. Ibid., 46.

90. Ibid., 50.

91. Ibid., 20–21.

92. Ibid., 54.

93. Ibid., 120.

94. Ibid., 94.

95. Ibid., 102.

96. Ibid., 180–81.

97. Ibid., 113.

98. Ibid., 154–55.

99. Ibid., 210–11.

100. Ibid., 197.

101. Ibid., 239–40.

102. Ibid., 137.

103. Hilary Holman, review of *Dead Man Walking* by Sister Helen Prejean, *Commonweal* 120 (November 19, 1993), 30–32.

104. *Dead Man Walking*, dir. Tim Robbins, 122 min., 1996.

105. John Simon, review of *Dead Man Walking* directed by Tim Robbins, *National Review* 48 (February 26, 1996), 64–66.

106. Austin Sarat, *When the State Kills: Capital Punishment and the American Condition* (Princeton, NJ: Princeton University Press, 2001), 220.

107. Ibid., 244–45.

108. Victoria Rebeck, review of *Dead Man Walking* directed by Tim Robbins, *The Christian Century* 113 (April 17, 1996), 431–32.

109. Christy Rodgers, review of *Dead Man Walking* directed by Tim Robbins, *Cineaste* 22 (1996), 42–44.

110. Ibid.

111. See David R. Dow, "Fictional Documentaries and Truthful Fictions: The Death Penalty in Recent American Films," *Constitutional Commentary* 17 (Winter 2000).

112. Brian D. Johnson, review of *Dead Man Walking* directed by Tim Robbins, *Maclean's* 109 (January 22, 1996), 62–63. See also reviews by Stuart Klawans, *The Nation* 262 (February 5, 1996), 35–37; David Ansen, *Newsweek*, January 8, 1996, 69.

113. See for example the review by Benjamin Irvy, "Staging Death Row: *Dead Man Walking* as Opera," *Commonweal* 129 (April 5, 2002), 24.

114. Sister Helen Prejean, "Letter from Death Row," *America* 180 (February 13, 1999), 24–25.

Chapter 4

1. See, for example, Jane McFann, "One City, One Book: Creating Community through Reading," *Reading Today* 20 (October–November 2002), 24.
2. Ernest J. Gaines, *A Lesson Before Dying* (New York: Vintage Books, 1993).
3. Philip Auger, "A Lesson About Manhood: Appropriating 'The Word' in Ernest Gaines's *A Lesson Before Dying*," *The Southern Literary Journal* 27 (Spring 1995), 74.
4. Gaines, *Lesson*, 4.
5. Ibid., 5.
6. *Powell v. Alabama*, 287 U.S. 45.
7. Gaines, *Lesson*, 7–8.
8. Ibid., 31.
9. Ibid., 140.
10. Ibid., 170.
11. Ibid., 88.
12. Ibid., 192.
13. Ibid., 220.
14. Ibid., 255.
15. Auger, "Lesson About Manhood."
16. William R. Nash, " 'You Think a Man Can't Kneel and Stand?' Ernest J. Gaines's Reassessment of Religion as a Positive Communal Influence in *A Lesson Before Dying*," *Callaloo* 24 (2001), 359.
17. Jeffrey J. Folks, "Communal Responsibility in Ernest J. Gaines's *A Lesson Before Dying*," *The Mississippi Quarterly* 52 (Spring 1999), 259–74.
18. *A Lesson Before Dying*, dir. Joseph Sargent, 105 min., 1999.
19. An editorial in the local paper compared the death of the defendant "to the senseless slaughter of songbirds by hunters and children." Harper Lee, *To Kill a Mockingbird* (New York: Warner Books, 1960), 243.
20. Christopher Metress, "*To Kill a Mockingbird*: Threatening Boundaries," *The Mississippi Quarterly* 48 (Spring 1995), 397–402.
21. Lee, *Mockingbird*, 9.
22. Ibid., 106.
23. Compare this attitude to the language in *A Time to Kill*, set fifty years later but where everyone in town uses the word incessantly. It is interesting to speculate whether the usage or the users were more common than in Harper Lee's Alabama.
24. Ibid., 80, 109.
25. Ibid., 154.
26. Ibid., 172–74.
27. Ibid., 190–94.
28. Ibid., 206–8.
29. Ibid., 214.
30. Ibid., 222.
31. Metress, "Threatening Boundaries."
32. Patrick Chura, "Prolepsis and Anachronism: Emmett Till and the Historicity of *To Kill a Mockingbird*," *The Southern Literary Journal* 32 (Spring 2000), 1–18.
33. *To Kill a Mockingbird*, dir. Robert Mulligan, 129 min., 1960.

34. Paul Bergman and Michael Asimow, *Reel Justice: The Courtroom Goes to the Movies* (Kansas City, MO: Andrews and McMeel, 1996), 141.
35. Ibid.
36. Stephen King, *The Green Mile* (New York: Pocket Books, 1999).
37. An exception is Percy, a politically connected guard, who is both sadistic and cowardly.
38. King, *Green Mile*, 440.
39. Ibid., 15–16.
40. Ibid., 113–14.
41. Ibid., 292.
42. Ibid., 293–98.
43. Ibid., 18–19.
44. Ibid., 119.
45. Ibid., 202–06.
46. Ibid., 350.
47. Ibid., 488.
48. Ibid., 491.
49. Ibid., 508.
50. Ibid., 535.
51. Ibid., 510.
52. *The Green Mile*, dir. Frank Darabont, 188 min., 1999.
53. Roger Ebert, review of *The Green Mile*, dir. Frank Darabont, *Chicago Sun-Times*, December 12, 1999.
54. The movie takes place in 1935 rather than 1932 as the book does. The only reason for the change seems to be so that the movie *Top Hat*, released in 1935, can be included.
55. See, for example, Andrew O'Hehir, review of *The Green Mile*, dir. Frank Darabont, [online at www.salon.com], December 10, 1999.
56. Ibid.
57. John Grisham, *A Time to Kill* (New York: Wynwood, 1989; Dell, 2003).
58. Ibid., ix–x.
59. Ibid., 27.
60. Ibid., 156.
61. Ibid., 194. The word "nigger" is used constantly in the novel. See discussion below.
62. Ibid., 47–48.
63. Ibid., 53–54.
64. Ibid., 62–63.
65. Ibid., 226.
66. Ibid., 108–9.
67. Ibid., 102.
68. Ibid., 391.
69. Ibid., 422.
70. Ibid., 482–84.
71. Ibid., 513.
72. Ibid., 509.
73. Ibid., 120.

74. Ibid., 232–33.
75. Ibid., 208.
76. Ibid., 161.
77. *A Time to Kill*, dir. Joel Schumacher, 149 min., 1996.
78. Wilda L. White, "Imagine . . . Justice," *Picturing Justice* [online at www.usfca.edu/pj].
79. John Grisham, *The Chamber* (New York: Doubleday, 1994).
80. Ibid., 76.
81. Ibid., 177–78.
82. Ibid., 186.
83. Ivan Solotaroff, *The Last Face You'll Ever See: The Private Life of the American Death Penalty* (New York: Harper Collins, 2001).
84. Grisham, *Chamber*, 191.
85. Ibid., 92.
86. Ibid., 72, 75.
87. Ibid., 65.
88. Ibid., 86–87.
89. Ibid., 89.
90. Ibid., 53.
91. Ibid., 493–94.
92. Ibid., 276.
93. Ibid., 392.
94. Ibid., 366.
95. Ibid.
96. Ibid., 508.
97. *The Chamber*, dir. James Foley, 113 min., 1996.
98. Barbara Shulgasser, "Latest from Grisham Factory," *San Francisco Examiner*, October 11, 1996.

Chapter 5

1. David R. Dow, "Fictional Documentaries and Truthful Fictions: The Death Penalty in Recent American Film," *Constitutional Commentary* 17 (Winter 2000).
2. *Last Light*, dir. Kiefer Sutherland, 104 min., 1993.
3. *Monster's Ball*, dir. Marc Foster, 111 min., 2001.
4. Robert Jay Lifton and Greg Mitchell, *Who Owns Death? Capital Punishment, the American Conscience, and the End of Executions* (New York: Perennial, 2002), 73.
5. Ibid., 77.
6. Rick Groen, "Southern Discomfort," *Toronto Globe and Mail*, February 1, 2002.
7. A. O. Scott, "Film Review: Courtesy and Decency Play Sneaky with a Tough Guy," *New York Times*, February 1, 2002.
8. Quoted in Ivan Solotaroff, *The Last Face You'll Ever See: The Private Life of the American Death Penalty* (New York: HarperCollins, 2001), 197–98.
9. Groen, "Southern Discomfort."
10. Elizabeth Rappaport, "Staying Alive: Executive Clemency, Equal Protection, and the Politics of Gender in Women's Capital Cases," *Buffalo Criminal Law Review* 4 (2001), 967–1007.
11. *I Want to Live*, dir. Robert Wise, 120 min., 1958.

12. *Dance with a Stranger,* dir. Mike Newell, 102 min., 1985.

13. *Last Dance,* dir. Bruce Beresford, 103 min., 1996.

14. Bosley Crowther, review of *I Want to Live,* dir. by Robert Wise, *New York Times,* November 19, 1958.

15. Jeremy Heilman, review of *I Want to Live* (May 15, 2002) [online at www.movie martyr.com].

16. Lawrence Russell, review of *I Want to Live* (September 28, 2000) [online at www.coastnet.com].

17. Vincent Canby, review of *Dance with a Stranger,* dir. by Mike Newell, *New York Times,* August 9, 1985.

18. "Ruth Ellis: The Last to Hang" [online at www.crimelibrary.com].

19. Jonathan Morris, "Ruth Ellis: Villain or Victim?" (November 30, 1999) [online at news.bbc.co.uk].

20. Richard Alleva, "Dead Woman Stumbles," *Commonweal,* June 14, 1996, 20–21.

21. Barbara Shulgasser, "Stone Loses a Step in Last Dance," *San Francisco Examiner,* May 3, 1996.

22. Brian D. Johnson, review of *Last Dance,* dir. by Bruce Beresford, *MacLean's* 109 (May 6, 1996), 60.

23. Jack Sommersby, "Life of David Gale" (April 21, 2003) [online at www.culture dose.net].

24. *The Life of David Gale,* dir. Alan Parker, 130 min., 2003.

25. Mark Steyn, "Who Cares? *The Life of David Gale,*" *Spectator* 291 (March 15, 2003), 68.

26. Roger Ebert, review of *The Life of David Gale,* dir. by Alan Parker, *Chicago Sun-Times,* February 21, 2003.

27. Desson Howe, review of *The Thin Blue Line,* dir. by Errol Morris, *Washington Post,* September 2, 1988.

28. *The Thin Blue Line,* dir. Errol Morris, 103 min., 1988.

29. Hal Hinson, review of *The Thin Blue* Line, dir. by Errol Morris, *Washington Post,* September 2, 1988.

30. *The Widow of St. Pierre,* dir. Patrice Leconte, 112 min., 2000.

31. David Sterritt, "Now Showing: Crusading Films," *Christian Science Monitor,* June 13, 2003.

Chapter 6

1. Barbara Parker, *Suspicion of Vengeance* (New York: Signet, 2003); Mary Willis Walker, *The Red Scream* (New York: Bantam, 1995); Michael Malone, *Time's Witness* (Napierville, IL: Sourcebooks, 2002); Scott Turow, *Reversible Errors* (New York: Farrar, Straus and Giroux, 2002).

2. Parker, *Suspicion,* 34.

3. Ibid., 428–30.

4. Ibid., 30.

5. Ibid., 108–09.

6. Ibid., 35.

7. See for example, *Burger v. Kemp,* 483 U.S. 776 (1987).

8. Parker, *Suspicion,* 33.

9. Ibid., 38–39.
10. Ibid., 277.
11. Ibid., 385.
12. Robert Croen, review of *Suspicion of Vengeance* by Barbara Parker, *Pittsburgh Post-Gazette*, October 25, 2001).
13. Review of *Suspicion of Vengeance* by Barbara Parker, *Publishers Weekly*, July 9, 2001.
14. Walker, *Red Scream*, 21–22.
15. Ibid., 71.
16. Ibid., 322.
17. Franklin E. Zimring and Gordon Hawkins, *Crime Is Not the Problem: Lethal Violence in America* (New York: Oxford University Press, 1997), Chapter 8.
18. Walker, *Red Scream*, 308–09.
19. Ibid., 315.
20. Ibid., 324.
21. Ibid., 325.
22. Ibid., 347.
23. Ibid., 348.
24. Ibid., 354. Italics added.
25. Ibid., 356–57.
26. Ibid., 359.
27. Ibid., 10, 71.
28. Ibid., 330.
29. Ibid., 90.
30. Malone, *Time's Witness*, 303.
31. Jill Baumgaertner, "A Literary Roudup," *The Christian Century* (November 15, 1989), 1049.
32. David E. Pitt, "Mystery is the Core of Fiction," *New York Times*, March 23, 1989.
33. Malone, *Time's Witness*, 8.
34. Ibid., 304.
35. Ibid., 129.
36. Ibid., 130.
37. Ibid., 245.
38. Ibid., 302–03.
39. Ibid., 414–15.
40. Ibid.
41. Ibid., 534.
42. Scott Turow, "To Kill or Not to Kill," *The New Yorker*, January 6, 2003, 40–47.
43. Robert McCrum, "To Hell with Perry Mason," *The Guardian*, November 23, 2002.
44. Turow, *Reversible Errors*, 6.
45. Ibid., 10.
46. Ibid., 132.
47. Ibid., 147.
48. Ibid., 320–21.
49. Turow, "To Kill or Not to Kill."
50. Turow, *Reversible Errors*, 409–10.
51. Sam Lieth, "It's All Perfectly Legal" (December 29, 2002) [online at www.arts.telegraph.co.uk]

52. Turow, *Reversible Errors*, 194.
53. Ibid., 421.
54. Ibid., 401.
55. Ibid., 427.
56. Julia E. Twarog, "Harvard Alum's New Novel Takes on Death Penalty" (February 7, 2003) [online at www.thecrimson.com].

Chapter 7

1. Adam Liptak, "The Death Penalty: Views of a Witness for the Prosecution," *New York Times*, February 15, 2003.
2. Anamona Hartocollis, "Steadfast Witness to Deaths Far Off," *New York Times*, May 18, 2003.
3. Linda Greenhouse, "In a Momentous Term, Justices Remake the Law, and the Court," *New York Times*, July 1, 2003.
4. Neil A. Lewis, "Ruling Allows Forcible Drugging of Inmate Before Execution," *New York Times*, October 7, 2003.
5. Adam Liptak, "Court Overturns 100 Death Sentences in 3 Western States," *New York Times*, September 2, 2003.
6. Linda Greenhouse, "Man on Death Row 24 Years Seems to Gain Before Justices," *New York Times*, December 9, 2003.
7. Adam Liptak, "Louisiana Sentence Renews Debate on the Death Penalty," *New York Times*, August 31, 2003.
8. Adam Liptak, "Prosecutors Fight DNA Use for Exoneration," *New York Times*, August 29, 2003.
9. Laura Masnerus, "States Seek Ways to Make Executions Error Free," *New York Times*, November 2, 2003.
10. Adam Liptak, "Critics Say Execution Drug May Hide Suffering," *New York Times*, October 7, 2003.
11. "Toward Death Penalty Reform," *New York Times*, October 13, 2003.
12. *Report of the Governor's Commission on Capital Punishment*, April 15, 2002 [online at www.idoc.state.il.us/ccp].
13. Scott Turow, *Ultimate Punishment: A Lawyer's Reflections on Dealing with the Death Penalty* (New York: Farrar, Straus and Giroux, 2003).
14. Ibid., 39.
15. Ibid., 23–24.
16. Ibid., 53–55.
17. Ibid., 64–65.
18. ACLU of Virginia et al., *Broken Justice: The Death Penalty in Virginia* (Richmond: American Civil Liberties Union of Virginia, 2003).
19. "Take This Sabbath Day," *The West Wing*, February 9, 2000.

BIBLIOGRAPHY

Acker, James R., Robert M. Bohm, and Charles S. Lanier, eds. *America's Experiment with Capital Punishment: Reflections on the Past, Present, and Future of the Ultimate Penal Sanction*. Durham, NC: Carolina Academic Press, 1998.

ACLU of Virginia et al. *Broken Justice: The Death Penalty in Virginia*. Richmond: American Civil Liberties Union of Virginia, 2003.

Alleva, Richard. "Dead Woman Stumbles: Beresford's *Last Dance*." *Commonweal* (June 14, 1996).

Anderson, Jeffrey. "Death Made Taxing." *San Francisco Examiner* (February 21, 2003).

Ansen, David. "Movie Review: *Dead Man Walking*." *Newsweek* (January 8, 1996).

Ashley, Victoria. "Death Penalty Redux: Justice Sandra Day O'Connor's Role on the Rehnquist Court and the Future of the Death Penalty in America." *Baylor Law Review* 54 (Spring 2002): 407–425.

Auger, Philip. "A Lesson about Manhood: Appropriating 'The Word' in Ernest Gaines's *A Lesson Before Dying*." *The Southern Literary Journal* 27 (Spring 1995): 74–86.

Baldus, David C., and George Woodworth. "Race Discrimination and the Death Penalty: An Empirical Overview." In *America's Experiment with Capital Punishment: Reflections on the Past, Present, and Future of the Ultimate Penal Sanction*, edited by James R. Acker, Robert M. Bohm, and Charles S. Lanier. Durham, NC: Carolina Academic Press, 1998.

Banner, Stuart. *The Death Penalty: An American History*. Cambridge, MA: Harvard University Press, 2002.

Baumgaertner, Jill. "A Literary Roundup." *The Christian Century* (November 15, 1989).

Bedau, Hugo Adam, ed. *The Death Penalty in America: Current Controversies*. New York: Oxford University Press, 1997.

———. "Habeas Corpus and Other Constitutional Controversies." In *The Death Penalty in America: Current Controversies*, edited by Hugo Adam Bedau. New York: Oxford University Press, 1997.

——. "Why the Death Penalty Is a Cruel and Unusual Punishment." In *The Death Penalty in America: Current Controversies*, edited by Hugo Adam Bedau. New York: Oxford University Press, 1997.

Bergman, Paul, and Michael Asimow. *Reel Justice: The Courtroom Goes to the Movies*. Kansas City, MO: Andrews and McMeel, 1996.

Berman, Paul Schiff. "Review Essay: The Cultural Life of Capital Punishment: Surveying the Benefits of Cultural Analysis of Law: When the State Kills and the American Condition." *Columbia Law Review* 102 (May 2002): 1129–1177.

Berry, Jason. Review of *Dead Man Walking* by Sister Helen Prejean. *National Catholic Reporter* (July 2, 1993).

Bohm, Robert M. "American Death Penalty Opinion: Past, Present, and Future." In *America's Experiment with Capital Punishment: Reflections on the Past, Present, and Future of the Ultimate Penal Sanction*, edited by James R. Acker, Robert M. Bohm, and Charles S. Lanier. Durham, NC: Carolina Academic Press, 1998.

Bowers, William J., and Benjamin D. Steiner. "Choosing Life or Death: Sentencing Dynamics in Capital Cases." In *America's Experiment with Capital Punishment: Reflections on the Past, Present, and Future of the Ultimate Penal Sanction*, edited by James R. Acker, Robert M. Bohm, and Charles S. Lanier. Durham, NC: Carolina Academic Press, 1998.

Bowman, David. "A Murder in Middle America: Truman Capote's Killer Instincts and the Making of the Sensational *In Cold Blood*." *Book* (November/December 2002).

Bright, Stephen B. "The Politics of Capital Punishment: The Sacrifice of Fairness for Executions." In *America's Experiment with Capital Punishment: Reflections on the Past, Present, and Future of the Ultimate Penal Sanction*, edited by James R. Acker, Robert M. Bohm, and Charles S. Lanier. Durham, NC: Carolina Academic Press, 1998.

——. "Sleeping on the Job." *National Law Journal* (December 4, 2000).

Brown, Dale. "A Lesson for Living: Interview with Ernest J. Gaines." *Sojourners* (September/October 2002).

Burtman, Bob. "Innocence Lost." In *Machinery of Death: The Reality of America's Death Penalty Regime*, edited by David R. Dow and Mark Dow. New York: Routledge, 2002.

Canby, Vincent. "Film review: *Dance with a Stranger*." *New York Times* (August 9, 1985).

Capote, Truman. *In Cold Blood*. New York: Random House, 1965; Vintage Books, 1994.

Chase, Anthony. *Movies on Trial: The Legal System on the Silver Screen*. New York: New Press, 2002.

Chura, Patrick. "Prolepsis and Anachronism: Emmett Till and the Historicity of *To Kill a Mockingbird*." *The Southern Literary Journal* 32 (Spring 2000): 1–18.

Clements, Marcelle. "Still Living with a Story of Death." *New York Times* (October 7, 2001).

Cole, David. *No Equal Justice: Race and Class in the American Criminal Justice System*. New York: New Press, 1999.

Conniff, Brian. "Psychological Accidents: *In Cold Blood* and Ritual Sacrifice." *The Midwestern Quarterly* 35 (Autumn 1993): 77–95.

Coyle, Marcia. "A Bizarre Murder Case Sharply Divides High Court." *National Law Journal* (April 1, 2002).

———. "Trimming Death Sentence Errors." *National Law Journal* (February 11, 2002).

Croan, Robert. "Review of *Suspicion of Vengeance* by Barbara Parker." *Pittsburgh Post-Gazette* (October 25, 2001).

Crocker, Phyllis L. "Is the Death Penalty Good for Women?" In *Machinery of Death: The Reality of America's Death Penalty Regime*, edited by David R. Dow and Mark Dow. New York: Routledge, 2002.

Crowther, Bosley. "Review of *I Want to Live*." *New York Times* (November 19, 1958).

Cullen, Francis T., Bonnie S. Fisher, and Brandon K. Applegate. "Public Opinion about Punishment and Corrections." *Crime and Justice* 27 (2000): 1–79.

"Dead Man Walking Out." *The Economist* (June 10, 2000).

Dee, Jonathan. "Review of *The Executioner's Song* by Norman Mailer." *Harper's* (June 1999).

DeLuca, Don. "Mikal Gilmore Delves into a Past That Gave Birth to a Murderer," Knight Ridder/Tribune News Service (July 20, 1994).

Dennis, Christopher, Marshall H. Medoff, and Michelle N. Gagnier. "The Impact of Racially Disproportionate Outcomes on Public Policy: The U.S. Senate and the Death Penalty." *Social Science Journal* 35 (April 1998): 169–174.

Denno, Deborah W. "Execution and the Forgotten Eighth Amendment." In *America's Experiment with Capital Punishment: Reflections on the Past, Present, and Future of the Ultimate Penal Solution*, edited by James R. Acker, Robert M. Bohm, and Charles S. Lanier. Durham, NC: Carolina Academic Press, 1998.

Denvir, John, ed. *Legal Reelism: Movies as Legal Texts*. Urbana, IL: University of Chicago Press, 1996.

Didion, Joan. " 'Let's Do It': Review of *The Executioner's Song* by Norman Mailer." *New York Times* (October 9, 1996).

Dorf, Michael C. "The Story Behind the Supreme Court's Refusal to Hear a Recent Death Penalty Case." *Findlaw's Writ* (September 4, 2002).

Dow, David R. "Fictional Documentaries and Truthful Fictions: The Death Penalty in Recent American Film." *Constitutional Commentary* 17 (Winter 2000): 511–553.

———. "How the Death Penalty Really Works." In *Machinery of Death: The Reality of America's Death Penalty Regime*, edited by David R. Dow and Mark Dow. New York: Routledge, 2002.

Dow, David R. and Mark Dow, eds. *Machinery of Death: The Reality of America's Death Penalty Regime*. New York: Routledge, 2002.

Dow, Mark. "The Line Between Us and Them: Interview with Warden Donald Cabana." In *Machinery of Death: The Reality of America's Death Penalty Regime*, edited by David R. Dow and Mark Dow. New York: Routledge, 2002.

Duffy, Michael. "HBO Film Does Justice to the Brothers Gilmore." Knight Ridder/Tribune News Service (November 12, 2001).

Ebert, Roger. "Film Review: *In Cold Blood*." (June 9, 2002). [Available online at www.suntimes.com].

———. "Film Review: *Last Dance*." *Chicago Sun-Times* (May 6, 1996).

———. "Film Review: *The Life of David Gale.*" *Chicago Sun-Times* (February 21, 2003).

———. "Film Review: *Monster's Ball.*" *Chicago Sun-Times* (February 1, 2002).

———. "Film Review: *The Thin Blue Line.*" *Chicago Sun-Times* (September 16, 1988).

———. "Film Review: *The Widow of St. Pierre.*" *Chicago Sun-Times* (March 30, 2001).

Folks, Jeffrey. J. "Communal Responsibility in Ernest J. Gaines's *A Lesson Before Dying.*" *Mississippi Quarterly* 52 (Spring 1999): 259–274.

Francke, Lizzie. "Film Review: *Dead Man Walking.*" *New Statesman and Society* (March 22, 1996).

Freedman, Eric M. "Earl Washington's Ordeal." *Hofstra Law Review* 29 (Summer 2001): 1089–1110.

———. "Federal Habeas Corpus in Capital Cases." In *America's Experiment with Capital Punishment: Reflections on the Past, Present, and Future of the Ultimate Penal Sanction,* edited by James R. Acker, Robert M. Bohm, and Charles S. Lanier. Durham, NC: Carolina Academic Press, 1998.

Friedman, Lawrence M. "Law, Lawyers, and Popular Culture." *Yale Law Journal* 98 (1989): 1579–1606.

Gaines, Ernest J. *A Lesson Before Dying.* New York: Vintage, 1993.

Galliher, John F., Larry W. Koch, Daniel Patrick Keys, and Teresa J. Guess. *America Without the Death Penalty: States Leading the Way.* Boston: Northeastern University Press, 2002.

Gilmore, Mikal. *Shot in the Heart.* New York: Random House, 1994.

Gleick, Elizabeth. "Seeing Ghosts: Gary's Brother Explains the Bleak Gilmore Past." *People Weekly* (June 13, 1994).

Greenhouse, Linda. "In a Momentous Term, Justices Remake the Law and the Court." *New York Times* (July 1, 2003).

———. "Justices Weigh Lawyers' Legal Obligations." *New York Times* (November 11, 2001).

———. "Man on Death Row 24 Years Seems to Gain Before Justices." *New York Times* (December 9, 2003).

Grisham, John. *The Chamber.* New York: Doubleday, 1994.

———. *A Time to Kill.* New York: Wynwood Press, 1989; Dell, 2003.

Groen, Rick. "Southern Discomfort." *Toronto Globe and Mail* (February 1, 2002).

Guest, David. *Sentenced to Death: The American Novel and Capital Punishment.* Jackson: University Press of Mississippi, 1997.

Hammel, Andrew. "Jousting with the Juggernaut." In *Machinery of Death: The Reality of America's Death Penalty Regime,* edited by David R. Dow and Mark Dow. New York: Routledge, 2002.

Haney, Craig. "Mitigation and the Study of Lives: On the Roots of Violent Criminality and the Nature of Capital Justice." In *America's Experiment with Capital Punishment: Reflections on the Past, Present, and Future of the Ultimate Penal Sanction,* edited by James R. Acker, Robert M. Bohm, and Charles S. Lanier. Durham, NC: Carolina Academic Press, 1998.

Hansen, Mark. "More for Moratorium." *American Bar Association Journal* (December 2000).

Hartocollis, Anemora. "Steadfast Witnesses to Deaths Far Off." *New York Times* (May 18, 2003).

Herbert, Bob. "Tainted Justice." *New York Times* (August 6, 2001).

———. "Texas Travesty." *New York Times* (August 2, 2001).

Hicks, Chris. "Film Review: *The Thin Blue Line*." *Deseret News* (December 28, 1988).

Hinson, Hal. "Film Review: *The Thin Blue Line*." *Washington Post* (September 2, 1988).

Holhman, Hilary. "Book Review: *Dead Man Walking* by Sister Helen Prejean." *Commonweal* (November 19, 1993).

Howe, Desson. "The Monster's Within." *Washington Post* (February 8, 2002).

———. "Film Review: *The Thin Blue Line*." *Washington Post* (September 2, 1988).

Howells, Gary N., Kelly A. Flanagan, and Vivian Hagan. "Does Viewing a Televised Execution Affect Attitudes Toward Capital Punishment?" *Criminal Justice and Behavior* 22 (December 1995), 411–424.

Ivry, Benjamin. "Staging Death Row: *Dead Man Walking* as Opera." *Commonweal* (April 5, 2002).

Jackson, Jesse L. Sr., Jesse L. Jackson Jr., and Bruce Shapiro. *Legal Lynching: The Death Penalty and America's Future*. New York: The New Press, 2001.

Jeffries, John C. Jr. *Justice Lewis F. Powell, Jr.: A Biography*. New York: Charles Scribner's Sons, 1994.

Johnson, Brian D. "Film Review: *Dead Man Walking*." *MacLean's* (January 22, 1996).

———. "Film Review: *Last Dance*." *MacLean's* (May 6, 1996).

Johnson, Robert. "Life Under Sentence of Death: Historical and Contemporary Perspectives." In *America's Experiment with Capital Punishment: Reflections on the Past, Present, and Future of the Ultimate Penal Sanction*, edited by James R. Acker, Robert M. Bohm, and Charles S. Lanier. Durham, NC: Carolina Academic Press, 1998.

Kaminer, Wendy. "The Switch." *New York Times* (July 7, 2002).

Kauffman, Stanley. "Film Review: *Last Dance*." *The New Republic* (May 20, 1996).

Kaveney, Roz. "Book Review: *Shot in the Heart*." *New Statesman and Society* (July 22, 1994).

King, Stephen. *The Green Mile*. New York: Pocket Books, 1999.

Kirchmeier, Jeffrey L. "Another Place Beyond Here: The Death Penalty Moratorium Movement in the United States." *Colorado Law Review* 73 (Summer 2002): 1–116.

Klawans, Stuart. "Film Review: *Dead Man Walking*." *The Nation* (February 5, 1996).

Kobil, Daniel T. "The Evolving Role of Clemency in Capital Cases." In *America's Experiment with Capital Punishment: Reflections on the Past, Present, and Future of the Ultimate Penal Sanction*, edited by James R. Acker, Robert M. Bohm, and Charles S. Lanier. Durham, NC: Carolina Academic Press, 1998.

Koestler, Arthur. *Reflections on Hanging*. New York: Macmillan, 1957.

Lazarus, Edward. "A Basic Death Penalty Paradox That Is Tearing the Supreme Court Apart." *Findlaw's Writ* (October 31, 2002).

———. "Death Penalty Polarization." *Findlaw's Writ* (April 17, 2001).

———. "Is There a First Amendment Right of the Public to View Preparations for Executions?" *Findlaw's Writ* (August 8, 2002).

Lee, Harper. *To Kill a Mockingbird*. New York: Warner Books, 1960.

Lewis, Neil A. "Ruling Allows Forcible Drugging of an Inmate Before Executions." *New York Times* (October 7, 2003).

Lifton, Robert Jay, and Greg Mitchell. *Who Owns Death? Capital Punishment, the American Conscience, and the End of Executions.* New York: Perennial, 2002.

Liptak, Adam. "Court Overturns 100 Death Sentences in 3 Western States." *New York Times* (September 2, 2003).

———. "Critics Say Executions May Hide Suffering." *New York Times* (October 7, 2003).

———. "The Death Penalty: Views of a Witness for the Prosecution." *New York Times* (February 15, 2003).

———. "Death Row Numbers Decline as Challenges to System Rise." *New York Times* (January 11, 2003).

———. "Louisiana Sentence Renews Debate on the Death Penalty." *New York Times* (August 31, 2003).

———. "Prosecutors Fight DNA Use for Exoneration." *New York Times* (August 29, 2003).

———. "Three Justices Call for Reviewing Death Sentences for Juveniles." *New York Times* (August 30, 2002).

Mailer, Norman. *The Executioner's Song.* Boston: Little, Brown, 1979; New York: Vintage Books, 1998.

Malone, Michael. *Time's Witness.* Naperville, IL: Sourcebooks, 2002.

Mansnerus, Laura. "States Seek Ways to Make Executions Error Free." *New York Times* (November 2, 2003).

Maslin, Janet. "Anatomy of a Murder: A Real Life Whodunit." *New York Times* (August 8, 1988).

———. "Death Row Diva: A Raw Sharon Stone." *New York Times* (May 3, 1996).

Masur, Louis P. *Rites of Execution: Capital Punishment and the Transformation of American Culture.* New York: Oxford University Press, 1989.

Mauro, Tony. "Court-Watchers See Subtle Shifts on Death Penalty." *National Law Journal* (February 21, 2000).

McCrum. Robert. "To Hell with Perry Mason" (November 23, 2002). [Available online at www.books.guardian.co.uk].

McGarrell, Edmund F., and Marla Sandys. "The Misperception of Public Opinion toward Capital Punishment: Examining the Spuriousness Explanation of Death Penalty Support." *American Behavioral Scientist* 39 (February 1996): 500–514.

McMillion, Rhonda. "Pulling the Plug on Executions." *American Bar Association Journal* (November 2000).

Mello, Michael, and Paul J. Perkins. "Closing the Circle: The Illusions of Lawyers for People Litigating for their Lives at the Fin de Siecle." In *America's Experiment with Capital Punishment: Reflections on the Past, Present, and Future of the Ultimate Penal Sanction,* edited by James R. Acker, Robert M. Bohm, and Charles S. Lanier. Durham, NC: Carolina Academic Press, 1998.

Metress, Christopher. "*To Kill a Mockingbird:* Threatening Boundaries." *The Mississippi Quarterly* 48 (Spring 1995): 397–402.

Mina, Antonio. "*Reversible Errors* Examines Detriments and the Role of Capital Punishment in U.S. Society" (January 17, 2003). [Available online at www.thehoya.com].

Mitchell, Elvis. "The Death Row System." *New York Times* (February 21, 2003).

Morris, Jonathan. "Ruth Ellis: Villain or Victim." *BBC News* (November 11, 1999).

Muaro, Victoria Tiffany. "Images of Crime and Criminals: How Media Creations Drive Public Opinion and Policy." Ph.D. dissertation, University of Minnesota, 1999.

Nance, William L. *The Worlds of Truman Capote*. New York: Stein and Day, 1970.

Narrander, Barbara. "The Multi-Layered Impact of Public Opinion on Capital Punishment Implementation in the American States." *Political Research Quarterly* 53 (December, 2000): 771–793.

Nash, William R. " 'You Think a Man Can't Kneel and Stand?' Ernest J. Gaines's Reassessment of Religion as a Positive Communal Influence in *A Lesson Before Dying*." *Callaloo* 24 (2001): 346–362.

Nelson, Lane, and Burk Foster, eds. *Death Watch: A Death Penalty Anthology*. Upper Saddle River, NJ: Prentice Hall, 2001.

O'Dell, Larry. "Conservative Republican Leads Anti-Death Penalty Push." Associated Press (January 20, 2001).

Parker, Barbara. *Suspicion of Vengeance*. New York: Signet, 2003.

Pinsker, Sanford. "Imagining American Reality." *The Southern Review* 29 (Autumn, 1993): 767–782.

Pitt, David E. "Mystery Is the Core of Fiction." *New York Times* (April 23, 1989).

Plimpton, George. *Truman Capote*. New York: Doubleday, 1997.

Popham, John N. "The Southern Writer's Search for Truth and Justice." *Georgia Law Review* 19 (Fall 1984): 227–232.

Prejean, Sister Helen. *Dead Man Walking*. New York: Vintage, 1994.

———. "Letter from Death Row." *America* (February 13, 1999).

Radelet, Michael L., and Hugh Adam Bedau. "The Execution of the Innocent." In *America's Experience with Capital Punishment: Reflections on the Past, Present, and Future of the Ultimate Penal Sanction*, edited by James L. Acker, Robert M. Bohm, and Charles S. Lanier. Durham, NC: Carolina Academic Press, 1998.

Radelet, Michael L., and Marian J. Borg. "The Changing Nature of the Death Penalty Debate." *Annual Review of Sociology* 26 (2000): 43–61.

Rebeck, Victoria A. "Movie Review: *Dead Man Walking*." *The Christian Century* (April 17, 1996).

Renaud, Trisha. "Electrocution as Cruel and Unusual." *National Law Journal* (July 23, 2001).

Report of the Governor's Commission on Capital Punishment (April 15, 2002) [Available online at www.idoc.state.il.us/ccp].

Rodgers, Christy. "Movie Review: *Dead Man Walking*." *Cineaste* (1996).

Rovella, David E. "Fixing the Penalty." *National Law Journal* (June 19, 2000).

———. "Pryor Defends Death Row Policies." *National Law Journal* (February 11, 2002).

Russell, Lawrence. "Dance with a Stranger." (August 15, 2000) [Available online at www.coastnet.com/~lwr/Fcourt].

———. "I Want to Live." (September 28, 2000) [Available online at www.coastnet.com/~lwr/Fcourt].

Sandys, Marla. "Stacking the Deck for Guilt and Death: The Failure of Death Qualification to Ensure Impartiality." In *America's Experiment with Capital Punishment: Reflections on the Past, Present, and Future of the Ultimate Penal Sanction*, edited by James R. Acker, Robert M. Bohm, and Charles S. Lanier. Durham, NC: Carolina Academic Press, 1998.

Sarat, Austin. *When the State Kills: Capital Punishment and the American Condition*. Princeton, NJ: Princeton University Press, 2001.

Sayers, Valerie. "A Good Old Boy in a Bad Old World." *New York Times* (April 23, 1989).

Scheck, Barry, Peter Neufeld, and Jim Dwyer. *Actual Innocence: When Justice Goes Wrong and How to Make It Right*. New York: Signet, 2001.

Schneider, William. "Growing Doubts about the Death Penalty." *National Journal* (June 10, 2000).

Schroth, Raymond A. "Book Review: *Dead Man Walking*." *America* (September 18, 1993).

Schulgasser, Barbara. "Latest from the Grisham Factory." *San Francisco Examiner* (October 11, 1996).

———. "Stone Loses a Step in *Last Dance*." *San Francisco Examiner* (May 3, 1996).

Scott, A. O. "Courtesy and Decency Play Sneaky with a Tough Guy." *New York Times* (February 8, 2002).

Semarro, Stephen. "Time for Reform of Death Penalty." *National Law Journal* (July 24, 2000).

"*Shot in the Heart:* Review." *The Economist* (July 9, 1994).

Silverstein, Ken. "The Judge as Lynch Mob." In *Machinery of Death: The Reality of America's Death Penalty Regime*, edited by David R. Dow and Mark Dow. New York: Routledge, 2002.

Simon, John. "Film Review: *Dead Man Walking*." *National Review* (February 26, 1996).

Smith, Patrick J. "Onstage Politics." *New Criterion* (December 2000).

Solotaroff, Ivan. *The Last Face You'll Ever See: The Private Life of the American Death Penalty*. New York: HarperCollins, 2001.

Sommersby, Jack. "Movie Review: *The Life of David Gale*" (April 21, 2003) [Available online at www.culturedose.net/review].

Steiker, Carol S., and Jordan M. Steiker. "Judicial Development in Capital Punishment Law." In *America's Experiment with Capital Punishment: Reflections on the Past, Present, and Future of the Ultimate Penal Sanction*, edited by James R. Acker, Robert M. Bohm, and Charles S. Lanier. Durham, NC: Carolina Academic Press, 1998.

Stern, Gary M. "Courtroom Life Imitates Art." *National Law Journal* (July 22, 2002).

Sterrett, David. "Now Showing: Crusading Films." *Christian Science Monitor* (June 13, 2003).

Steyn, Mark. "Who Cares? *The Life of David Gale*." *Spectator* (March 15, 2003).

Sullivan, Thomas P. "Think First, Execute Later." *National Law Journal* (July 8, 2002).

"Suspicion of Vengeance: Review." *Publishers Weekly* (July 9, 2001).

Swanson, William. "Murder, He Wrote." *Minneapolis-St. Paul Magazine* (November 1995).

Toumarkine. Doris. "Film Review: *The Widow of St. Pierre.*" *Film Journal* (September 5, 2003).

"Toward Death Penalty Reform." *New York Times* (October 13, 2003).

Turbide, Diane. "Book Review: *Shot in the Heart.*" *MacLean's* (July 18, 1994).

Turow, Scott. *Reversible Errors*. New York: Farrar, Straus and Giroux, 2002.

———. "To Kill or Not to Kill." *New Yorker* (January 6, 2003).

———. *Ultimate Punishment: A Lawyer's Reflections on Dealing with the Death Penalty.* New York: Farrar, Straus and Giroux, 2003.

Twarog, Julia. "Harvard Alum's New Novel Takes on Death Penalty" (February 7, 2003) [Available online at www.thecrimson.com].

U.S. General Accounting Office. "Death Penalty Sentencing: Research Indicates Pattern of Racial Disparities." In *The Death Penalty in America: Current Controversies*, edited by Hugo Adam Bedau. New York: Oxford University Press, 1997.

Vancil, David E. "Redemption According to Ernest Gaines." *African American Review* 28 (Autumn 1994): 489–491.

Vandiver, Margaret. "The Impact of the Death Penalty on the Families of Homicide Victims and Condemned Prisoners." In *America's Experiment with Capital Punishment: Reflections on the Past, Present, and Future of the Ultimate Penal Sanction*, edited by James R. Acker, Robert M. Bohm, and Charles S. Lanier. Durham, NC: Carolina Academic Press, 1998.

Von Drehle, David. *Among the Lowest of the Dead: The Culture of the Condemned*. New York: Random House, 1994.

Walker, Mary Willis. *The Red Scream*. New York: Bantam, 1994.

Welch, Mandy, and Richard Burr. "The Politics of Finality and the Execution of the Innocent: The Case of Gary Graham." In *Machinery of Death: The Reality of America's Death Penalty Regime*, edited by David R. Dow and Mark Dow. New York: Routledge, 2002.

White, Penny J. "Errors and Ethics: Dilemmas in Death." *Hofstra Law Review* 29 (Summer 2001): 1265–1299.

Whitehead, John T., and Michael B. Blankenship. "The Gender Gap in Capital Punishment Attitudes: An Analysis of Support and Opposition." *American Journal of Criminal Justice* 25 (2000): 1–13.

Wilgoren, Jodi. "Appeals Process in Illinois Includes the Exonerated." *New York Times* (December 17, 2002).

———. "Governor Assails System's Errors as He Empties Illinois Death Row." *New York Times* (January 12, 2003).

———. "Illinois Panel: Death Sentence Needs Overhaul." *New York Times* (April 15, 2002).

Williamson, Sam. "Why Scott Turow's New Novel Will Appeal to Legal Geeks and a More General Audience." *Findlaw's Writ* (October 25, 2002).

Yardley, Jim. "Texas Death Row Appeals Lawyers Criticized." *New York Times* (December 3, 2002).

———. "Texas Retooling Criminal Justice in Wake of Furor." *New York Times* (June 1, 2001).

Young, Gary. "When Jurors, Judges, and Lawyers Snooze, Do Clients Have Recourse?" *New Jersey Law Journal* (August 26, 2002).

Zimring, Franklin E., and Gordon Hawkins. *Crime Is Not the Problem: Lethal Violence in America*. New York: Oxford University Press, 1997.

Politics,
Media &
Popular Culture

David A. Schultz, *General Editor*

This series is devoted to both scholarly and teaching materials that examine the ways politics, the media, and popular culture interact and influence social and political behavior. Subject matters to be addressed in this series include, but will not be limited to: media and politics; political communication; television, politics, and mass culture; mass media and political behavior; and politics and alternative media and telecommunications such as computers. Submission of single-author and collaborative studies, as well as collections of essays are invited.

Authors wishing to have works considered for this series should contact:

Peter Lang Publishing
Acquisitions Department
275 Seventh Avenue, 28th floor
New York, New York 10001

To order other books in this series, please contact our Customer Service Department at:

800-770-LANG (within the U.S.)
(212) 647-7706 (outside the U.S.)
(212) 647-7707 FAX

or browse online by series at:

WWW.PETERLANGUSA.COM